This volume brings together a set of conversations between the editors and some of the world's leading educational thinkers about issues that are not only philosophical but also practical. Each of these thinkers is challenged to clarify the ways in which they conceptualize the relationship between theory and research, the empirical and the normative, and theory and practice. What emerges from these conversations are insights that are perceptive, thoughtful and engaging, and also incredibly helpful to early career and established scholars alike.

**Fazal Rizvi**
Professor of Global Studies in Education, University of Melbourne, Australia and Emeritus Professor, University of Illinois, Urbana-Champaign, USA

*Theory and Philosophy in Education Research: Methodological Dialogues* is ideal reading for new education researchers – and those who are not so new. The dialogic structure provides an innovative scaffold into further reading about theory and research.

**Annette Woods**
Professor, Queensland University of Technology, Australia, and President, Australian Association for Research in Education

# THEORY AND PHILOSOPHY IN EDUCATION RESEARCH

The issue of methodology is a fundamental concern for all who engage in educational research. Presenting a series of methodological dialogues between eminent education researchers including Michael Apple, Gert Biesta, Penny Enslin, John Hattie, Nel Noddings, Michael Peters, Richard Pring and Paul Smeyers, this book explores the ways in which they have chosen and developed research methods to style their investigations and frame their arguments.

These dialogues address the specialized and technical aspects of conducting educational research, conceptualize the relationship between methodology and theory, and provide in-depth discussion of concerns including falsifiability, openness, interpretation and researcher judgement. Foregrounding the researchers' first-hand experience and knowledge, this book will provide future and current researchers with a deeper comprehension of the place of theory in education research.

An illuminating resource for undergraduate and postgraduate researchers alike, *Theory and Philosophy in Education Research* confronts the intricate complexities of conducting education research in a highly engaging and accessible way.

**John Quay** is an associate professor in the Graduate School of Education at the University of Melbourne, Australia.

**Jennifer Bleazby** is a lecturer in the Faculty of Education at Monash University, Australia.

**Steven A. Stolz** is a senior lecturer in the School of Education at La Trobe University, Australia.

**Maurizio Toscano** is a lecturer in the Graduate School of Education at the University of Melbourne, Australia.

**R. Scott Webster** is an associate professor in the Faculty of Education at Deakin University, Australia.

# THEORY AND PHILOSOPHY IN EDUCATION RESEARCH

Methodological Dialogues

Edited by John Quay, Jennifer Bleazby,
Steven A. Stolz, Maurizio Toscano and
R. Scott Webster

LONDON AND NEW YORK

First published 2018
by Routledge
2 Park Square, Milton Park, Abingdon, Oxon OX14 4RN

and by Routledge
711 Third Avenue, New York, NY 10017

*Routledge is an imprint of the Taylor & Francis Group, an informa business*

© 2018 selection and editorial matter, John Quay, Jennifer Bleazby, Steven
A. Stolz, Maurizio Toscano and R. Scott Webster; individual chapters,
the contributors

The right of John Quay, Jennifer Bleazby, Steven A. Stolz, Maurizio Toscano and
R. Scott Webster to be identified as the authors of the editorial material, and of
the authors for their individual chapters, has been asserted in accordance with
sections 77 and 78 of the Copyright, Designs and Patents Act 1988.

All rights reserved. No part of this book may be reprinted or reproduced or
utilized in any form or by any electronic, mechanical, or other means, now
known or hereafter invented, including photocopying and recording, or in any
information storage or retrieval system, without permission in writing from
the publishers.

*Trademark notice*: Product or corporate names may be trademarks or registered
trademarks, and are used only for identification and explanation without intent
to infringe.

*British Library Cataloguing-in-Publication data:*
A catalogue record for this book is available from the British Library

*Library of Congress Cataloguing-in-Publication data:*
Names: Quay, John, editor.
Title: Theory and philosophy in education research: methodological dialogues /
edited by John Quay, Jennifer Bleazby, Steven A. Stolz, Maurizio Toscano,
Scott Webster; foreword by David Beckett.
Description: Abingdon, Oxon; New York, NY: Routledge, 2018. |
Includes bibliographical references.
Identifiers: LCCN 2017051804 (print) | LCCN 2017060102 (ebook) |
ISBN 9781351176118 (eb) | ISBN 9780815386018 (hb) |
ISBN 9780815386025 (pb)
Subjects: LCSH: Education–Research–Methodology.
Classification: LCC LB1028 (ebook) | LCC LB1028 .T439 2018 (print) |
DDC 370.72–dc23
LC record available at https://lccn.loc.gov/2017051804

ISBN: 978-0-8153-8601-8 (hbk)
ISBN: 978-0-8153-8602-5 (pbk)
ISBN: 978-1-351-17611-8 (ebk)

Typeset in Bembo
by Deanta Global Publishing Services, Chennai, India
Printed and bound by CPI Group (UK) Ltd, Croydon, CR0 4YY

# CONTENTS

| | |
|---|---|
| *Acknowledgements* | *ix* |
| *Contributors* | *xi* |
| *Foreword by David Beckett* | *xviii* |

1 Locating theory in research: opening a conversation     1
*John Quay, Jennifer Bleazby, Steven A. Stolz, Maurizio Toscano*
*and R. Scott Webster*

2 Theory as research: philosophical work in education     23
*Peter Roberts*

3 Michael Apple on praxis, rhetoric and educational research:
in dialogue with Jennifer Bleazby     36
*Jennifer Bleazby and Michael Apple*

4 Gert Biesta on thinking philosophically about education;
thinking educationally about philosophy in education and
educational research: in dialogue with Steven A. Stolz     53
*Steven A. Stolz and Gert Biesta*

5 Penny Enslin on liberal feminism, justice and education:
in dialogue with Jennifer Bleazby     68
*Jennifer Bleazby and Penny Enslin*

**viii** Contents

6 John Hattie on interpretation, the story of research and the
necessity of falsifiability: in dialogue with Maurizio Toscano     85
*Maurizio Toscano and John Hattie*

7 Nel Noddings on care theory and caring practice: in dialogue
with John Quay     101
*John Quay and Nel Noddings*

8 Michael Peters on science, genealogy and openness in
educational research: in dialogue with Steven A. Stolz     114
*Steven A. Stolz and Michael Peters*

9 Richard Pring on making research *educational* research:
in dialogue with R. Scott Webster     129
*R. Scott Webster and Richard Pring*

10 Paul Smeyers and a perspective on educational research:
in dialogue with Maurizio Toscano     144
*Maurizio Toscano and Paul Smeyers*

11 Becoming a good education researcher     158
*Lyn Yates*

*Index*     *169*

# ACKNOWLEDGEMENTS

This book originated from a one-day conference, held in 2015, sponsored by the Australian Association for Research in Education (AARE) and the Melbourne Graduate School of Education (MGSE). We, the organizers of the conference and editors of this book, are all members of the AARE Special Interest Group: "Educational Theory and Philosophy". We sincerely thank both organizations for supporting this event, with funds to cover transcriptions and conference expenses (AARE), and ICT assistance and spaces to conduct the conference itself (MGSE). The aim of the conference was to support education researchers, and, with this in mind, all author proceeds from this book will be directed to AARE to assist future initiatives aiding education researchers. Further support for the book was provided by the Philosophy of Education Society of Australasia (PESA) in the form of a grant to help produce the book's index. Our sincere thanks to our colleagues in PESA.

All of the contributors to this book gave of their time freely and generously. The dialogues were initially interviews, recorded either via telephone or online. We thank each and every one of the eight interviewees, all of whom shared details of their lives and work: Michael Apple, Gert Biesta, Penny Enslin, John Hattie, Nel Noddings, Michael Peters, Richard Pring and Paul Smeyers. Each one was selected by their interviewer as an international expert who could make a contribution to this question of theory and education research, and as someone whose work they were familiar with. During the conference, the recorded interviews were re-played and discussed.

The two bookend chapters from Peter Roberts and Lyn Yates were based on their keynote presentations, where they addressed in broader terms the issue of theory in education research. Both chapters provide a sense of coherence across the dialogues. We thank both Peter and Lyn for accepting our invitation to headline this conference and for sharing aspects of their life's work in education research to support others in this endeavour.

**x** Acknowledgements

We thank David Beckett for opening the conference with a series of important remarks that situated the question of theory and research in both practical and philosophical terms. His foreword to this book draws on his opening remarks, setting the scene for the research conversation and the content to follow.

Another person we thank is Sarah Tomasetti, whose art adorns the cover of this book. Sarah's generous sharing of her work enabled us to show the book in a way which stepped outside norms for academic texts. This is something personal and important to all the editors.

Finally, we acknowledge those who attended the one-day conference and those who may read this book. We undertook both tasks to forward the work of education research amongst colleagues and students alike.

John Quay
Jennifer Bleazby
Steven A. Stolz
Maurizio Toscano
R. Scott Webster

# CONTRIBUTORS

**Michael Apple** is the John Bascom Professor of Curriculum and Instruction and Educational Policy Studies at the University of Wisconsin, Madison, where he has taught since 1970. Prior to completing his doctorate at Teachers College, Columbia University, Professor Apple was a school teacher in New Jersey, where he was the president of his local teachers' union and a political activist involved in anti-racism and anti-corporate movements, as well as in efforts to improve conditions for teachers and students in disadvantaged schools. Professor Apple's research interests include critical theory and critical pedagogy, education and inequality, curriculum theory and development, the sociology of curriculum, the relationship between culture and power in education, and democratizing educational policy and practice. He is one of the most influential and prolific scholars in the field of education, having published over 50 books and more than 300 articles and chapters, many of which have become seminal texts. Some of his publications include: *Ideology and Curriculum* (Routledge, 1979, 1990, 2004), *Education and Power* (Routledge, 1982, 1995, 2012), *Official Knowledge: Democratic Education in a Conservative Age* (Routledge, 1993, 2000, 2014), *Cultural Politics and Education* (Teachers College Press, 1996), *Educating the Right Way: Markets, Standards, God, and Inequality* (Routledge, 2001, 2006), *Can Education Change Society?* (Routledge, 2013), and *Knowledge, Power, and Education* (Routledge, 2013). He is the recipient of numerous awards, including the Lifetime Achievement Award by the American Educational Research Association, the UCLA Medal for Outstanding Academic Achievement, and thirteen honorary doctorates from universities around the world.

**David Beckett** is an Honorary Professorial Fellow in the Melbourne Graduate School of Education, The University of Melbourne, having recently retired from the Deputy Deanship. Research on the epistemological and ontological significance of innovative professional practices and formations continues, as do many

**xii** Contributors

doctoral supervisions. Professor Beckett is a Fellow of the Australian Council for Educational Leaders and a Fellow of the Philosophy of Education Society of Australasia.

**Gert Biesta** (www.gertbiesta.com) is Professor of Education and Director of Research at the Department of Education of Brunel University London, United Kingdom, NIVOZ Professor for Education at the University for Humanistic Studies, Utrecht, the Netherlands, and Visiting Professor at NLA University College, Bergen, Norway. He served as Editor-in-Chief of the journal *Studies in Philosophy and Education* from 1999 to 2014 and is currently Associate Editor of the journal *Educational Theory*. His work focuses on the theory and philosophy of education and the theory and philosophy of educational and social research. His recent work has focused particularly on curriculum, teachers and teaching. Recent books include *The Beautiful Risk of Education* (Routledge, 2014), *Teacher Agency: An Ecological Approach* (with Mark Priestley and Sarah Robinson; Bloomsbury, 2015) and *The Rediscovery of Teaching* (Routledge, 2017). He is also co-author, with Barbara Stengel, of the contribution on the philosophy of teaching in the fifth edition of the *Handbook of Research on Teaching* of the American Educational Research Association (AERA) (2016).

**Jennifer Bleazby** has been a lecturer in the Faculty of Education, Monash University, Australia since 2010. Prior to taking up her position at Monash University, Dr Bleazby worked as a philosophy, history, humanities and media studies teacher in secondary schools. In 2008, she completed a PhD in the School of Philosophy at the University of New South Wales, Australia. Her main areas of research are philosophy of education, philosophy for children, feminist philosophy, and pragmatism, especially the philosophy of John Dewey. She is the author of the book *Social Reconstruction Learning: Dualism, Dewey and Philosophy in Schools* (Routledge, 2013). Other recent publications include: 'Why some school subjects have a higher status than others: The epistemology of the traditional curriculum hierarchy', *Oxford Review of Education*, 41(5), and the forthcoming 'Education', in G. Oppy (Ed.), *A Companion to Atheism and Philosophy* (Wiley Blackwell, 2018).

**Penny Enslin** is Professor of Education in the School of Education at the University of Glasgow. Prior to joining the University of Glasgow, Professor Enslin worked in the School of Education at the University of Witwatersrand, Johannesburg, where she is now an Emeritus Professor. She has also taught History and Religious Instruction in secondary schools in Johannesburg. A central focus of Professor Enslin's research has been the defence of liberal autonomy as a key aim of education and defending liberal theory against attacks from Marxism, postmodernism, and those multiculturalists and Africanists who oppose liberalism. Her research interests include education for democratic citizenship, gender and education, liberalism, higher education, cosmopolitanism, peace education, and social justice. Professor Enslin has authored over 100 journal articles, book

Contributors **xiii**

chapters and conference papers and edited two book collections in the field of education. Some of her more recent publications include: 'Rethinking the "western tradition"' (co-authored with Kai Horsthemke), in M. A. Peters and C. Mika (Eds.), *The Dilemma of Western Philosophy* (Routledge, 2017); 'Getting the measure of measurement: global educational opportunity' (co-authored with Mary Tjiattas), *Educational Philosophy and Theory*, 49(4); 'Liberalism and education: Between diversity and universalism', in L. J. Waks (Ed.), *Leaders in Philosophy of Education* (Sense, 2014); 'Citizenship Education in Post-Apartheid South Africa', *Cambridge Journal of Education*, 33(1); and 'Deliberative Democracy, Diversity and the Challenges of Citizenship Education' (co-authored with Shirley Pendlebury and Mary Tjiattas), *Journal of Philosophy of Education*, 35(1).

**John Hattie**'s work is internationally acclaimed. His influential 2008 book *Visible Learning: A Synthesis of over 800 Meta-Analyses Relating to Achievement* is believed to be the world's largest evidence-based study into the factors that improve student learning. Hailed by the Times Education Supplement as "teaching's Holy Grail", this ground-breaking study involved more than 80 million students from around the world and brought together 50,000 smaller studies. *Visible Learning* found that positive teacher–student interaction is the most important factor in effective teaching. Since 2011, Laureate Professor Hattie has been Director of the Melbourne Education Research Institute at the University of Melbourne. He is also the Chair of the Australian Institute for Teaching and School Leadership (AITSL), through which he provides national leadership in promoting excellence so that teachers and school leaders have maximum impact on learning. He is also past-president of the International Test Commission and Associate Editor of the *British Journal of Educational Psychology* and *American Educational Research Journal*. Professor Hattie was awarded the New Zealand Order of Merit in the 2011 Queen's Birthday Honours, is a Fellow of the Australian Council for Educational Leaders and the American Psychological Association, and has published and presented over 500 papers, and supervised 190 thesis students.

**Nel Noddings** is Lee L. Jacks Professor of Education, Emerita, at Stanford University. She is past-president of the National Academy of Education, the Philosophy of Education Society and the John Dewey Society. In addition to 22 books – among them *Caring: A Feminine Approach to Ethics and Moral Education* (University of California Press, 1984), *Women and Evil* (University of California Press, 1989), *The Challenge to Care in Schools* (Teachers College Press, 1992), *Educating for Intelligent Belief or Unbelief* (Teachers College Press, 1993), and *Philosophy of Education* (Westview Press, 1995) – she is the author of more than 300 articles and chapters on various topics ranging from the ethics of care to mathematical problem solving. Her latest books are *Happiness and Education* (Cambridge University Press, 2003), *Educating Citizens for Global Awareness* (Teachers College Press, 2005), *Critical Lessons: What Our Schools Should Teach* (Cambridge University Press, 2006), *When School Reform Goes Wrong* (Teachers College Press, 2007), *The Maternal Factor: Two*

*Paths to Morality* (University of California Press, 2010), *Peace Education* (Cambridge University Press, 2011), *Education and Democracy in the 21st Century* (Teachers College Press, 2013) (named Outstanding Book of the Year 2015 by the American Association of Colleges for Teacher Education), *A Richer, Brighter Vision for American High Schools* (Cambridge University Press, 2015), and *Teaching Controversial Issues* (co-authored with Laurie Brooks) (Teachers College Press, 2016). Her work has so far been translated into 14 languages. Nel spent 15 years as a teacher, administrator, and curriculum supervisor in public schools; she served as a mathematics department chairperson in New Jersey and as Director of the Laboratory Schools at the University of Chicago. At Stanford, she received the Award for Teaching Excellence three times. She also served as Associate Dean and as Acting Dean at Stanford for four years. Nel is a Laureate member of Kappa Delta Pi, and holds a number of awards, among them the Anne Rowe Award for contributions to the education of women (Harvard University), the Willystine Goodsell Award for contributions to the education of women (American Educational Research Association), Medal for Distinguished Service (Teachers College Columbia University), Lifetime Achievement Award (American Educational Research Association (Division B), the Award for Distinguished Leadership in Education (Rutgers University), and honorary doctorates from Columbia College, Montclair State University, Queen's University, Canada, Lewis and Clark College, and Manhattan College.

**Michael Peters** is Professor of Education at the University of Waikato, New Zealand and Emeritus Professor in Educational Policy, Organization, and Leadership at the University of Illinois at Urbana–Champaign, United States of America. He is Executive Editor of the journal *Educational Philosophy and Theory*, and Founding Editor of five international journals: *Policy Futures in Education* (SAGE), *E-Learning and Digital Media* (SAGE), *Knowledge Cultures* (Addleton), *The Video Journal of Education and Pedagogy* (Springer), and *Open Review of Education Research* (T&F). His interests are in philosophy, education and social policy and he has written over eighty books, including most recently: *A Companion to Wittgenstein on Education: Pedagogical Investigations* (Springer, 2017) with Jeff Stickney, *The Global Financial Crisis and Educational Restructuring* (Peter Lang, 2015) and *Paulo Freire: The Global Legacy* (Peter Lang, 2014) both with Tina Besley, *Education Philosophy and Politics: The Selected Works of Michael A. Peters* (Routledge, 2012), *Cognitive Capitalism, Education, and Digital Labour* (Peter Lang, 2011) with Ergin Bulut, and *Neoliberalism and After? Education, Social Policy and the Crisis of Western Capitalism* (Peter Lang, 2011). He has acted as an advisor to governments and UNESCO on these and related matters in the United States of America, Scotland, New Zealand, South Africa and the European Union. He was made an Honorary Fellow of the Royal Society of New Zealand in 2010 and awarded honorary doctorates by State University of New York (SUNY) in 2012 and University of Aalborg in 2015.

**Richard Pring** holds the following degrees: MA Oxon, PhD London, Hon. D.Litt (U. of Kent) and Hon D.Litt (IoE/U. of London). From 1989 to 2003, he was the first Professor of Education at the University of Oxford and Director of the Department of Education, before becoming the 2003–2009 Director of the £1 million Nuffield Review of 14–19 Education and Training (report published by T&F). His work focuses on the philosophy of education and some of his books include: *The Philosophy of Educational Research* (3rd edn., Bloomsbury, 2015), *The Life and Death of Secondary Education for All* (Routledge, 2013), *John Dewey* (Bloomsbury, 2007) and *Philosophy of Education* (Continuum, 2004). Presently, Richard is writing a book entitled *The Future of Publicly Funded State Schools* (Routledge, forthcoming).

**John Quay** is Associate Professor in the Melbourne Graduate School of Education at the University of Melbourne. Prior to his academic career, he was a school teacher in outdoor and environmental education, and physical education. John's areas of research interest stem from his teaching experience, where awareness of a core academic curriculum existing literally in parallel with a co-curricular program illuminated an issue at the heart of education. His research focus brings this and other practical issues connected with schools and education into conversation with theoretical perspectives emanating primarily from the philosophical work of Dewey, Heidegger and Peirce. John's contributions revolve around various understandings of experience, building on the notion that education is a human endeavour and thus cannot be understood apart from conceptions of human existence. He has published *Education, Experience and Existence: Engaging Dewey, Peirce and Heidegger* (Routledge, 2013), *John Dewey and Education Outdoors* (with Jayson Seaman, Sense, 2013) and *Understanding Life in School* (Palgrave, 2015).

**Peter Roberts** is Professor of Education and Director of the Educational Theory, Policy and Practice Research Hub at the University of Canterbury in New Zealand. His primary areas of scholarship are philosophy of education and educational policy studies. His most recent books include *Happiness, Hope, and Despair: Rethinking the Role of Education* (Peter Lang, 2015), *Education, Ethics and Existence: Camus and the Human Condition* (with Andrew Gibbons and Richard Heraud, Routledge, 2015), *Better Worlds: Education, Art, and Utopia* (with John Freeman-Moir, Lexington Books, 2013), *The Virtues of Openness: Education, Science, and Scholarship in the Digital Age* (with Michael Peters, Paradigm Publishers, 2012), *Paulo Freire in the 21st Century: Education, Dialogue, and Transformation* (Paradigm Publishers, 2010) and *Neoliberalism, Higher Education and Research* (with Michael Peters, Sense Publishers, 2008). In 2012, Peter was a Rutherford Visiting Scholar at Trinity College, Cambridge, and in 2016 he was a Canterbury Fellow at the University of Oxford. He is the Immediate Past-President of the Philosophy of Education Society of Australasia.

**Paul Smeyers** is Research Professor for Philosophy of Education at Ghent University, Belgium, Extraordinary Professor at K.U. Leuven, Belgium, and Honorary Extraordinary Professor at Stellenbosch University, South Africa. He teaches philosophy of education and qualitative/interpretative research methods.

**xvi** Contributors

He has a wide involvement in philosophy of education (around 300 publications). He holds, or has held, several positions in the International Network of Philosophers of Education (President since 2006) and is Link-Convenor (Programme Chair) of Network 13, Philosophy of Education, of the European Educational Research Association. He is Associate Editor of *Educational Theory*, and a member of the Editorial Board of *Studies in Philosophy and Education* (Springer), the *Journal of Philosophy of Education* (Wiley), and *Ethics and Education* (T&F). For more than a decade he has been the Chair of the Research Community Philosophy and History of the Discipline of Education established by the Research Foundation Flanders, Belgium. His major publications and co-publications include: *Thinking Again: Education after Postmodernism* (Bergin & Garvey, 1998), *Education in an Age of Nihilism* (Falmer Press, 2000), *The Therapy of Education* (Palgrave Macmillan, 2007), *Blackwell Guide to the Philosophy of Education* (Wiley, 2003), *Showing and Doing: Wittgenstein as a Pedagogical Philosopher* (Paradigm Publishers, 2008), *Understanding Education and Educational Research* (Cambridge University Press, 2013), and a co-edited collection, the *International Handbook of Interpretation in Educational Research Methods* (Springer, 2014).

**Steven A. Stolz** is Senior Lecturer in Education at La Trobe University, Australia. Before he became an academic, he taught for ten years as a secondary school teacher in the following curriculum areas: mathematics, science, religious education, health and physical education. He also has a background in analytical and continental traditions of philosophy, which has led to a diverse array of research interests that include: philosophy of action, moral philosophy, aesthetics, epistemology, and phenomenology. At the moment, his primary area of scholarship is concerned with educational philosophy and theory, but he also has a particular interest in the areas of embodied cognition, narrative enquiry, and learning theories in psychology. His scholarship is best described as being located at the intersection between education and philosophy, particularly how theory informs practice and/or how practice informs theory. Recent publications of note include: 'MacIntyre, rival traditions and education', *Discourse: Studies in the Cultural Politics of Education* (2015), 'Nietzsche on aesthetics, educators and education', *Studies in Philosophy and Education* (2016), 'MacIntyre, managerialism and universities', *Educational Philosophy and Theory* (2016), and 'MacIntyre, rationality, and universities', *Civil Society, Education and Human Formation* (2017). Some of Steven's notable academic awards and distinctions include the following: Philosophy of Education Society of Australasia doctoral scholarship (2011), the La Trobe University Faculty of Education emerging researcher award (2013), and various invitations to be a visiting scholar at the University of Stirling (United Kingdom), University of New Orleans (United States of America), and the University of Illinois at Urbana-Champaign (United States of America). Currently, he is the convener of the "Educational Theory and Philosophy" special interest group (2016–present), which is part of the Australian Association for Research in Education.

**Maurizio Toscano** is a Lecturer in Science Education in the Graduate School of Education at the University of Melbourne. Maurizio's academic research and teaching work focuses on understanding the metaphysical relationships between science, art, the environment, philosophy and education. His work is informed by his wide-ranging academic experiences: his doctoral training was in astrophysics, he has undertaken and supervised research into aesthetics, the scientific imagination and artistic practice, and he has exhibited artworks, collaborated with artists and written about the art-science nexus. His publications examine philosophical perspectives on science and education that draw upon the works of Heidegger, Wittgenstein, Cavell, Nietzsche and Sloterdijk.

**R. Scott Webster** is an associate professor in the School of Education at Deakin University where he is the coordinator of the Curriculum, Pedagogy and Professional Learning teaching and learning group. He studied for his Master's degree at Oxford University, United Kingdom and completed his PhD studies at the University of Queensland and Griffith University in Australia. Scott was awarded a Research Fellowship at Monash University, Australia for 2006 and 2007, in which he wrote the book *Educating for Meaningful Lives* (Sense, 2009). Scott's main areas of research interest include: education theory, philosophy of education, curriculum theory, ethics, values, spirituality, meaning of life, Dewey, Kierkegaard, Nietzsche and Heidegger. He has several articles published in journals and books relating to teacher education, the philosophy of education and spirituality.

**Lyn Yates** is Redmond Barry Distinguished Professor of Curriculum in the Melbourne Graduate School of Education, University of Melbourne. She is a past-president and honorary life member of the Australian Association for Research in Education, and a Fellow of the Australian Academy of Social Sciences. Her books include *Theory/Practice Dilemmas* (Deakin University, 1993), *The Education of Girls: Policy, Research and the Question of Gender* (ACER, 1993), *Feminism and Education* (La Trobe University Press, 1993), *What Does Good Education Research Look Like?* (Open University Press, 2004), *Making Modern Lives* (SUNY, 2006), *Australia's Curriculum Dilemmas: State Policies and the Big Issues* (Melbourne University Press, 2011), *Curriculum in Today's World: Configuring Knowledge, Identities, Work and Politics* (Routledge, 2011), and *Knowledge at the Crossroads?* (Springer, 2017).

# FOREWORD

*David Beckett*

Let me provoke some big-picture thinking, as a way in to the richness of this book. The *Stanford Encyclopedia of Philosophy* has an entry on the 'Underdetermination of Scientific Theory' which should be provocative for educationalists:

> At the heart of the underdetermination of scientific theory by evidence is the simple idea that the evidence available to us at a given time may be insufficient to determine what beliefs we should hold in response to it.
>
> *(Stanford, 2017, p. 1)*

Most of us in education as practitioners and as researchers would recoil from the notion that 'evidence' (as such) would alone 'determine' anything. For us, and for anyone in the social sciences and the humanities (as contrasts with the physical sciences), 'facts' (as an example of 'evidence') never speak for themselves. However, the Stanford entry then loosens up:

> a single scientific hypothesis does not by itself carry any implications about what we should expect to observe in nature; rather, we can derive empirical consequences from an hypothesis only when it is conjoined with many other beliefs and hypotheses, including background assumptions about the world, beliefs about how measuring instruments operate, further hypotheses about the interactions between objects in the original hypothesis' field of study and the surrounding environment, etc.
>
> *(Stanford, 2017, p. 1)*

And from here we can be fellow travellers with scientists. In the social sciences, and in the humanities, we are "conjoined with many other beliefs and hypotheses" (Stanford, 2017, p. 1), since our work is inevitably normative. Education research is

Foreword **xix**

embedded in both the social sciences and the humanities, so, at its most general, we deal with the conditions of humankind in the world (whatever these are taken to be). For us, there is no such thing as the 'innocent eye'. Nor is there such a thing as a 'brute fact'. Humans inevitably experience *perception* (or 'seeing') as falling under a *conception* (of what we are 'looking for'). And, equally, our concepts (of what we are 'looking' for) shape what we then perceive. Thus, what we 'see' is shaped by what we 'look for', and vice versa. As Kant (1929) put it, "Thoughts without content are empty, intuitions without concepts are blind" (p. 93: perception and conception).

This book takes *education* research as one particular side of that Yin-and-Yang relationship endemic to *all* research, and acknowledges the 'underdetermination' of evidence as an epistemological feature of it. Within these pages, there are significant 'methodological dialogues' where some of the world's leading education researchers interrogate the *relational* nature of their work.

Each dialogue invites the reader into the space of theorisation. In such spaces, how the world – or a specific issue within it – is framed as an object of educational inquiry already implicates what is valued and sought in the inquiry process. To emphasise: *all* research is relational in the Kantian sense, but the educational version is more turbo-charged. This is because *education* research exists to improve human learning; thus, it is intensely normative. Power and knowledge coalesce around ideologically framed provisions of learning, typically through systemic structures such as schooling. So teaching, classrooms, assessments, and vocational formation are some main elements in the normative nature of research, where what researchers are 'looking for' and what they are 'seeing' are co-implicated.

Furthermore, education research takes normativity into 'rough ground'. This terrain is the contested and contestable topography where even the nature of the inquiry, and its epistemological assumptions, are part of the inquiry itself, as the 'percepts and concepts' relationship reveals. Wittgenstein, in discussing the relationship of language to the wider world, gives us a metaphor for the enactment of education research:

> We have got on to slippery ice where there is no friction and so in a certain sense the conditions are ideal, but also, just because of that, we are unable to walk. We want to walk: so we need *friction*. Back to the rough ground!
> *(Wittgenstein, 1953, quoted in O'Toole and Beckett, 2010, p. 38)*

To get traction in the turbo-charged and often over-heated world of education research, we need to rub up against settled assumptions. This friction will add to the heat, but there will be movement.

Heat is essential in cooking, too. In Chapter 1 of this book, *Locating Theory in Research: Opening a Conversation*, John Quay, Jennifer Bleazby, Steven A. Stolz, Maurizio Toscano and R. Scott Webster work the correspondences between research and catering. Opening a conversation around locating theory is a little like opening a cookbook: there are many recipes for many tantalising dishes, and many ingredients and techniques involved in making them. But for both research, and catering, the danger is that a reductive technicism may ensue. Just pick a theory (or

**xx**  David Beckett

a recipe) and follow the process! Their metaphorical warning is significant: research, like catering, is, in my terms, 'underdetermined by evidence'. There is the purpose, the context, and judgements of 'taste' all of which add mightily to the prospect of catering success, as it does in research activities. What you 'see' (the percept) is intimately related to what you are 'looking for' (the concept).

This book originated in an innovative and well-attended conference held at The University of Melbourne on May 29, 2015. The event was co-sponsored by the Australian Association for Research in Education (AARE), and the Melbourne Graduate School of Education (MGSE), Australia, and keynote presentations were given by Professor Lyn Yates (MGSE) and Professor Peter Roberts (University of Canterbury, New Zealand). This book is shaped around the 45-minute recorded presentations from our esteemed colleagues in various parts of the world and the following 45-minute facilitated discussions, which took place locally in the MGSE, amongst conference participants.

For each of these 45-minute recorded presentations, the brief was to address a theoretical framework which situates an education phenomenon, problem or issue, and to outline a methodology which clarifies the approaches applied in investigating specific education research questions. The dialogues you can now read have therefore arisen within quite specific, but epistemologically profound, circumstances; there is no such thing as the 'innocent eye' in education research.

The conference, and this book, take us into what Spinoza called the 'sphere of ideas', and he meant that in a way that many of us in education research find helpful. Rather than follow Cartesian dualism (the famous mind over the body philosophical proposition put forward by Descartes, summarised in *cogito ergo sum*), Spinoza was a monist – and a naturalist. He argued for what we today can call the Yin-and-Yang of percepts and concepts, in the melding of thinking and the will (or the conative), all in an embodied person. It sounds wonderfully contemporary, in its monism:

> You see… how and why I think that the human body is a part of nature. As regards the human mind, I believe it is also a part of nature, for I maintain that there exists in nature an infinite power of thinking… which contains subjectively the whole of nature, and its thoughts proceed in the same manner as nature – that is, in the sphere of ideas.
>
> *(Spinoza, 1966, pp. 21–22)*

I was delighted to open the 2015 conference, and, in my remarks on that day, I used this quotation, to emphasise the innovative design of the event, drawing as it did upon embodied (local) and disembodied (recorded) experiences, to generate the 'infinite power of thinking' present in the natural world.

I also believe Spinoza's ontology should be taken more widely. He is reminding us that human experience is not only monist, but also *holist*: we encounter the world from amidst our whole relationality, which is never 'blind' (because we 'see' relations through our willpower), nor 'empty' (because we 'think' our way about).

Holism is traditionally a fundamental educational ideal. Whole persons, 'learning' nations and inclusive cultures are prominently turbo-charged norms for many of us. As you dip into this book and engage the methodological dialogues, bear in mind the 'big picture' thinking which is going on: it is onto-epistemological. Simply, how can research improve us, as humans, educationally? And how can it improve you?

David Beckett, FPESA, FACEL
Professor of Education
The University of Melbourne

## References

Kant, I. (1929). *Critique of Pure Reason* (N. Kemp-Smith, Trans.). London: Macmillan. (Original work published 1787.)

O'Toole, J. and Beckett, D. (2010). *Educational Research: Creative Thinking and Doing.* Melbourne, Australia: Oxford University Press.

Spinoza, B. (1966). *Letters to Friend and Foe.* New York, NY: Philosophical Library.

Stanford, K. (2017). Underdetermination of Scientific Theory. *The Stanford Encyclopedia of Philosophy* (Winter 2017 Edition). Stanford, CA: Metaphysics Research Lab, Stanford University. Available online at https://plato.stanford.edu/archives/win2017/entries/scientific-underdetermination (accessed 19 September 2017).

Wittgenstein, L. (1953). *Philosophical Investigations* (G.E.M. Anscombe, Trans.). Oxford: Basil Blackwell.

# 1

# LOCATING THEORY IN RESEARCH

## Opening a conversation

*John Quay, Jennifer Bleazby, Steven A. Stolz,*
*Maurizio Toscano and R. Scott Webster*

### Correspondences between researching and catering

This introductory chapter is specifically intended to support those newer to research, such as graduate researchers, by offering a propaedeutic – a teaching orientated introduction – to help scaffold a way into the multifaceted conversation about theory and research that unfolds in the chapters to come. For this reason, we have designed the first chapter around a series of analogies between researching and catering. It may appear incongruous to bring researching – which most would consider to be a highbrow and specialized enterprise – together with the seemingly commonplace, everyday task of catering a shared meal. However, this everydayness is valuable because it supports the notion of "'carrying over' – *metapherein*" (Arendt, 1978, p. 103) from something familiar to something seemingly more complex. The resulting juxtaposition assists in making visible what is commonly taken for granted. Positioning both researching and catering as inquiries, and drawing correspondences between them on this basis, supports improved comprehension of the nature of researching and specifically the place of theory in education research.

We begin where we believe many graduate researchers begin: in their confrontation with the specialized and sometimes technical aspects of the task of doing research.[1] However, we do not mean to convey that either researching or catering are merely mechanistic, which may sometimes be assumed when the notion of a "recipe" is used. Both catering and researching involve much more than mechanical steps prescribed by instructional procedures. Our position here will become clearer as the chapter progresses to its conclusion, leading into the broader conversation about the place of theory in research that makes up the bulk of this book.

The first section of this chapter expands on the analogy by highlighting correspondences between the tasks and materials involved in researching and catering. The aim here is to raise awareness of the *complexities* that lie beneath a technical

**2** John Quay et al.

orientation. These complexities illuminate the presence of three levels of inquiry – inquiries within inquiries within inquiries – debunking the notion that either researching or catering are simple and straightforward procedural undertakings. This section is, of course, itself underpinned by a particular theoretical perspective articulated in greater detail elsewhere (see Quay, 2013, 2015).

The second section of this chapter delves deeper to unfold this perspective in relation to some of the *intricacies* that characterize these complexities of inquiry. In doing so, this section brings together the philosophical work of Charles S. Peirce and John Dewey, both steeped in the pragmatic tradition. We note that other theorists could just as readily be employed here to offer a different understanding of the logic of inquiry and challenge or support the position we have articulated. However, we have chosen to privilege the pragmatic perspectives of Peirce and Dewey in this circumstance because we consider their work to proffer important insights regarding the nature of both theory and inquiry.

The first and second sections lead from a concern with the complexities and intricacies of inquiring to the much broader question of how *judgments* are made within inquiring. In this way, the third section of this chapter, itself founded in a further theoretical perspective, illuminates the importance of comprehending the way theories situate ideas and practices historically, geographically, philosophically and politically – thus predisposing judgment. As Karl Popper argued, "there are no uninterpreted visual sense data, … whatever is 'given' to us is already interpreted, decoded" (1976, p. 139). Theories are, after all, human creations. Applying our culinary analogy, judgments made through inquiring are responses based on particular "tastes" that must be acknowledged and explained. "Theory here, then, refers to the articulation of the framework of beliefs and understandings which are embedded in the practice we engage in" (Pring, 2015, p. 96). Locating theory in research is not a matter of finding a needle in a haystack, but rather of understanding how every aspect of researching is imbued with theory.

This third section of the chapter is perhaps the most important, as it highlights how arguing for the place of theory in inquiry is itself a theoretically framed endeavor, thus segueing into the conversation on theory and research that comprises the remainder of the book. We acknowledge without reservation that theoretical positions frame the way we have presented all sections of this chapter, evoking certain theoretical perspectives. No account is of itself so universal that it could not be challenged or supported by way of other theoretical frameworks, as Thomas Kuhn (1970) so eloquently emphasized in his exploration of scientific revolutions.

## Complexities of researching and catering: primary, secondary and tertiary level inquiries

A closer look at the act of catering a shared meal for family or friends reveals that what may appear to be a singular inquiry is actually a primary level inquiry comprised of two interdependent secondary level inquiries. The primary level inquiry of catering a shared meal is comprised of both *preparing* the menu, including choice and cooking of dishes, as well as *presenting* the dishes, including plating and serving of the dishes. Applying our analogy, the primary level inquiry of researching an issue can be seen to be comprised of two secondary level inquiries: one is focused on *investigating* the question that pinpoints this issue, while the other is focused on *communicating* the argument that is developed via investigation of this question. The shift from question to argument, from investigating to communicating, corresponds with the shift from preparing the menu to presenting the dishes. The extent of this shift is revealed in some of the basic features of each secondary level inquiry which, when juxtaposed, further highlight correspondences between researching and catering (see Table 1.1).

It is important to note that the two secondary level inquires actually inform and shape each other. They are not merely distinct steps in a sequence. Investigation of a question already involves considering the generation of an argument and communication of this argument. Furthermore, as we think about the argument in more detail we may also redefine the initial question. Question and argument co-inform each other. The same can be said for preparation of a menu and presentation of the dishes. Our choice of menu informs the way we plate and serve the dishes and vice versa. For example, we may reconsider our decision to make soup when we realize we don't have enough soup bowls for everyone.

**TABLE 1.1** Correspondences between catering and researching at the very basic level of tasks and materials, highlighting the presence of two secondary level inquiries within a primary level inquiry.

| Catering a shared meal | Researching an issue? |
| --- | --- |
| *Menu to be prepared?* | *Question to be investigated?* |
| Cooking procedures (integrated recipes with detailed accounts of preparation for multiple dishes, including ingredient sourcing and cooking, that is reproducible) | Research methods (detailed accounts of data collection and analysis procedures that are reproducible) |
| Cooking techniques (e.g., searing, marinating, poaching) | Research techniques (e.g., participant observing, interviewing, structural equation modeling, videoing) |
| Cooking ingredients – need to be sourced and worked with (e.g., field mushrooms) | Data – need to be collected and worked with (e.g., online survey responses) |
| Cooking tools/equipment (e.g., utensils, oven, saucepans) | Tools/equipment (e.g., research hardware such as measuring and recording equipment, research software such as NVIVO) |
| *Dishes to be presented?* | *Argument to be communicated?* |
| Table and room settings for dining (e.g., formal, casual, buffet) | Document forms (e.g., thesis, report, article) |
| Plating techniques (e.g., classical, landscape, finger foods, sharing platters) | Writing/formatting/referencing styles (e.g., Harvard, APA, Chicago, Oxford) |

4  John Quay et al.

## *What, how and who questions*

Digging deeper reveals a further tertiary level of inquiry, denoted by three question types: what, how and who questions (see Figure 1.1).[2] Each secondary level inquiry is informed by these three interrelated questions. Most obvious is how both secondary level inquiries involve what and how questions: "What is the …?" and "How is the …?". These questions articulate the particular tertiary inquiries that constitute the main elements of each secondary level inquiry. In preparing a shared meal, these may be: "What is the menu to be prepared?" and "How is the menu to be prepared?", followed by "What are the dishes to be presented?" and "How are the dishes to be presented?". When researching, these equate to: "What is the question to be investigated?" and "How is the question to be investigated?", followed

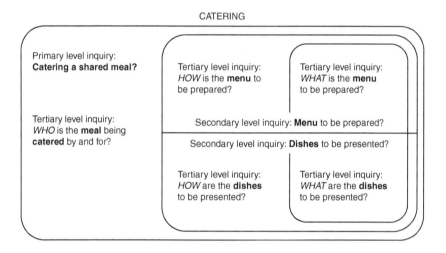

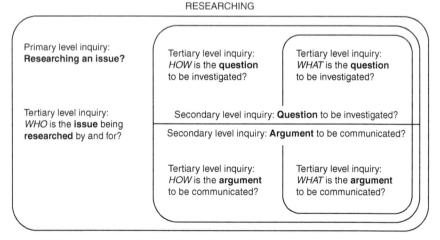

**FIGURE 1.1**  Catering and researching, illuminating primary, secondary and tertiary level inquiries and the what, how and who questions informing them.

Locating theory in research **5**

by "What is the argument to be communicated?" and "How is the argument to be communicated?".

A further tertiary level question is focused on "Who …?". This question emphasizes the context within which the research or catering is taking place, characterized by the needs and interests of particular groups of people. In catering, the who question can be articulated for each secondary level inquiry: "Who is the menu being prepared by and for?" and "Who are the dishes being presented by and for?". For example, one might ask questions like: "What dish can I prepare for my vegan, gluten-intolerant friend who is coming to dinner?", "Should I use penne pasta instead of spaghetti and cut the meatballs into small pieces so it's easier for the baby to eat?", "Can I just use readymade gravy since I'm no good at making it myself or can I get someone else to make this part of the meal?". These questions show the prevalence of "who" in catering deliberations. In researching we ask analogous questions, such as: "Who does the issue affect and what are their needs and interests (e.g., school students, parents, teachers, curriculum developers, teacher education providers, governments, society at large)?". We also need to ask: "Who is the issue being investigated by and what relevant skills and knowledge do they possess?". This is closely related to another question: "Who needs to be involved in the investigation of the issue and communication of the argument – that is, who should collaborate?". For example, if the research could be improved by the collection of quantitative data and I have little expertise in this methodology, I may want to collaborate with a statistician or, perhaps, adjust my research focus so that the project can be completed to a high standard without the collection of such data. Other important "who" questions are: "Who is communicating the argument and to whom is it being communicated?" and "How can it be communicated in such a way that it will persuade this particular group of people?".

These various questions, discerning "Who …?" at the secondary level of inquiry, come together at the primary level of inquiry: "Who is the meal being catered by and for?". In researching it is similar, with the primary who question asking: "Who is the issue being researched by and for?". This who question reveals how the secondary level inquiries come together as the one primary inquiry via the needs and interests of particular groups of people. These groups together constitute the broad community of stakeholders involved in any researching or catering project.

To elaborate, all research involves a situation or a project, wherein a range of people have a stake in resolving a shared issue – for example, a research project seeking funding to resource it. Here a group of researchers, often organised as chief and partner investigators, including doctoral candidates and supported by research assistants, will develop a funding submission that articulates an issue to be researched via investigation of a specific question or questions. This submission may involve input from others beyond the core research team who have a stake in this issue, others who are not researchers per se, widening the range of people identified in the submission. This is important as the question must appeal to a funding body, such as a government department or a philanthropic organisation, as expressive of an issue which they believe is of enough concern to their constituents that it is

**6** John Quay et al.

worthy of funding in a competitive process. The research team must also convince the funding body that, as a team, they possess all the skills and knowledge needed to effectively complete the proposed project. If there is agreement, then the question will be investigated in a way suggested by the researchers, managed within the financial constraints of the funding made available. The means of communicating the argument generated will be a part of the submission. These means may include, for instance, journal articles, conference presentations, theses, reports, and professional learning workshops. All will be developed by the researchers, perhaps with support from other stakeholders, to meet the express needs of the funding body within the timeframe specified in the successful submission.

In the case of a research doctorate, the project is usually funded by the student's candidature, which may draw on some form of government support for the university where it is being undertaken. There are a range of people involved, including the supervisors, the broader faculty, academics from other institutions, research participants as co-researchers, and unnamed examiners, who will have an interest in some aspect of the project. The question will be investigated and an argument generated, within a timeframe commensurate with the conditions of the candidature. The argument will be communicated initially as a formal thesis, for the examiners. Other avenues of communication may be journal papers, a book or books, conference papers, and any further means of conveying the argument or aspects of it to a range of stakeholder audiences. In this scenario, the question "Who is the research being conducted by and for?" can answered from multiple angles. From one perspective, it is the research student who is conducting the project, with the support of supervisors and others, for the examiners. From another perspective, it is the supervisors guiding the research student conducting the project for the examiners, but also for the benefit of the faculty and the university, supporting access to future funding for doctoral candidates and other research. From a further perspective, it is the government that is enabling the research through the funding provided, for the purposes of helping the community advance its research agenda and benefit from the outcomes. All of these various perspectives highlight the ways in which the who question draws all involved parties together as part of the primary inquiry.

The interdependence of these three levels of inquiry – primary, secondary and tertiary – reveals a complexity that one must be conscious of in researching to comprehend the extent of the task at hand. Awareness of these three levels of inquiry reveals an array of multiple interdependent inquiries: inquiries within inquiries. Interdependent what, how and who questions together constitute two interdependent secondary level inquiries which conjointly constitute the primary level inquiry. This complexity often goes unnoticed in other forms of everyday inquiry, including the inquiry involved in catering a shared meal, perhaps due to the familiarity, repetitiveness and habitual actions involved in this daily task.

Our task now is to locate theory more explicitly within this complexity to understand its role. We can do this by drawing on the logical investigations of

Charles S. Peirce and John Dewey, whose logical theories, it must be noted, are informed by the philosophical tradition of pragmatism, of which they are sometimes described as the founders. Peirce engaged in a "logical study of the theory of inquiry" which he described as the "general theory of how research must be performed" (CP 2.106).[3] Building on Peirce, Dewey undertook an "inquiry into inquiry" (1938, p. 20), in pursuit of "a unified logic, a theory of inquiry" (p. 79). Through an understanding of these two general theories of inquiry, we aim to illuminate the place of theory within the complexities of inquiry which we have detailed above.

## Intricacies of researching and catering: abduction-deduction-induction as entwined stages of inquiring

### Inquiring as transforming

A key concern for Dewey and Peirce was how we think, how we inquire, and how we reason logically when confronted with an issue requiring some resolution. In this sense, the work of Peirce and Dewey informs both catering and researching. Dewey defined inquiry as "the controlled or directed transformation of an indeterminate situation into one that is so determinate in its constituent distinctions and relations as to convert the elements of the original situation into a unified whole" (1938, pp. 104–105). In basic terms, inquiry aims to deal with an issue (such as catering a meal for a hungry family or group of friends) so that it is no longer an issue. As such, inquiry enables and achieves a transformation. But how does this transformation occur? In short, what is the logic of inquiring?

Dewey articulated a mature version of his account of inquiry in *Logic: The Theory of Inquiry*, a book which was "a development of ideas regarding the nature of logical theory" (1938, p. iii). Adherents of Dewey will be aware that these ideas concerned him over much of his working life. They were first presented some forty years previously, "in *Studies in Logical Theory* [1903]", then "somewhat expanded in *Essays in Experimental Logic* [1916a]", and "briefly summarized with special reference to education in *How We Think* [1933, first edition 1910]" (Dewey, 1938, p. iii). In this summary, Dewey referred to "five phases, or aspects, of reflective thought" (1933, p. 107). These ideas were also briefly summarized in *Democracy and Education* (1916b, p. 176), where Dewey spoke of the "general features" of "reflective experience". Reflective thought and reflective experience were the same for Dewey, highlighting how he did not draw a distinction between experiencing and thinking. Juxtaposing both summaries reveals the continuity over time of Dewey's ideas on reflecting:

> (1) *suggestions*, in which the mind leaps forward to a possible solution; (2) an intellectualization of the difficulty or perplexity that has been *felt* (directly experienced) into a *problem* to be solved, a question for which the answer must be sought; (3) the use of one suggestion after another as a leading

**8** John Quay et al.

idea, or *hypothesis*, to initiate and guide observation and other operations in collection of factual material; (4) the mental elaboration of the idea or supposition as an idea or supposition (*reasoning*, in the sense in which reasoning is a part, not the whole, of inference); and (5) testing the hypothesis by overt or imaginative action.

*(Dewey, 1933, p. 107)*

(*i*) perplexity, confusion, doubt, due to the fact that one is implicated in an incomplete situation whose full character is not yet determined; (*ii*) a conjectural anticipation – a tentative interpretation of the given elements, attributing to them a tendency to effect certain consequences; (*iii*) a careful survey (examination, inspection, exploration, analysis) of all attainable consideration which will define and clarify the problem in hand; (*iv*) a consequent elaboration of the tentative hypothesis to make it more precise and more consistent, because squaring with a wider range of facts; (*v*) taking one stand upon the projected hypothesis as a plan of action which is applied to the existing state of affairs: doing something overtly to bring about the anticipated result, and thereby testing the hypothesis.

*(Dewey, 1916b, p. 176)*

The steps and phases Dewey identified in these summaries do not align perfectly, as they were published 17 years apart, yet they do reveal a marked continuation in his work, discernible in how, from beginning to end of an inquiry, inquiring is intent on transforming a situation via the generation and application of theory. Theory is here embraced as "hypo-thesis": a possibility which has yet to be confirmed as a "thesis" through adequate testing. However, this is not to say that inquiring must involve explicit identification of a particular hypothesis as is often the case in the natural sciences. Theory generation via hypotheses, plural, is the engine of inquiring; testing is when the rubber meets the road. Both inform each other.

### Inquiring as theory generation

Within the accounts of reflecting presented above, it is notable that Dewey saw a further distinction between two types of reflective experience, distinguished "according to the proportion of reflection found in them" (1916b, p. 169). The type with less reflection he called "trial and error method": "we simply do something, and when it fails, we do something else, and keep on trying till we hit upon something which works, and then we adopt that method as a rule-of-thumb measure in subsequent procedure" (pp. 169–170). He considered some experiences to "have very little else in them than this hit and miss or succeed process" (p. 170). However, this trial and error method neglected steps three and four in reflective experience, prompting Dewey to point out that "it is the extent and accuracy of steps three and four which mark off a distinctive reflective experience from one on the trial and error plane. They make *thinking* itself into an experience" (p. 176). Elsewhere Dewey framed this as "the distinction ... between what is experienced as the result of a minimum of incidental reflection and what is experienced in consequence of continued and regulated reflective inquiry" (1929, pp, 6–7). Taking a trial and error approach means that reflective experience moves from step two straight to step five, omitting steps three and four, those steps which embrace more focused reflecting. Dewey was clear that these steps "do not follow one another in set order" (1933, p. 115). In practice, there is a much more intricate to-ing and fro-ing occurring between and amongst the various "steps".

A consequence of this difference between two types of reflection can be seen in the generation of hypotheses. Hypotheses wrap facts up inside tentative ideas, derived imaginatively. Dewey referred to these as "suggested meanings" which "present themselves as the means of restoring unity, coherence and consistency to the particulars" (1922, p. 31). When involved in catering or researching, suggested meanings frequently emerge in response to the questions posed. For example, a child tells her father that she is hungry, prompting her father to check the time to see if it is, indeed, time for a meal. The father forms the preliminary hypothesis that he ought to prepare lunch and begins to imagine some possible meals that can be prepared quickly, with the ingredients and food preparation tools on hand, to satisfy his daughter's hunger and nutritional needs. The imagined meals are the ideas or hypotheses, wrapping up the facts of the situation coherently: the child's hunger, nutritional needs, the ingredients in the fridge, the food preparation tools available, and the fact that it is lunchtime. The imagined ideas (i.e. the possible meals to be created), if applied, could integrate all the facts and solve the issue at hand, transforming the fragmented, problematic experience into a coherent, meaningful whole.

Importantly, a hypothesis is not something one needs to consider only at the primary level of inquiry. Because of the interdependent nature of the various levels of inquiry, hypotheses are worked with in each level, connected with the questions that arise as one digs below the surface of the primary inquiry to the questions arising at secondary and tertiary levels (see Figure 1.1). Generation of hypotheses is thus a key aspect of any inquiry, arising throughout. Peirce recognised the importance of generating hypotheses as one of the "three stages of inquiry" (CP 6.469), which are comprised of "three kinds of reasoning" (CP 5.145): "abduction, deduction and induction ... the key of logic" (CP 2.98). While reasoning is often considered to be composed of induction and deduction alone, Peirce's insight revealed another form of reasoning he called abduction, which concerns the generation of, or the creation of, a hypothesis as the first stage of inquiry.[4] For Peirce, deduction tests a previously created hypothesis by elaborating on its conceivable meanings in thought, asking after the possibilities attributable to it; whereas induction tests a pre-existing hypothesis by applying it experimentally in the world, asking whether the claim to validity of the hypothesis can be justified. Both deduction and induction, according to Peirce, require a hypothesis to begin with, which is generated through abduction. It is worth noting that Dewey did not use the term abduction[5] and instead labelled this first stage of inquiry as "*inference*": the "process of arriving at an idea of what is absent on the basis of what is at hand" (1933, p. 95).

As mentioned above in Dewey's summaries, inference (or abduction – the generation of hypotheses) can be conducted more critically or less critically, with the less thorough version equating to trial and error. In the trial and error method of inquiring, generation of a hypothesis isn't a markedly critical process; the aim is to simply generate a hypothesis, almost any hypothesis, and to then pursue it as a possible solution. Hence, "one of the most marked differences between poor thinking and good thinking is the former's premature acceptance and assertion of suggested meanings" (Dewey, 1922, p. 31) or hypotheses; in contrast, "one of the marks of controlled thinking is postponement of such acceptance" (Dewey, 1922, p. 31). This postponement of acceptance in inference, or abduction, enables progress through steps three and four in Dewey's account of reflective experience before taking step five. Steps three and four engage more focused deliberation, offering a more rigorous approach because they "make *thinking* itself into an experience" (Dewey, 1916b, p. 176). The result is generation of hypotheses, or theories, characterised by a higher level of precision and consistency, because the facts are more extensively and exhaustively attended to when seeking a possible explanation.

Step four is deduction, Peirce's stage two of inquiry, and deduction works to support abduction. Dewey equates this step with "the process of developing the bearings – or, as they are more technically termed, the *implications* – of any idea with respect to any problem" (1910, p. 75). These implications arise from hypotheses which have been tested in thought for their possibilities in offering adequate responses. At this hypothetical stage, "meaning is only suggested", because "we hold it in suspense as a possibility rather than accept it as an actuality"; as such "the meaning is an *idea*" and thus "an idea … stands midway between assured understanding and mental confusion and bafflement" (Dewey, 1933, p. 132). Peirce's stage three of inquiry, induction, is step five in Dewey's account of reflective experience, taking thinking back to an engagement with what is at hand, through experimental testing in the world. This testing engages with facts, but facts which are now potentially transformed via a fresh theory.

This brief pragmatic outline of inquiry highlights its main features via an exploration of the synergies between the work of Peirce and Dewey in this area. However, further detail is required if these stages and steps are to be more fully comprehended, especially in relation to how they inform understanding of the place of theory in inquiry. It is important to again highlight that while both Dewey and Peirce have used process descriptors in order to convey how inquiry proceeds – terms such as steps, stages and phases – this does not mean that inquiry unfolds in a neat and orderly progression. The next sections in this chapter expand the treatment of each stage of inquiry, but do not intend to cement in place a unidirectional linear progression, as presented in Figure 1.2.

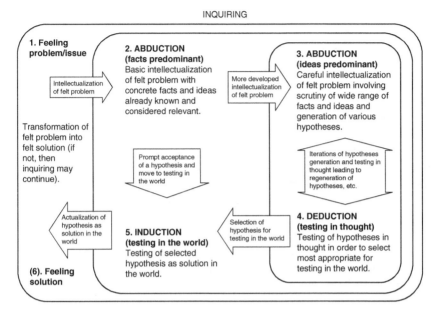

**FIGURE 1.2** A diagrammatic representation of the intricacies of inquiring bringing together the philosophical work of Peirce and Dewey. Note that Dewey did not mention a step 6, so this has been included in brackets.

## *Stage one of inquiring: abduction*

Like Dewey, Peirce saw the origin of inquiry in some perplexity, confusion or doubt. "Every inquiry whatsoever takes its rise in the observation ... of some surprising phenomenon, some experience which either disappoints an expectation, or breaks in upon some habit of expectation" (CP 6.469). It is this emotional state that engenders inquiry, propelling it forward toward generation of a hypothesis, a fresh theory or way of understanding. In this sense, catering only becomes an inquiry if it is not a habitual exercise. If catering a meal, say breakfast for the family, involves a very set and stable routine – every morning with the same foods, amounts, timing, setting of the table, etc. – the prevailing emotional state does not include surprise, perplexity, or confusion, and thus there is no perceived need for inquiry. Catering becomes inquiring when it is not routine, which may occur with the slightest change of habit or expectation, such as, perhaps, when someone expresses dislike for the food presented, or when one recognises that they are out of eggs which are needed to make the regular breakfast menu. An emotional state is aroused which is the starting point of an inquiry. Then "the inquiry begins with pondering these phenomena in all their aspects, in the search of some point of view whence the wonder shall be resolved" (CP 6.469). It should be noted again that such inquiring could follow a trial and error method, at least initially – such as merely substituting some different but accessible foods. If this is unsuccessful the unresolved issue and

**12** John Quay et al.

further inquiry may involve more focused reflecting, perhaps involving discussions, to generate further facts and hypotheses.

The beginning of inquiry in pondering – characterised by wonder and engagement with the phenomena or facts that are seen to comprise the issue – is, for Peirce, a form of reasoning: it is abduction, the first stage of inquiry. Wonder is thus another emotional state that may lead to inquiring, beginning as pondering. In pondering, "abduction makes its start from the facts, without, at the outset, having any particular theory in view, though it is motivated by the feeling that a theory is needed to explain the surprising facts" (CP 7.218). Abduction searches for a possible explanation, a hypothesis, a tentative theory, one that is better than whatever understanding might have been in place before. Thus "in abduction the consideration of the facts suggests the hypothesis", and in this way "abduction seeks a theory" (CP 7.218) to better explain the situation. The aim of abduction is to draw the facts of the situation together in a meaningful way, as a hypothesis. Peirce described the experience of abduction as consisting of "the whole series of mental performances between the notice of the wonderful phenomenon and the acceptance of the hypothesis" (CP 6.469), which could then be tested via deduction and then induction:

> The search for pertinent circumstances and the laying hold of them, sometimes without our cognizance, the scrutiny of them, the dark laboring, the bursting out of the startling conjecture, the remarking of its smooth fitting to the anomaly, as it is turned back and forth like a key in a lock, and the final estimation of its plausibility.
>
> *(CP 6.469)*

This labouring with the facts in search of a theory is built on the "hope that, although the possible explanations of our facts may be strictly innumerable, yet our mind will be able, in some finite number of guesses, to guess the sole true explanation of them" (CP 7.219). Peirce recognised that a person "before whom a scientific problem is placed immediately begins to make guesses, not wildly remote from the true guess" (CP 2.86). Hence his belief that "the human mind is akin to the truth in the sense that in a finite number of guesses it will light upon the correct hypothesis" (CP 7.220). These guesses, however, are aimed at achieving the purposes of the inquiry. And abduction thus comes to a head when "a conjecture arises that furnishes a possible explanation", enabling "the inquirer … to regard his [sic] conjecture, or hypothesis, with favour", thereby holding it "to be plausible" (CP 6.469).

The importance of abduction as the source of explanation, theory, hypothesis, or meaning is underlined by Peirce's claim that "all the ideas of science come to it by the way of abduction" (CP 5.145). Philosopher of science Norwood Russell Hanson, drawing on Peirce's work, also employs a culinary analogy to describe the importance of abduction to the generation of a hypothesis in science. The meal Hanson has in mind incorporates the meat of a hare as the main ingredient. Referring to the (historically) popular *Mrs Beeton's Book of Household Management*, published in 1861, Hanson noted that "Mrs Beeton's recipes begin with the hare as given" (1958, p. 72). His point is that some recipes of the day assumed the hare as given, as sitting ready on the kitchen table, akin to when a hypothesis is accepted as already given in some understandings of researching. But, of course, the hare must be caught before the meal preparation can progress, as the hypothesis must be generated before the researching can advance. Highlighting this difference, Hanson observed that "a preliminary instruction in many cookery books … reads 'First catch your hare'" ( 1958, p. 72). Drawing on this correspondence of "catching" in both situations, Hanson suggests that "the ingenuity, tenacity, imagination and conceptual boldness which has marked physics since Galileo shows itself more clearly in hypothesis-catching than in the deductive elaboration of caught hypotheses" (1958, p. 72). Such hypothesis-catching is abduction, which is required as the first stage of inquiry, before deduction or induction can become involved.

## *Stage two of inquiring: deduction*

"Abduction having suggested a theory" (CP 8.209) – one that is accepted as plausible, but which is still an idea – a move to stage two of inquiry is needed, because "the hypothesis must be tested" (CP 6.470). And the first phase of testing is deduction. In this stage "we employ deduction to deduce from that ideal theory [arrived at via abduction] a promiscuous variety of consequences to the effect that if we perform certain acts we shall find ourselves confronted with certain experiences" (CP 8.209). Dewey referred to these consequences as *implications* (1910, p. 75) of the idea, if applied to the problematic situation. Thus, a basic sentence stem of deductive reasoning may be something like: "Given this hypothesis, then the possible implications include: …". For example, when deciding on a menu for a weekend family lunch, one concern may be the location. The hypothesis generated via abduction is that lunch with the extended family *could* be a picnic in a city park. In order to evaluate how effective this hypothesis might be, possible implications of applying it need to be considered, which involves drawing on the relevant facts. For example, someone would need to organize who is bringing what dishes and what crockery and cutlery (which may or may not be simple, depending on the other people involved); Elizabeth could bring drinks (as she is not a very good cook); the menu would need to cope with the weather forecast (hot day expected), which means an ice box will probably be needed; those preparing the food will need to remember that gluten free dishes are required (as Grandma is gluten intolerant); someone may need to get there early to secure a good spot in the park with a table in the shade (as it could be busy); etc. This deductive reasoning extends understanding of the hypothesis: developing it, expanding it, explaining it.

The shift from stage one (abduction) to stage two (deduction) of inquiry is thus from: (1) reasoning with the phenomena, the limited initial facts, in order to find some meaning, or a hypothesis, to (2) reasoning with a hypothesis, a theory, by way of its implications and possibilities, opening up awareness of further facts in an "examination of the hypothesis, and a muster of all sorts of conditional experiential consequences which would follow from its truth" (CP 6.470). Hence this is "reasoning concerning probabilities" (CP 5.145). In short, deductive reasoning with a hypothesis can lead to identification of further relevant facts and hypotheses or further growth of the hypothesis in question.

Dewey was very aware that such reasoning depends "upon the store of knowledge" (1933, p. 111) of those conducting the inquiry. "And this depends not only upon the prior experience and special education" of this individual or group, "but also upon the state of culture and science of the age and place" (Dewey, 1933, p. 111). In other words, deductive reasoning "depends upon what is already known and upon the facilities that exist for communicating knowledge and for making it a public, open resource" (Dewey, 1933, p. 112). For example, in the picnic situation above, someone with prior experience of organising picnics will do a much better job of considering all the implications of holding the picnic – i.e. they can perform the deduction associated with this abduction better than someone who has little knowledge of picnics. This highlights the importance of accessing other sources of knowledge when deductively testing the implications of a hypothesis. Deduction thus works with abduction to enable generation of a more plausible hypothesis.

The movement between abduction and deduction is a move from reasoning with the facts to generate ideas and eventually a plausible idea, to then testing that hypothesis by reasoning with the possible implications that accrue to it – and in the process identifying further relevant facts and improving or dismissing the hypothesis. Both are necessary. Hence Dewey's position that "data (facts) and ideas (suggestions, possible solutions) … form the two indispensable and correlative factors in all reflective activity" (1933, p. 104). It is important to recognise that the movement between abduction and deduction, involving both facts and ideas, is not unidirectional. Deduction can lead to further abduction in an interplay involving multiple iterations that improves the hypotheses in question, enabling deduction of the one "most plausible" hypothesis. In the picnic example above, the process of deduction may lead an inquirer to adjust their original hypothesis by imagining a barbeque in the back garden as easier logistically and more accommodating of everyone's needs. Peirce therefore aligns deduction – because it is primarily working with hypotheses, with suggested meanings, with ideas – with "the reasoning of mathematics" (CP 5.145). Another stage is required to move beyond ideas to ascertain "how far those consequents accord with experience, and of judging accordingly whether the hypothesis is sensibly correct, or requires some inessential modification, or must be entirely rejected" (CP 6.472); a move that takes inquiry into its third stage, another phase of testing, that of induction.

### *Stage three of inquiring: induction*

Where abduction reasons from facts in search of a theory, in a form of reasoning Peirce described as "after all, nothing but guessing" (CP 7.219), and deduction

Locating theory in research **15**

tests a theory via its possible implications in thought, induction reasons from a theory back to facts by testing this theory experimentally. Thus Dewey argued that "we never get wholly beyond the trial and error situation" (1916b, p. 177) because a hypothesis must always face the trial of experiment; "our most elaborate and rationally consistent thought has to be tried in the world and thereby tried out" (1916b, p. 177). Peirce similarly claimed that "induction is the experimental testing of a theory" (CP 5.145). "In induction the study of the hypothesis suggests the experiments which bring to light the very facts to which the hypothesis had pointed" (CP 7.218). Thus, the basic sentence stem of inductive reasoning may be something like: "Given this selected hypothesis, then a test of its suitability would be …".

Remember that this hypothesis may not have been tested in deductive reasoning, as the proponent of inquiry may be attempting to resolve the issue via trial and error method. In the example of the family picnic lunch, with no deductive reasoning, the experiment may be to simply have a go: just arrange a menu for a picnic lunch that might work. But having been through a phase of deductive reasoning, there may be multiple forms of experiment which can attest to the validity of the selected hypothesis. One experiment may be to ask around to see if anyone might volunteer to organize who will bring what dishes; if no one is willing, then the hypothesis – that the lunch on Saturday with the extended family *could* be a picnic in a city park – is placed in doubt. Another experiment might be to try out the gluten free pasta salad recipe for dinner at home beforehand to see if it tastes good and is likely to satisfy Grandma. However, other experiments could also be undertaken to test this hypothesis, and these could also succeed. "We then proceed to try these experiments", Peirce acknowledged, "and if the predictions of the theory are verified, we have a proportionate confidence that the experiments that remain to be tried [as in, any other experiments devised] will [also] confirm the theory" (CP 8.209). In short, induction "sets out with a theory and it measures the degree of concordance of that theory with fact" (CP 5.145). The key point here is that such concordance may not be complete or universal, but may be contingent. Such "measuring" to ascertain this degree of truth positions induction as "the concluding step" (CP 7.218) in inquiry.

It is not beyond probability that this step may deny a suitable degree of concordance of the theory with fact, thereby falsifying the hypothesis and classing the inquiry as a failure. Yet, as Dewey recognised:

> A great advantage of possession of the habit of reflective activity is that failure is not *mere* failure. It is instructive. For a failure indicates … what further observations should be made. It suggests … what modifications should be introduced in the hypothesis.
>
> *(1933, p. 114)*

Like deduction, induction is working with abduction. All three stages of inquiry are entwined and are intent on generation of theory.

## Judgments of researching and catering: methodologies, cuisines and theoretical frameworks

Up to this point we have focused on raising awareness of the *complexities* inherent to working with three levels of inquiry, as well as the *intricacies* of abduction, deduction and induction operating within these levels to generate and test theories. Such drilling down into the details, aimed at locating theory, presents a challenge to comprehending researching and catering that can appear quite daunting. Yet such attention to detail also illuminates the source (not sources, plural) of the coherence that binds all aspects of a research project or a catering enterprise together, so that each (complexity and intricacy) can be approached with a greater degree of understanding and confidence. One way of comprehending this source is flagged by Dewey and Peirce in the origins of inquiry: in "feeling" (see Figure 1.2), of which we shall say more later in this section. Another way, not separate from feeling, was alluded to in our first section of this chapter on the complexities of researching and catering. Here the coherence lay in the who question that characterized the primary level inquiry: "Who is the meal being catered by and for?" and "Who is the issue being researched by and for?". The tertiary level who question *situates* the primary level inquiry in the relevant context. "Who" and "feeling" come together as the source for this coherence.

Beginning with the who question, identification of the specific people who comprise this "who" is quite concrete. These are the particular family or friends for whom the meal is being catered, and also includes those doing the catering. They are the specific stakeholders for whom the issue is being researched, as well as those doing the researching. Yet these people can be positioned within larger identifiable social groupings revealing shared characteristics, especially those characteristics that inform and condition the *judgments* members of this social group will tend to make when involved in an inquiry. As Hans-Georg Gadamer argued, this is "why the prejudices of the individual, far more than his [sic] judgments, constitute the historical reality of his being" (1989, pp. 276–277). But then how do these prejudices or pre-judgments work? Here we enlist Wittgenstein's discussion of aesthetic judgment:

> The words we call expressions of aesthetic judgment play a very complicated role, but a very definite role, in what we call a culture of a period. To describe their use or to describe what you mean by a cultured taste, you have to describe a culture.
>
> *(Wittgenstein, 1966, p. 8)*

Aesthetic judgment is always pre-informed by socially and culturally derived prejudices; and social and cultural prejudices have their aesthetic judgment. "Feeling" and "who" come together in this way. It is worth pointing out that aesthetic does not here simply refer to beauty or other artistic categorizations. The etymology of the word aesthetic lies in the Greek *aisthesis*, which means perception. Hence,

Locating theory in research **17**

judgment in a catering situation relates to perception of flavors, achieved via taste or "cultured taste" (Wittgenstein, 1996, p. 8). Taste, involving prejudice, informs and conditions the judgments that discern flavors. The menu and dishes must fulfil flavor expectations, as judged via taste. Catering and researching expectations thus rest on complexes of shared "agreements in judgment", as Cavell (1979, p. 359) put it; agreements that must be continually re-affirmed by the social and cultural group that enacts them, which, on occasion, calls for revisions or outright rejection. One might see these agreements in judgment as securing a particular culinary tradition and the development over time of a corresponding set of stable and identifiable methods and practices, and even a set of legitimate, prescribed or canonical ingredients. In culinary language this points to cuisines, as highlighted by sociologist Priscilla Parkhurst Ferguson:

> The cornerstone of culinary discourse and the discipline that it represents is cuisine – the code that structures the practice of food and allows us to discuss and to represent taste. Cuisine places culinary practices in a social context by sharing the experience of taste in an idiom that allows articulation of the present and reproduction in the future.... Cuisine specifies the conditions between the general and the particular as it negotiates the gap between collective taste and idiosyncratic tastes. Above all, by socializing appetite and taste, cuisine turns the individual relationship with food into a collective bond.
>
> *(Parkhurst Ferguson, 2004, pp. 18–19)*

Cuisines express a style or manner of culinary practice associated with taste. The who question is then not only referring to a grouping of particular individuals, but also the nature of their social and cultural cohesion, which informs the generation of hypotheses. A cuisine, as a style or manner, is a way of being someone, a way of doing something, and a way of knowing something or someone. In research terms a cuisine is synonymous with a methodology. In fact, we can show the similarities here between catering and researching by replacing culinary words in the above paragraph with research words:

> The cornerstone of *research* discourse and the discipline that it represents is *methodology* – the code that structures the practice of *researching* and allows us to discuss and to represent *judgment*. *Methodology* places *research* practices in a social context by sharing the experience of *judging* in an idiom that allows articulation of the present and reproduction in the future.... *Methodology* specifies the conditions between the general and the particular as it negotiates the gap between collective *judgment* and idiosyncratic *judgments*. Above all, by socializing *inclination* and *judgment*, *methodology* turns the individual relationship with *research* into a collective bond.

Cuisines function in catering as methodologies function in researching. Both situate specific "whats" and "hows" in a "who" as a system of theories and practices which frame understanding. Cuisines and methodologies can in this sense be understood as "whos"; constituting, as Gadamer highlighted, the prejudices of judgments. Agreements in judgment are aesthetic or perceptual prejudices which define the conditions of membership to a particular "who" and the values shared. Cuisines are often named for social and cultural groups, such as people from a particular region or religion – like Italian cuisine or Buddhist cuisine. Such regions can be much more specific than nation states however, such as Cajun cuisine or Sami cuisine. Cuisines can also develop from mixtures of cuisines, such as Malaysian-Chinese cuisine. As well as geographies, cuisines have histories, philosophies, biologies, ecologies, and, of course, politics and economics. In her study of the evolution of cuisines, Rachel Laudan remarks on how "the creation of new cuisines followed adoption of new culinary philosophies" which "came from new ideas about politics and economics, religion, the human body, and the environment" (2013, p. 6).

Similarly, methodologies can be traced to particular social and cultural groups, being developed by people and thus having their own histories, geographies, philosophies, biologies, ecologies, politics, and economics. Indeed, Michael Apple draws attention to the unobtrusive and hence largely hidden influence of social ideologies in this regard (see Chapter 3). Such influence is "hegemonic" in that these social ideologies dominate thinking, values and beliefs, without an explicit awareness that they are shaping the making of judgments, as they are embedded in an aesthetic as prejudices. This hegemonic work is conducted covertly with "whats" and "hows" such that development of a distinctive "who" is an outcome, as a system of coherent theories and practices. Hegemony can be made visible by highlighting issues of gender, as Nel Noddings argues (see Chapter 7), and race, as Penny Enslin attests (see Chapter 5). Richard Pring and Gert Biesta both point out that in education research this hegemony commonly involves conceptions of what education is or is not (see Chapters 9 and 4 respectively).

Yet such boundaries are not fixed for all time, as Michael Peters argues in terms of "openness" (see Chapter 8). Whilst traditionalists might try to hold on to set ways of doing things, the more adventurous continue to explore culinary fusions (e.g., TexMex, Yoshoku) or establish new territories (e.g., molecular gastronomy). The possibility for plurality, evolution and novelty in culinary practices and products derives from an understanding that establishing, hybridizing, re-affirming and contesting cuisines relies upon a higher level of abstraction, one that in research would correspond to a theoretical or philosophical tradition that informs one's research practice. In the realm of catering this shows up as recognition of the "aesthetic experience" (Dewey, 1950) of consuming and preparing food. Beyond the point of fulfilling a brute biological need for nutrition – the intake of calories, pure and simple – our sensual, perceptual, affectual and embodied relationships with food point to an aesthetic necessity that shapes what we do in preparing and partaking of meals.

No one who undertakes research and reflects upon its personal significance or its significance for others would fail to recognize the aesthetic dimension of

Locating theory in research **19**

research. Without awareness of it, there is merely the instrumental application of methods and techniques. Aesthetic experience brings the origin of aesthetic judgment – in bodies, perceptions and experiences – back into the field of what constitutes research. In fact, the revolutions and evolutions in education research over the past century attest to the need to give such aesthetic experience greater or lesser prominence in what we claim is the proper orientation toward the world – that is, the degree to which our judgments are attuned to the world appropriately in an objective, subjective, narrative, symbolic, archaeological or other mode. This is captured in John Hattie's insistence on the primacy of stories and interpretations: the need to take the aesthetic experience of research seriously (see Chapter 6). Likewise, we can read in Paul Smeyers' work the invitation to understand the broad aesthetic that prevails in the academy today and the aesthetic that it has displaced (see Chapter 10).

It is for this reason, perhaps, that the aesthetic experience of research – the feeling of profound necessity that drives us to undertake research, which itself is synonymous with theories and philosophies – is so elusive and so easy to ignore. Such aesthetic experience is grasped via a cuisine or methodology, expressive of aesthetic judgment, but its intellectual comprehension lies in a theoretical framework that elucidates the way the ideas come together coherently. As Peter Roberts argues in Chapter 2 of this book, "'theory' precedes 'method' in the sense that all methods presuppose a certain orientation to the world" (p. 30). He therefore claims that "a 'theoretical framework' is more than a 'methodology'" (p. 30), pointing to the significance of the who question in comprehending theory:

> A theoretical framework provides a lens through which to pose problems, address questions, and analyse data, but it is not merely a means toward these ends. If we take seriously the notion of working with theory as discussed in the first part of this chapter, we will also have a concern with the *theorists* who inform a framework. We will want to know something of their lives, their contexts, their struggles. If we engage their ideas deeply, we form a kind of intellectual relationship with theorists, regardless of whether we "agree" or "disagree" with them.
>
> *(Roberts, Chapter 2, pp. 30–31)*

Comprehension of a theoretical framework involves history, geography, philosophy, biology, ecology, politics and economics, because theory is a creation emerging from discourse amongst people, perhaps crossing centuries and many borders. The dialogues presented in this book offer insight into the work of particular theorists who have grappled with issues in education emanating from their own histories, geographies, philosophies, biologies, ecologies, politics and economics. This grappling suggests that a theoretical framework is not simply "chosen" by a researcher as if from a supermarket shelf of possibilities. While some of the theories mentioned may be considered more suitable for investigating certain phenomena than others, theory is never finished or complete as it is continually being renegotiated. To some

**20** John Quay et al.

extent, every thesis remains a hypothesis. As Lyn Yates argues in Chapter 11 of this book, every research argument (thesis) both challenges and reinforces understandings of theory:

> A good thesis which works with theory or theories should end up not only using those theories to focus and provide ways of making progress and critical perspective, but with something to say about those theories (their adequacy, their limitations, what else might be needed).
>
> *(Yates, Chapter 11, p. 165)*

While a theory may enable us to set a particular research endeavor within a frame so that it can be comprehended, every attempt to do so further positions and problematizes that theory, developing it further in specific ways and directions and thus contributing to the various associated discourses. Theories situate because they are positioned in ever changing historical, geographical, philosophical, biological, ecological, political and economic contexts. This points to the challenge of engaging with and developing theory. It is not the case that a theoretical framework is decided upon and implemented at the beginning of any research project, as we have shown via the complexities, intricacies and judgments involved in inquiry. Theory must be grappled with at each level of inquiry – primary, secondary and tertiary – via abduction, deduction and induction, acknowledging the need to "rethink some of the ideas with which we started as those ideas are put to the test, either empirically or via the development of an argument" (Roberts, Chapter 2, p. 30).

This book draws together accounts from noted education theorists with the express aim of further exposing the importance of theory and how to engage with it. The chapters we have helped craft in dialogue with Michael Apple, Gert Biesta, Penny Enslin, John Hattie, Nel Noddings, Michael Peters, Richard Pring, and Paul Smeyers each offer history, geography, philosophy, and politics – implicating economics, biology and ecology – highlighting the way theory has been generated in approaches to the particular issues of education that have gripped these people. In these chapters a wide range of theories and theorists are discussed, such as critical theory, pragmatism, feminism, liberalism, care theory, Marxism and neo-Marxism, post-colonialism, poststructuralism, logical positivism, genealogy, etc. These names may seem to suggest neat pigeonholes, but in actuality they are characterised by shared notions and often subtle distinctions, like cuisines. Chapters from Peter Roberts and Lyn Yates bookend these dialogue chapters, drawing theories together with theorists to offer further insights into how theory and philosophy contribute to education research. Our hope is that all the chapters in this book, including this current chapter, support improved understanding of the place of theory in research, making researching in education a more open and accessible task, just like catering a shared meal for family or friends.

## Notes

1 A narrative investigation of this positioning of graduate researchers is undertaken in Stolz & Ozolins (forthcoming).

Locating theory in research  **21**

2 For further theoretical and philosophical exposition of the relation between what, how and who, please see Quay (2013, 2015).
3 "CP" with volume and section numbers follows a recognized reference convention for citing text in the *Collected Papers of Charles Sanders Peirce*. See reference list.
4 There are many philosophical accounts of reasoning, of which Peirce's is one and Dewey's another. They are brought together here in their complementarity, although they are not identical.
5 "It should first be admitted that Dewey, though acknowledging his intellectual debt to Peirce, does not actually use either the term 'abduction' or 'abductive inference' in any of his writings on logic. Still, the presence of the activity these terms are invoked to represent is unmistakable in Dewey's approach to logic" (Marcio, 2001, p. 102).

## References

Arendt, H. (1978). *The life of the mind*. San Diego, CA: Harcourt.

Beeton, S. O. (1861). *Mrs Beeton's book of household management*. London: S. O. Beeton Publishing.

Cavell, S. (1979). *The claim of reason: Wittgenstein, skepticism, morality and tragedy*. Oxford, UK: Oxford University Press.

Dewey, J. (1903). *Studies in logical theory*. Chicago, IL: The University of Chicago Press.

Dewey, J. (1910). *How we think*. Boston, MA: D. C. Heath & Co.

Dewey, J. (1916a). *Essays in experimental logic*. New York: Dover Publications.

Dewey, J. (1916b). *Democracy and education*. New York: The Free Press.

Dewey, J. (1922). An analysis of reflective thought. *The Journal of Philosophy*, *19*(2), 29–38.

Dewey, J. (1929). *Experience and nature* (2nd edn.). Chicago, IL: Open Court Publishing.

Dewey, J. (1933). *How we think: A restatement of the relation of reflective thinking to the educative process* (rev. edn.). Boston, MA: D. C. Heath and Company.

Dewey, J. (1938). *Logic: The theory of inquiry*. New York: Holt, Rinehart and Winston.

Dewey, J. (1950). Aesthetic experience as a primary phase and as artistic development. *Journal of Aesthetics and Art Criticism*, *9*, 56–58.

Gadamer, H. G. (1989). *Truth and method* (2nd, rev. edn.). New York: Continuum.

Hanson, N. R. (1958). *Patterns of discovery: An inquiry into the conceptual foundations of science*. London: Cambridge University Press.

Kuhn, T. S. (1970). *The structure of scientific revolutions* (2nd edn.). Chicago, IL: University of Chicago Press.

Laudan, R. (2013). *Cuisine and empire: Cooking in world history*. Berkeley, CA: University of California Press.

Marcio, J. J. (2001). Abductive inference, design science, and Dewey's theory of inquiry. *Transactions of the Charles S. Peirce Society*, *37*(1), 97–121.

Parkhurst Ferguson, P. (2004). *Accounting for taste: The triumph of French cuisine*. Chicago, IL: University of Chicago Press.

Peirce, C. S. (1931–1935; 1958) Collected Papers of Charles Sanders Peirce (Vol. 1–6, C. Hartshorne and P. Weiss, Eds.; Vol. 7–8, A. Burks, Ed.). Cambridge, MA: Harvard University Press. [Cited as CP.]

Popper, K. (1976). *Unended quest: An intellectual autobiography*. London: Routledge.

Pring, R. (2015). *Philosophy of educational research* (3rd edn.). London: Bloomsbury Publishing.

Quay, J. (2013). *Education, experience and existence: Engaging Dewey, Peirce and Heidegger*. London: Routledge.

Quay, J. (2015). *Understanding life in school: From academic classroom to outdoor education*. New York: Palgrave Macmillan.

Roberts, P. (2018). Theory as research: philosophical work in education. In Quay, J., Bleazby, J., Stolz, S.A., Toscano, M. & Scott Webster, R. (Eds.). *Theory and philosophy in education research: Methodological dialogues.* (pp. 23–35). London: Routledge.

Stolz, S. A. & Ozolins, J. T. (forthcoming). A narrative approach exploring philosophy in education and educational research. *Educational Studies.* Advance online publication. doi: 10.1080/03055698.2017.1388215.

Wittgenstein, L. (1966). Lectures on aesthetics. In C. Barrett (Ed.). *Lectures and conversations on aesthetics, psychology and religious belief.* (pp. 1–36). Oxford, UK: Basil Blackwell.

Yates, L. (2018). Becoming a good education researcher. In Quay, J., Bleazby, J., Stolz, S.A., Toscano, M. & Scott Webster, R. (Eds.). *Theory and philosophy in education research: Methodological dialogues.* (pp. 158–168). London: Routledge.

# 2

# THEORY AS RESEARCH

## Philosophical work in education

*Peter Roberts*

### Introduction

This chapter sets questions pertaining to theory, philosophy and research in their broader contexts. Beginning with brief reflections on the meaning and significance of key terms, I argue for a shift from "theory *and* research" to "theory *as* research" in education. I stress the importance of ideas and intellectual kinship in pushing back against the dominant policy trends of our time, ask how we might make philosophy of education a way of life, and explore some of the possible consequences of serious engagement with theory. This chapter also considers some of the practical dimensions of the research process, with particular attention to methods, methodologies and theoretical frameworks. I conclude with a few remarks on the value of expanding the range of sources we consult in addressing philosophical and educational questions.

### From "theory *and* research" to "theory *as* research"

Many years ago, I was asked as a young scholar what I was doing in my thesis. I explained that I was focusing on the educational philosophy of Paulo Freire and commented briefly on the questions I was addressing and the argument I was developing. It was, I recall, a congenial conversation, near the end of which my interlocutor inquired: "But are you doing any research?" I was somewhat ill-prepared to respond at the time, but I now see this as an early signal of a problem that persists to the present day. In Education, as in many other fields of study, we often assume that theoretical or philosophical work is merely preparatory to, supplementary to, or a way of making sense of, what really matters: the data gathered through empirical research (cf. Standish, 2001). To work with theory, it seems, is somehow not "real" research. Acknowledgement may be made of the importance of a well-developed theoretical framework in informing the methodology of an investigation or in analysing data, but engaging and applying theory in this manner is often distinguished from, and accorded a different status than, the "research itself." In short, we tend to talk of theory *and* research; what is needed is an approach that recognises theory *as* research. The difference between these two ways of thinking about "theory" and "research" is not merely a matter of language, it is also a question of what we value and why (cf. Bridges, 2003; Suissa, 2007). More than this, it has to do with the ontology that guides our work as researchers; how we understand research depends on how we understand ourselves.

Books on research methodology are among the most popular produced by academic publishers, and often go through multiple editions.[1] While some texts are devoted principally to the "how to" of research (and will often be cited by postgraduate students in the "Methodology" sections of their theses), others are concerned more with debates over the nature of research (e.g., Bridges & Smith, 2007; Reid, Hart & Peters, 2014). The field of Education, more than many other areas of inquiry, has long been characterised by tensions and divisions between different groups of researchers. These differences are sometimes depicted as a battle between quantitative and qualitative paradigms. While there is no denying the fact that such conceptual and methodological differences exist, the divide between quantitative and qualitative investigation is, in Richard Pring's words, ultimately a "false dualism" (2015, p. 67). Quantitative research relies upon qualitative understanding (Alexander, 2014, p. 13), and qualitative inquiry will also sometimes employ statistics and figures to support an argument. A somewhat narrower way of capturing what is under dispute is to see this as a divide between empirical and theoretical research. That, too, is not without its problems. All theory, we might say, is informed by the empirical "data" generated through human experience. At the same time, all forms of empirical investigation pre-suppose, and draw upon, implied or explicit theories. And, of course, philosophical and empirical work can be deliberately combined.[2] Whatever approach is taken – whether quantitative or qualitative, theoretical or empirical – research is not simply any form of inquiry; it is, as Stenhouse argued more than three decades ago, "*systematic inquiry made public*" (cited in Biesta & Burbules, 2003, p. 70).

In examining the nature of educational inquiry, the terms "theory" and "philosophy" are sometimes used interchangeably. "Theory" is the more expansive of the two terms, but there are no rigid boundaries between the theorising philosophers of education engage in and that undertaken by, say, sociologists of education. Avoiding a sharp distinction between the two is consistent with the growing diversity of voices in philosophy of education, where many who may not initially have seen themselves as part of this international community have made important contributions (Roberts, 2015a). To be a little more precise, however, we might say that a focus on *philosophies* suggests a concern not merely with theory in and of itself but with something more holistic: a philosophical worldview with ontological, epistemological and ethical dimensions, together with an interest in *philosophers* (their contexts, their lives, their connections with other thinkers, their bodies of

Theory as research **25**

work). Theory as research of this kind does not separate the thinker from what is thought. This is in keeping with the approach adopted by Miguel de Unamuno, who, in reflecting on the ideas of Spinoza, deliberately referred to him as the "the *man* Benedict Spinoza" (1972, p. 9, emphasis added). Unamuno's point was that if we are to understand the philosophy, we must begin with the philosopher – a human being who, like the rest of us, must struggle with his or her faults and frailties and whose thought is inextricably linked with the particulars of his or her time and circumstances.

It must be remembered also that our interest here is not just in "philosophy" or "philosophers" but in "philosophies of *education*," and this implies something more again. Work in this domain has a direct or indirect concern with teaching and/or learning, and with processes of human formation; it is necessarily non-neutral; and it is practical as well as theoretical (Griffiths, 1998; O'Toole & Beckett, 2013). Philosophy of education is not simply a "branch" of philosophy or a form of "applied philosophy." Seeing oneself as an educationist implies a form of ethical commitment that need not be there for a philosopher. There is, moreover, no "branch" of philosophy *not* relevant to philosophy of education (Standish, 2007, p. 162).[3] The title of this chapter refers to philosophical *work* in education, and this too is worth emphasising. Philosophical inquiry is difficult and demanding. It requires effort and persistence, and it is often uncomfortable. In undertaking philosophical activity as educationists, we work not only on research problems, questions and projects but also *on ourselves*. Work of this kind is not easily "contained"; it is seldom finite and it refuses to be cleanly separated from other parts of human life. To take this task seriously, then, is no easy matter and we must be prepared to live with the existential consequences of our philosophical endeavours.

## Policy, politics and educational research

The multidisciplinary nature of Education as a field of inquiry is potentially one of its great strengths. Realising that potential, however, is not merely a question of epistemology; it is also a matter of *politics*. How we understand education, and ourselves as educational researchers (or not), can, for example, have a significant bearing on funding decisions (cf. Yates, 2012). Research never occurs in a vacuum. We are shaped in our research activities by the policies and politics of our time. Policy never fully *determines* what we do, but it does have an important bearing on how we understand and engage in research, why we do so, and for whom. Differences between policies in the degree to which, and ways in which, they shape conceptions and practices of educational research are not simply the result of chance. Processes of policy development, interpretation and application are often typified not by harmony and consensus, but by struggle and contestation. No one can escape from the policy net; it entangles us all. For this reason, among others, critical engagement with policy remains a key task for educational researchers (see further: Gale, 2003; McLaughlin, 2000).

The key role that policy plays in shaping conceptions and practices of research is especially evident when the dominant policy narrative of our time – neoliberalism – is examined. For more than three decades, neoliberal ideas have exerted a powerful influence over higher education and research policy (Giroux, 2002; Ozga, Popkewitz & Seddon, 2006; Roberts & Peters, 2008). Neoliberalism has taken different forms in different contexts over time (Harvey, 2005). Elements of neoliberal policy and politics particularly relevant to the work of educational researchers include the dominance of economic goals, the commodification of knowledge, the logic of performativity, a prevailing ethos of competition, and the emphasis on marketing and "branding." These features of contemporary neoliberal life are consistent with the broad trends identified by Lyotard in his classic work, *The Postmodern Condition* (1984). They are exemplified in a number of specific policy developments, including the growth of research assessment regimes, such as the Research Assessment Exercise (2008) and Research Excellence Framework (2014) in the United Kingdom, the Excellence in Research for Australia evaluation framework (Australian Research Council, 2015), and the Performance-Based Research Fund (Tertiary Education Commission, 2016) in New Zealand. This is an "age of measurement" (Biesta, 2009), where the obsession with performance, rankings, and comparisons has exerted a significant influence on how and why educational researchers go about their work.

Research has increasingly been driven by, and largely reduced to, the language of "outputs." Performance-based research funding schemes have promoted both a form of individualism and a kind of conformity (Roberts, 2013). In pitting one researcher against another and fostering a spirit of academic self-promotion, they uphold the individualistic values that are central to neoliberal philosophy. At the same time, by creating rather rigid, standardised systems for categorising, capturing and evaluating research activity, they encourage a certain conformity. All aspects of research, from the publication of books and articles to the mentoring of colleagues, must, if they are to count in performance-based assessment exercises, ultimately be reconfigured as "outputs." Academics, thesis students, and others involved in the research process sometimes end up being seen this way: as measurable outputs in a system focused not on knowledge, research relationships or research cultures but on measured *performance*. The rankings generated by such systems come to define the worth of the researcher and the activities in which he or she engages. Research assessment regimes are just one example of how, under neoliberalism, there is too little trust in academics and too much trust in systems of performance management and measurement (Woelert & Yates, 2014).

In working environments structured by the logic of performativity, celebrating the *immeasurability* of much that matters in education, and in educational research, becomes a subversive act. Indeed, the very notion of taking philosophical work in education seriously can be seen as a form of implied resistance against the dominant policy trends of our time. There is, however, no one best way to "push back." Here I want to stress the importance of a sense of community and connection in helping us to see the world otherwise. The notion of *intellectual kinship* encapsulates what I have in mind.[4] Intellectual kinship is a key ingredient in building strong scholarly communities. Collegiality, not competition, is the ethical glue that holds such communities together. Kindred spirits in a research community, like kinfolk in an extended family, can "fight" with one another, but tensions can sometimes be helpful in allowing thought to advance. Intellectual kinship, by returning us to the roots of academic life, is a "radical" concept. It suggests a coming together of scholars (these days, this might be virtually), with some kind of common purpose but also with a respect for difference and constructive debate.

*Ideas* are central to intellectual kinship. In pushing back against neoliberalism, ideas are not enough on their own, but they still matter in today's world – perhaps more than ever. Ideas provide the connecting points that allow us to build and sustain intellectual communities across generations. There is no single, universally accepted definition of an "intellectual," and job advertisements that read "intellectuals wanted" are rare! Intellectuals need not work in universities or other tertiary education institutions; they may occupy any number of different roles in a society. But most accounts of what it means to be an intellectual involve some reference to ideas, and if ideas are to be nurtured, nourished and tested, connections with others are vital. There are numerous examples from across the centuries of thinkers valuing ideas so highly that they have been willing to die for them (Bradatan, 2015). Making ideas pivotal in our lives demands a shift from the logic of performativity and the language of outputs to a deep concern with knowledge and understanding. This is not just an epistemological shift but an ontological transformation: in working with ideas, we simultaneously work on ourselves. This process does not reach an endpoint where we can say we know all that needs be known; instead, it requires commitment to a lifelong process of reflection and ongoing change.

## Philosophy (of education) as a way of life

The notion of intellectual kinship sketched above is closely aligned with what Pierre Hadot calls "philosophy as a way of life" (1995, p. 29).[5] Hadot argues that for the ancient Greeks and Romans it was not enough to simply study ethics or logic; philosophy had to be *lived*. It was "a method of spiritual progress which demanded a radical conversion and transformation of the individual's way of being" (Hadot, 1995, p. 265). The goal was wisdom, and through wisdom, the ancients believed, peace, freedom and cosmic consciousness could be attained (p. 265). Philosophy conceived in these terms is something to be practised in every moment of life. It demands constant attention to the present and a certain calmness and presence of mind, regardless of political conditions and social circumstances. Seeing philosophy in this light is not a self-centred, isolated, individualistic process; it requires mutual commitment and support among a community of kindred spirits. Far from seeking to escape from the world, those who make philosophy a way of life strive to serve their fellow citizens and to change the social world for the better. Wisdom becomes intimately connected with social justice.

**28** Peter Roberts

Across the centuries, the ideal of philosophy as a way of life has been eroded. The scholasticism of the Middle Ages linked philosophy with theology and involved the training of specialists by other specialists. The birth of the medieval university witnessed a shift toward more abstract philosophical activity. Hadot maintains that this approach, with some exceptions, has continued to the present day. Philosophy of education provides an interesting test case in considering this claim. In some respects, the field exhibits key features of the scholasticism discussed by Hadot, with specialised discourses, books, journals, and courses devoted to the subject. Still, something of the ancient ideal to which Hadot refers remains. There is no one way to undertake philosophical work in education. The range of discourses in evidence among contemporary philosophers of education is a source of dismay for some (e.g., Wilson, 2003) but is largely celebrated by others (e.g., Roberts, 2015a). Many who participate in these conversations are employed in universities, but this does not mean all who fall into this category were hired specifically as philosophers of education. In today's academic world, where philosophy of education is taught at all, it will often be in other guises (e.g., via courses in curriculum, policy, or "teacher education"). There is no one methodology or tradition of inquiry in philosophy of education; instead, the field is informed and structured by a rich variety of different methodologies and theoretical orientations. Nonetheless, there are questions, themes and problems many philosophers of education, whatever their different perspectives and approaches to research, have in common as key concerns. Most are concerned, in one way or another, with the meaning and purposes of education, with how we come to know and understand ourselves, others and the world, and with what we value (and why) in our educational endeavours.

The ancient Greek and Roman thinkers to whom Hadot refers were, for the most part, relatively privileged, and in many cases enjoyed rights (as "citizens") that were denied many others (e.g., slaves) in their societies. Being able to debate ideas about knowledge, virtue, and the nature of reality, in an extended way in the company of other like-minded souls, demanded forms of leisure and spaces for participation that were simply not available to all. How does this compare with the contemporary situation for philosophers of education? Few can afford to devote themselves to philosophical work in education without also having to face the gritty realities of earning a living. But the imperative to generate an income need not be in direct conflict with deeper philosophical commitments. For those employed in university positions, a philosophical life in education is invariably more than a matter of upholding professional obligations; it also has to do with how we understand ourselves, interact with others, and pursue our ideals. We cannot step "outside" the politics and policies that frame our time, but must negotiate spaces for philosophical activity within the constraints imposed by a neoliberal world. In making philosophy of *education* a way of life, we commit ourselves to a lifelong process of learning, and this demands a certain openness and humility. We need to recognise that there is much that we do not know, and be willing to live with uncertainty, incompleteness, and the restlessness that comes from deep reflection and a probing, inquiring, and investigative frame of mind.

A serious commitment to philosophy as a way of life is no easy undertaking. It is, in some senses, a 24/7 process. In working with theory – in making ideas central to our lives – we must serve a kind of life sentence! There is no complete "escape" from the ideas we confront and construct, and insomnia is a real possibility. Life becomes not simpler and easier but more complicated, difficult and uncomfortable. Philosophy of education as a way of life means learning how to *live with* ideas, and with oneself. Once we go down this path, there is no going back. Having encountered ideas that shake the foundations of our thoughts or challenge the assumptions that guide our lives, we cannot simply decide we've had enough and return to our earlier selves. A life of this kind involves despair as well as joy, and the two will often be more closely connected with each other than we realise.[6] The suffering engendered by a philosophical life in education is one consequence of developing our capacity for reflective consciousness (cf. Unamuno, 1972), but this need not be merely "useless pain" (Ozolins, 2003). Suffering can have educative value (Roberts, 2016). It can enable forms of intellectual growth that would otherwise remain underdeveloped, and it can allow us to enter into communicative relationships with others in a more compassionate and balanced manner.[7] Making a breakthrough in understanding is sometimes only possible once we have come right to the edge of an existential abyss, a situation that can be terrifying but also ultimately uplifting.

Working with theory is, to some extent, always a struggle with time. This is sometimes experienced as a kind of anxiety associated with pressures to perform under neoliberalism (e.g., "I must come up with a great idea by Monday …"). But we can also see "worked time" as the soil through which theory grows and takes shape. Conceived in this way, time can become both oppressive and subversive. Its relentless march can be debilitating; it can seem as though time is "controlling" us. Equally, however, we can make time work for us in resisting some of the demands of a performance-driven world. Nietzsche (1997), conscious of the hastening pace of life in the nineteenth century, saw himself as an advocate of slow reading and writing. We can speak of *slow theory* in similar terms.[8] If theory can prompt us to pause and to ponder, it acts, quietly but insistently, against the frenetic push to produce, more and more, faster and faster, for larger and larger groups of people.

Slowing down allows us to better develop the key human faculty of *attention*. Working with theory, as research and as a process of human formation, can be seen as both a means and an end in pursuing this goal. The concept of attention was central to the philosophy of Simone Weil (1997, 2001) and her interpreters (e.g., Murdoch, 2001). Attention for Weil has both epistemological and moral import (Roberts, 2011). It is both a form of concentration and a mode of responding to others. The ability to focus, to listen, and to attend to another human being is, as Weil sees it, a kind of miracle. Attention to the Other is often the most important but most difficult task we face. Attention, like intellectual kinship, runs counter to the self-centredness that characterises our age. Theory as research cultivates our ability to attend but it does not always do so in a linear or predictable way. We may find ourselves immersed in an attentive state when we least expect it, our previous efforts having finally born visible fruit where hitherto we had experienced

**30** Peter Roberts

only frustration. Slow, attentive work with theory goes to the heart of educational inquiry; it allows us to address the deeper "why?" questions that must always be asked, whatever our specific field of inquiry (see Webster, 2009).

## Some practical considerations

The idea of slowing down is also important in thinking about some of the practical challenges of completing a thesis or any other substantial research project. Among today's postgraduate students, there is sometimes a premature concern with methods. This goes further in some cases and becomes a kind of "methods anxiety." A helpful step in responding to this, as a supervisor, is to say "slow down!" Students are sometimes convinced they want to conduct interviews, or complete a case study, or undertake statistical analysis, before they have done virtually anything else in advancing their study! It is important to avoid an inflexible, strict linearity in the development and progression of a research project. Nevertheless, there is merit in asking students, before they confirm their research methods, to consider other questions: What have others said/done that might be relevant to my area of research interest? What are some of the gaps, tensions, points of overlap, and key themes/concerns in the existing literature(s) relevant to my topic? What is the "problem" that prompts investigation? What are my key research questions? When a student has reached a point where he or she can delineate well-formed research questions, some methods will be ruled out as possibilities while others will remain open.

I advise the thesis students with whom I work to "write, write and write," from the beginning. Writing is more than words; it is at once a form of (re)reading the self and the world. Writing of the kind demanded by doctoral study is difficult and demanding; it is a constant process of struggle. But writing, challenging though it may be, can also play a pivotal role in helping to clarify ideas and impart a stronger sense of structure and direction to a thesis investigation. Writing is a form of systematic work that both harnesses and further develops our capacity for attention. We scholars create the words on the page (or screen) but those words, once formed, also work on us. Writing is a process of human formation. We never write alone, even if no one else is physically present in the room with us. We are always beholden to those who have gone before us (and who accompany us contemporaneously) for their words, their struggles to make sense of themselves and the world. Intellectuals often love books, but even if we abhor them, the words of others recorded through the ages exert a silent influence on how we think, on what questions we ask, and on who we seek out as kindred spirits in pursuing our inquiries.

In a thesis, "theory" precedes "method" in the sense that all methods presuppose a certain orientation to the world. As a research investigation unfolds, however, theory also follows from the methods employed. We may rethink some of the ideas with which we started as those ideas are put to the test, either empirically or via the development of an argument. As is often noted, a "methodology" is more than "methods," but I would go further than this and stress that a "theoretical framework" is more than a "methodology." A theoretical framework provides a lens through which to

Theory as research **31**

pose problems, address questions, and analyse data, but it is not merely a means toward these ends. If we take seriously the notion of working with theory as discussed in the first part of this chapter, we will also have a concern with the *theorists* who inform a framework. We will want to know something of their lives, their contexts, their struggles. If we engage their ideas deeply, we form a kind of intellectual relationship with the theorists, regardless of whether we "agree" or "disagree" with them. Yet, just as a theoretical framework is not reducible to a "methodology," so too should a "methodology" chapter in a thesis or book not *exclude* theory. This form of exclusion is by no means unusual, particularly in theses that involve empirical investigation. A methodology chapter will often provide details on the research design, the ethics approval processes, the ways in which data have been gathered, and so on, neglecting altogether the role of theory in structuring the investigation.

In completing any major piece of academic work, there are dangers in both excessive narrowness and excessive breadth. Being too certain of one's certainties, as Paulo Freire (1997) warned, can impede the openness necessary to consider other ideas, other people, and other perspectives on questions of importance. Even our sense of what counts as an important question can be constrained by excessive narrowness in our thinking about theory. In the academic world, we are all eclectics to some degree. Thesis students sometimes believe they must focus on just one theorist and become an expert on his or her work. But the very act of attending properly to one thinker demands of us that we draw on others. This point has wider significance when we consider the standard requirement that a doctoral thesis make "an original contribution to knowledge." In one sense, *no* theory is original; we are, as noted above, always indebted to others who have engaged in the act of theorising before us. In another sense, however, short of direct copying of someone else's work, *all* theory is original. Originality emerges in the way we interpret, synthesise, compare, contest, and apply ideas. Postgraduate students may want to know how many theorists they should consider (if it is to be more than one), and there is no simple answer to this question. It is not the number of theorists that matters so much as the *cohesiveness, coherence* and *clarity* of the framework or argument that is developed. A "smorgasbord" approach with a shallow sampling of myriad ideas is unhelpful, but so is an approach that is so narrow, so tightly constrained, that it is impossible for the scholar to "see the wood for the trees." *Both* breadth and depth are important. Breadth gives a sense of perspective. It can allow us to begin to grasp and appreciate the history of thought relevant to a particular problem. It can help us to place ideas into their wider contexts. Depth is also vital, however, in probing further, in pushing theory, and oneself as the researcher, in new directions.

Let me conclude this section with a few comments on how our horizons for research might be expanded, with potentially fruitful results. In Education, we tend to rely almost exclusively on non-fiction sources in addressing our research questions. Such sources can include journal articles, academic books, research reports, and other written documents. But we need not limit ourselves to such texts. Ontological, epistemological, ethical, aesthetic, political, and educational questions can be addressed via critical engagement with novels, short stories, plays, film, painting, photography,

32 Peter Roberts

sculpture, and dance. The potential value of literary fiction for philosophers has been well established.[9] Indeed, some of the most accomplished novelists of the last two centuries – Dostoevsky, Tolstoy, Unamuno, Camus, Beauvoir, Sartre, and Murdoch, among others – were also fine thinkers and philosophers. Examples of educationists blending references to fictional works with citations from more traditional non-fiction sources can be found from the early 1970s onwards,[10] but there is scope for further work of this kind. The boundaries between different genres of writing are often not as rigid as we believe them to be, and literary works (as well as other non-traditional sources) can often allow us to pursue forms of philosophical understanding that would otherwise be difficult or impossible. Literature focuses on the *particulars* of ethical life; on the messy realities characters must negotiate as they make their way in the world. Novels, short stories, and plays enable us to see how abstract principles might be enacted, contradicted, and rendered more complex through human relationships, decisions, and actions. Literature is not a substitute for traditional non-fiction sources, but it can work in complementary ways with those sources in deepening and extending theoretical understanding.

## Conclusion

Educational research is a complex, contested terrain. As a multidisciplinary field of inquiry, Education includes many more specialised areas of research, each with their own histories of scholarly evolution and debate. The rich diversity that is evident among Educational researchers can be a strength, provided tensions between scholars serve not as intractable divisions but as the basis for careful reflection and ongoing dialogue. In seeking to understand why and how some domains of inquiry and some approaches to educational research come to be valued more than others, questions of context are vital. Research in Education is a non-neutral, ethical and political activity. Philosophy of education has much to offer our current age, not only in developing skills in argumentation and analysis but also in applying those skills to the constructive critique of policy. We must be prepared for the existential consequences of a shift from "theory *and* research" to "theory *as* research." Philosophical work in education is demanding and difficult. To commit to philosophy of education not just for professional reasons but as a way of life requires a willingness to embrace discomfort, uncertainty and wakefulness. Philosophy of education not only tolerates but celebrates the immeasurability of much that matters most in education. Seeking out spaces for quietly subversive "slow theory" in a frenetic, performance-driven world is unlikely to get any easier in the foreseeable future, but work of this kind will remain crucial in the years ahead.

## Notes

1  Well known examples include: Cohen, Manion and Morrison (2007), Creswell (2009), Denzin & Lincoln (2005), and Punch (2005).
2  This point is readily illustrated in these sources, among others: Anyon (2009), Lingard (2015), O'Toole and Beckett (2013), and Pring (2015). See also a recent special issue of *Studies in Philosophy and Education*, introduced by Wilson and Santoro (2015).

3 These are matters for ongoing discussion and debate. See: Feinberg (2006), Howe (2014), Laverty (2014), Noddings (2012), Roberts (2015a), Siegel (2009), Standish (2007), and White (2013).
4 This concept is explored in some depth in Roberts (2015b).
5 The ideas considered in the first two paragraphs of this section are developed in greater detail in Roberts (2015a).
6 There is an extensive literature germane to this point. Among many other helpful sources, see: Beauvoir (1948), Camus (1968), Cioran (1995), Dostoevsky (2004), Kierkegaard (1989), Unamuno (1972), and Weil (1997).
7 Outdoor activities and exercise can also be crucial in helping to maintain a sense of balance and perspective, and in allowing us to work more creatively and productively with theory. For a thoughtful examination of the connections between outdoor experiences and intellectual life, see Quay (2015).
8 See also Berg and Seeber (2016) on the idea of the "slow professor."
9 Compare: Nussbaum (1990), Cunningham (2001), Murdoch (1999), Novitz (1987), Palmer (1992), and Weston (2001).
10 Maxine Greene was a pioneer in this respect. See, for example, Greene (1973). For two attempts to continue this legacy, see Roberts and Freeman-Moir (2013) and Roberts (2015c).

## References

Alexander, H. A. (2014). Traditions of inquiry in education: Engaging the paradigms of educational research. In A. D. Reid, E. P. Hart & M. A. Peters (Eds.) *A companion to research in education* (pp. 13–25). Dordrecht, Netherlands: Springer.

Anyon, J. (2009). Introduction: Critical social theory, educational research, and intellectual agency. In J. Anyon, with M. J. Dumas, D. Linville, K. Nolan, M. Perez, E. Tuck, & J. Weiss (Eds.) *Theory and educational research: Toward critical social explanation* (pp. 1–23). New York: Routledge.

Australian Research Council (2015). *Excellence in research for Australia*. Available online at www.arc.gov.au/excellence-research-australia.

Beauvoir, S. de (1948). *The ethics of ambiguity* (B. Frechtman, Trans.). New York: Citadel Press.

Berg, M. & Seeber, B. K. (2016). *The slow professor: Challenging the culture of speed in the academy.* Toronto, Canada: University of Toronto Press.

Biesta, G. (2009). Good education in an age of measurement: On the need to reconnect with the question of purpose in education. *Educational Assessment, Evaluation and Accountability, 21*(1), 33–46.

Biesta, G. J. J. & Burbules, N. C. (2003). *Pragmatism and educational research.* Lanham, MD: Rowman & Littlefield.

Bradatan, C. (2015). *Dying for ideas: The dangerous lives of the philosophers.* London: Bloomsbury.

Bridges, D. (2003). *Fiction written under oath? Essays in philosophy and educational research.* Dordrecht, Netherlands: Kluwer.

Bridges, D. & Smith, R. (Eds.) (2007). *Philosophy, methodology and educational research.* Oxford, UK: Blackwell.

Camus, A. (1968). Love of life. In A. Camus, *Lyrical and critical essays* (E. C. Kennedy, Trans.). New York: Vintage Books.

Cioran, E. M. (1995). *Tears and saints* (I. Zarifopol-Johnston, Trans.). Chicago, IL: University of Chicago Press.

Cohen, L., Manion, L. & Morrison, K. (2007). *Research methods in education* (6th ed.). London: Routledge.

Creswell, J. W. (2009). *Research design: Qualitative, quantitative, and mixed methods approaches* (3rd ed.). Thousand Oaks, CA: Sage.

## 34 Peter Roberts

Cunningham, A. (2001). *The heart of what matters: The role for literature in moral philosophy.* Berkeley, CA: University of California Press.

Denzin, N. K. & Lincoln, Y. S. (Eds.) (2005). *The Sage handbook of qualitative research* (3rd ed.). Thousand Oaks, CA: Sage.

Dostoevsky, F. (2004). *Notes from underground* (R. Pevear & L. Volokhonsky, Trans.). New York: Everyman's Library.

Feinberg, W. (2006). "Back to the future": Philosophy of education as an instrument of its time. *Education and Culture, 22*(2), 7–18.

Freire, P. (1997). *Pedagogy of the heart.* New York: Continuum.

Gale, T. (2003). Realising policy: The *who* and *how* of policy production. *Discourse: Studies in the Cultural Politics of Education, 24*(1), 51–65.

Giroux, H. A. (2002). Neoliberalism, corporate culture, and the promise of higher education: The university as a democratic public sphere. *Harvard Educational Review, 72*(4), 424–463.

Greene, M. (1973). *Teacher as stranger.* Belmont, CA: Wadsworth.

Griffiths, M. (1998). *Educational research for social justice: Getting off the fence.* Buckingham, UK: Open University Press.

Hadot, P. (1995). *Philosophy as a way of life* (M. Chase, Trans.). Oxford: Blackwell.

Harvey, D. (2005). *A brief history of neoliberalism.* Oxford, UK: Oxford University Press.

Howe, K. R. (2014). Philosophy of education and other educational sciences. *Theory and Research in Education, 12*(1), 77–87.

Kierkegaard, S. (1989). *The sickness unto death* (A. Hannay, Trans.). London: Penguin.

Laverty, M. J. (2014). Conceiving education: The creative task before us. *Theory and Research in Education, 12*(1), 109–119.

Lingard, B. (2015). Thinking about theory in educational research: Fieldwork in philosophy. *Educational Philosophy and Theory, 47*(2), 173–191.

Lyotard, J.-F. (1984). *The postmodern condition: A report on knowledge* (G. Bennington & B. Massumi, Trans.). Minneapolis, MN: University of Minnesota Press.

McLaughlin, T. H. (2000). Philosophy and educational policy: Possibilities, tensions and tasks. *Journal of Education Policy, 15*(4), 441–457.

Murdoch, I. (1999). *Existentialists and mystics: Writings on philosophy and literature.* London: Penguin.

Murdoch, I. (2001). *The sovereignty of good.* London and New York: Routledge.

Nietzsche, F. (1997a). *Daybreak: Thoughts on the prejudices of morality.* R. J. Hollingdale, Trans.; M. Clark & B. Leiter (Eds.). Cambridge, UK: Cambridge University Press.

Noddings, N. (2012). *Philosophy of education* (3rd ed.). Boulder, CO: Westview Press.

Novitz, D. (1987). *Knowledge, fiction and imagination.* Philadelphia, PA: Temple University Press.

Nussbaum, M. (1990). *Love's knowledge: Essays on philosophy and literature.* New York: Oxford University Press.

O'Toole, J. & Beckett, D. (2013). *Educational research: Creative thinking and doing* (2nd ed.). South Melbourne, Vic: Oxford University Press.

Ozga, J., Popkewitz, T. and Seddon, T. (Eds.) (2006). *World yearbook of education 2006: Education research and policy.* London: Routledge.

Ozolins, J. (2003). Suffering: Valuable or just useless pain? *Sophia, 42*(2), 53–77.

Palmer, F. (1992). *Literature and moral understanding: A philosophical essay on ethics, aesthetics, education, and culture.* Oxford, UK: Clarendon Press.

Pring, R. (2015). *Philosophy of educational research* (3rd ed.). London: Bloomsbury.

Punch, K. F. (2005). *Introduction to social research: Quantitative and qualitative approaches* (2nd ed.). London: Sage.

Quay, J. (2015). *Understanding life in school: From academic classroom to outdoor education.* London: Palgrave Macmillan.

Reid, A. D., Hart, E. P. & Peters, M. A. (Eds.) (2014). *A companion to research in education*. Dordrecht, Netherlands: Springer.

Research Assessment Exercise (2008). *RAE2008*. Available online at www.rae.ac.uk.

Research Excellence Framework (2014). *REF2014*. Available online at www.ref.ac.uk.

Roberts, P. (2011). Attention, asceticism and grace: Simone Weil and higher education. *Arts and Humanities in Higher Education, 10*(3), 315–328.

Roberts, P. (2013). Academic dystopia: Knowledge, performativity and tertiary education. *The Review of Education, Pedagogy, and Cultural Studies, 35*(1), 27–43.

Roberts, P. (2015a). "It was the best of times, it was the worst of times": Philosophy of education in the contemporary world. *Studies in Philosophy and Education, 34*, 623–634.

Roberts, P. (2015b). Partnership as intellectual kinship. *Knowledge Cultures, 3*(5), 42–48.

Roberts, P. (Ed.) (2015c). *Shifting focus: Strangers and strangeness in literature and education*. London: Routledge.

Roberts, P. (2016). *Happiness, hope, and despair: Rethinking the role of education*. New York: Peter Lang.

Roberts, P. & Freeman-Moir, J. (2013). *Better worlds: Education, art, and utopia*. Lanham, MD: Lexington Books.

Roberts, P. & Peters, M. A. (2008). *Neoliberalism, higher education and research*. Rotterdam, Netherlands: Sense Publishers.

Siegel, H. (Ed.) (2009). *The Oxford handbook of philosophy of education*. Oxford, UK: Oxford University Press.

Standish, P. (2001). Data return: The sense of the given in educational research. *Journal of Philosophy of Education, 35*(3), 497–518.

Standish, P. (2007). Rival conceptions of the philosophy of education. *Ethics and Education, 2*(2), 159–171.

Suissa, J. (2007). Shovelling smoke? The experience of being a philosopher on an educational research training programme. In D. Bridges & R. Smith (Eds.). *Philosophy, methodology and educational research* (pp. 283–297). Oxford, UK: Blackwell.

Tertiary Education Commission (2016). *Performance-based research fund*. Available online at www.tec.govt.nz/funding/funding-and-performance/.

Unamuno, M. de (1972). *The tragic sense of life in men and nations* (A. Kerrigan, Trans.). Princeton, NJ: Princeton University Press.

Webster, S. (2009). *Educating for meaningful lives through existential spirituality*. Rotterdam, Netherlands: Sense Publishers.

Weil, S. (1997). *Gravity and grace* (A. Wills, Trans.). Lincoln, UK: Bison Books.

Weil, S. (2001). *Waiting for God* (E. Craufurd, Trans.). New York: Perennial Classics.

Weston, M. (Ed.) (2001). *Philosophy, literature and the human good*. London: Routledge.

White, J. (2013). Philosophy, philosophy of education, and economic realities. *Theory and Research in Education. 11*(3), 294–303.

Wilson, J. (2003). Perspectives on the philosophy of education. *Oxford Review of Education, 29*(2), 279–303.

Wilson, T. S. & Santoro, D. A. (2015). Philosophy pursued through empirical research: Introduction to the special issue. *Studies in Philosophy and Education, 34*, 115–124.

Woelert, P & Yates, L. (2014). Too little and too much trust: Performance measurement in Australian higher education. *Critical Studies in Education, 56*(2), 175–189.

Yates, L. (2012). *My school, my university, my country, my world, my google, myself ...* What is education for now? *Australian Education Researcher, 39*(3), 259–274.

# 3

# MICHAEL APPLE ON PRAXIS, RHETORIC AND EDUCATIONAL RESEARCH

In dialogue with Jennifer Bleazby

*Jennifer Bleazby and Michael Apple*

## Introduction

Michael Apple is probably best known as one of the founders of critical pedagogy in the United States. For over forty years, he has critiqued the "New Right", a powerful social and political movement that incorporates the ideologies of neo-liberalism and neo-conservatism. His research examines the influence of these ideologies on education. A particular focus has been an examination of the ways in which schools perpetuate racial, class, and gender inequalities and other social injustices. In the following dialogue, Apple discusses the theories and methodologies that have shaped his work. Given the focus of his research, it is not surprising that he has made extensive use of neo-Marxists and critical theorists, including Jürgen Habermas, Herbert Marcuse, Theodore Adorno, Walter Benjamin, Antonio Gramsci, Andre Gorz and Paulo Freire. However, as Apple states in this dialogue, "labels are lazy," and referring to him as merely a neo-Marxist may obscure the wide range of theorists that have shaped his thought. This includes many feminist theorists, critical race theorists, pragmatists and post-structuralists. He has also made use of a diverse range of interdisciplinary research methods and forms of data, including qualitative and quantitative research, as well as the tools of both analytic and continental philosophy.

A dogmatic adherence to any one theoretical framework or research methodology would be inconsistent with Apple's research aims. As a scholar-activist, the primary aim of his research is to respond, in a critical and transformative manner, to real educational problems and social injustices. This implies a willingness to use any tools that will enable one to effectively respond to the problem at hand. For example, even though quantitative research methods, like standardized testing, are used by the New Right to justify a neo-liberal agenda, it would be a mistake for progressives to simply dismiss such methods. Apple argues that many progressive

Michael Apple on praxis **37**

researchers have "deskilled themselves" in quantitative methods and, consequently, they are not able to provide sophisticated critiques of the Right's use of statistics. Nor are they able to use statistics to justify their alternative viewpoints. This does not mean we can use such theoretical and methodological tools uncritically. Critical theorists remain aware of the origins and limitations of the theories and methods they use and of the capacity these tools have to be utilized in problematic ways.

Apple's openness to using a wide range of theories and methodologies follows from his commitment to praxis – reflective, socially transformative action, which integrates theory and practice. As discussed in the dialogue, praxis is an overarching concept in all of Apple's work. It is a foundational idea in Marxist theory, critical theory and pragmatism, as well as in the work of Aristotle, Hannah Arendt, Martin Heidegger and many others.[1] Praxis is sometimes thought to mean merely the process of applying a theory, especially in order to transform society. However, praxis actually rejects the theory/practice dichotomy this implies, where theories are developed in isolation from concrete experience and then applied to the real world. With praxis, the theories themselves are produced through our transformative interactions with our social-cultural environment. The very reason such theories can be effectively applied to real social problems is because the theories themselves have emerged from participants in these very same concrete experiences. They are not abstract ideas constructed by scholars sitting in ivory towers. Praxis requires that educators and scholars be activists – transformative intellectuals who work with communities to develop and enact theories that have the potential to improve people's lives. Most of the theorists mentioned in the following dialogue exemplify scholar-activism. This is the understanding of educators that Gramsci and Freire proposed. Apple's commitment to praxis and activism seems second nature to him. Throughout the dialogue, he contextualizes his beliefs and research with reference to his family background and his experience as a school teacher, president of a teachers' union and political activist. He exhibits a constant, critical, self-awareness of the way his research interacts with material realities beyond academia.

Another definitive feature of Apple's work is his ongoing analysis of how language is used by different groups to shape consciousness and justify particular social, moral and political ideals. Apple discusses the importance of identifying and critiquing rhetoric. Research becomes rhetorical when it is not connected to practice or material realities. Thus, theories that do not emerge through praxis are rhetorical. Apple has even criticized critical pedagogy for its "rhetorical flourishes" because it fails to "base its utopian visions and theories in an unromantic appraisal of the material and discursive terrain that now exists" (2006, pp. 53–54). As such, the critical pedagogy literature often fails to outline real strategies for challenging the increasingly powerful Right. This problem is reflected in the way many school teachers attempt to implement critical pedagogy. They simply incorporate some "alternative culture" into the existing curriculum, such as teaching elements of hip hop culture (e.g., graffiti in art class, rap music in English literature). Not only does this fail to transform unjust educational systems, it may actually reinforce them. It is most commonly students from disadvantaged backgrounds who

## 38 Jennifer Bleazby and Michael Apple

are taught such alternative curricula, while students from more privileged groups are typically taught more traditional academic curricula (e.g., literary classics). The traditional academic curriculum is more elite and better prepares students for entry into high status university courses and careers and the "high culture" of the middle classes. Thus, a superficial adoption of elements of critical pedagogy may simply help maintain existing social inequalities. This problem is not merely a result of teachers failing to properly understand critical pedagogy. It results from the overly theoretical and utopian nature of much of the critical pedagogy literature. As Apple suggests, praxis acts as a corrective to such rhetoric because it entails theories that outline real strategies for dismantling unjust education systems and structures – systems and structures that can undermine efforts made by individual teachers in the classroom. In the following dialogue, Apple's commitment to praxis, and to deconstructing rhetoric, are discussed in relation to a range of current educational issues.

## The dialogue

**Jennifer Bleazby (JB):**    When educational researchers engage with philosophies it is usually for one of two purposes: (1) to outline a theoretical framework that situates the educational problem or the issue; (2) to outline a methodology in order to investigate specific educational research questions. How have you used philosophy to support your educational research?

**Michael Apple (MA):**    I think it may be important to first understand some of my background. Some of my philosophical training comes from my family, not only academic work. I am the first generation finishing secondary school in my family. Yet, on the other hand, I come from a communist family, with a mother who was deeply involved in antiracist mobilisations and a grandfather who was a political exile from Russia, though he never finished primary school. I come from a family of printers, where, in Europe and the United States, printing was the most radical craft union. By the time I was 11, I was expected to have read volumes I and II of *Capital* (Marx, 1974) and to talk about it. Even though I didn't understand more than half. In my family, the expectation was that children would have something to say. Therefore, my understanding of what I call relational analysis, of seeing things not at the surface, but the deeper structures underneath, comes from a family tradition, not just academic training.

My formal background in philosophy is both analytic and continental. I had been a school teacher for many years and was admitted to the philosophy of education program at Columbia University. That was largely an analytic program. We did not read Dewey (*Collected Works, 1969–1991*). He was not considered a strong philosopher. I didn't read Dewey until much later in my career. My schooling was with people like Jonas Soltis (Soltis 1984; Fenstermacher & Soltis, 2004; Feinberg, W. & Soltis 2004;

Walker & Soltis, 2009; Strike and Soltis 2009), who was my professor at the time, and Israel Scheffler (1960, 1965, 1973, 1974, 1985, 1991); two of the founders of analytic philosophy of education. Thus I developed analytic tools and a distrust of rhetoric. Through having read Wittgenstein (1922, 2010) and Austin (1962), I understood that language does a variety of things: control, explain, describe, legitimate, mobilise. That actually had a very important influence on my later work, when I looked at the way in which language is used, the way in which the Right mobilises particular concepts, such as "democracy" and changes its very meaning. It also makes me mistrust a number of the people in what is called "critical pedagogy." Although I am one of the founders of critical pedagogy in the United States, too much of the work in that area is simply rhetorical. I want to demand more than rhetoric.

**JB:**  You have argued that the critical pedagogy literature is rhetorical because it does not always respond to changing ideological and material realities.[2] In particular, you state that it fails to suggest real strategies for responding to dominant neo-liberal ideas and practices. Can you elaborate on this notion of rhetoric and how you respond to it in your research?

**MA:**  I am strongly influenced by a concept called praxis. It has a very long history, as you know.[3] To me, it is an epistemological commitment – a commitment to theory that is done in relationship to its object. That requires an epistemology of interaction, so I am a little mistrustful of those people who engage in philosophical "slumming." By that, what I mean is they are in education as a way of making a set of arguments, but their arguments are not connected to the material realities of schools, literacy programs, unions and materialities of existence. In that sense, their research is rhetorical. Do not misunderstand me. I think rhetoric is crucial in some circumstances. As a former union president, I think we have to be good at learning to speak in different registers to different groups of people. But I think it has to go further. I think the most sophisticated theory is done in interaction with reality.

**JB:**  Praxis is a key aspect of the educational theory of Dewey, who is indebted to the philosopher Charles Peirce (*Collected Papers*, 1932-1958). Peirce originally named his philosophy "pragmatism" (1905, p. 165), which is an indication of the importance he placed on practice as a key element in the inquiry process. Praxis is also a key feature of the educational and political ideas of Paulo Freire (1970), who was influenced by Gramsci, Marxists and critical theorists. Those people are important figures in critical pedagogy. However, I'm not sure that everyone who claims to be a proponent of critical pedagogy has a good understanding of people like Dewey and Freire. It seems that some educational researchers want to use critical pedagogy as their theoretical framework, but they do not fully understand the ideas upon which it is based. Do you think it is important that educational researchers go back and read these key theorists?

**40** Jennifer Bleazby and Michael Apple

**MA:** I think it is crucial. In part, because I don't think we should be reinventing the wheel, but I also think it is important to ground yourself. Both Freire and Dewey were political activists. I spent a lot of time with Paulo Freire in Brazil. Some of my books became movement books during the dictatorship and thus I spent a lot of time working with the Workers Party in Brazil. I could not do my work well unless I had read someone like Paulo Freire. However in saying that, I did not read either Freire or Dewey during the initial stages of my work; it was probably not until I was finishing my doctorate that I read them. I was initially more familiar with the writing of Du Bois (1961, 1998)[4] than I was with Dewey and Freire. I come from an antiracist background and a labourer's background. There is a tradition of what we now call critical pedagogy within the labourers' tradition in the United States and certainly within the antiracist tradition in the United States.

**JB:** What are some other philosophies or theories that have shaped your educational research?

**MA:** I was lucky enough to work with Dwayne Huebner (1999) and Maxine Greene (1986, 1988, 1995). They demanded that I explore other philosophies besides analytic philosophy. Analytic philosophy is quite sophisticated as a methodology. However, I found it increasingly boring and, given my background politically, I was very disheartened by it. It didn't give me what I wanted, which was an organic connection to political theories and movements. Given this, I was sent by Huebner and Greene to The New School to take courses in continental philosophy. These courses were taught by people who had been students of Habermas (1987, 1989a, 1989b, 1996) and who had worked with Arendt (1967, 1998). I was formed in this odd interstice between analytic sophistication, not connected to anything in the world, and things that were deeply connected to an epistemological and political position. However, even given my immense respect for him, I had many worries about Habermas. An example would be his definition of the public sphere, which is fully classed, raced and gendered. Even before Nancy Fraser (1990) wrote her brilliant material elaborating that critique, many of us understood that there was something wrong with the critical theory tradition coming out of post-holocaust Europe. These are the kinds of things that tended to form me: a cultural-studies form of the social theory of Habermas, Marcuse (1964), Adorno (Adorno, *et al.*, 1950; Horkheimer & Adorno, 1973), and Benjamin (2008),[5] and a recognition that even though it was exceptionally powerful and illuminating it still had to be dealt with reflectively as well.

**JB:** There is often quite a division between continental philosophy and analytic philosophy. Although, the categories of analytic and continental philosophy are somewhat problematic and a bit ambiguous. I am a pragmatist, so it has never been clear as to which of these two philosophical traditions I belong. I don't think that pragmatism clearly belongs within either one of

Michael Apple on praxis **41**

these traditions, which is fitting given that much of pragmatism is focused on rejecting various false dichotomies. You draw on theorists and methods from both analytic and continental philosophy, despite the common assumption that these traditions are opposed to one and other. Can ideas from continental and analytic philosophy be effectively integrated?

**MA:** Your position is exactly the position to take, it seems to me. I think it is the tension between those traditions that is important. No, they cannot be integrated easily. Some people see me as more neo-Marxist than Marxist and in many ways that is true. But I think labels are lazy. I have also been influenced by some post-structural theories, for example I think Foucault (1980, 1995) is brilliant, but also needs to be approached critically. So I would prefer to work in between traditions: Marxist, neo-Marxist, and some post-structural forms. I don't think they can be merged. The sparks fly from where they rub against each other epistemologically and politically, in terms of their forms of explanation.

**JB:** Many progressive educational researchers critique the neo-liberal ideology inherent in much educational policy and practice. Do the negative connotations of neo-liberalism mean that researchers should avoid *all* aspects of liberalism? Does liberalism, as a philosophical and political theory, have anything of value to offer educational researchers and political activists today? It seems to me that there are many valuable elements of liberalism, such as sophisticated notions of equality, justice, democracy and rights, which may be overlooked by researchers who are wary of anything associated with liberalism.

**MA:** I would be less worried about whether I *am* using liberalism, rather than whether I'm *not*. In part because I think many people on the Left have forgotten the specificities of the United States. Marx was not translated and available in the United States until much later than Europe. Most poststructuralism comes out of a debate with Stalinism and essentialism in Europe. We never had that in the United States. Class was hardly on the agenda. The issue of political economy was hardly on the agenda, theoretically. Thus liberalism was the dominant discourse and many, many groups radicalized it. So I prefer to be a little more honest and nuanced about the history of liberalism, as the discourse that was used for counter-hegemonic purposes. Let me give you an example. Women's movements in the United States used liberalism – the right to contract and the demand to be treated as an individual – as a counter-hegemonic form. The demand for teachers to be treated as individual professionals, with autonomy and respect, is a response to the fact that women's labour was treated as throwaway. Women teachers had no pensions. They were paid one-third of what a male teacher made. Liberalism's notion of the autonomous individual, who is able to contract out one's labour, was actually radicalized in terms of the history of gender specificities. Given this, I think that it is a misreading of liberalism to see it as only this reformist tradition. I think that it was used in the United States

**42** Jennifer Bleazby and Michael Apple

in different ways than Australia and then in England, Germany and France. I think history becomes very important as we think about these kinds of things. So I am a little more comfortable with it, provided I remember that it is very limited in its reforms.

**JB:** What do you think about rights discourse as a tool for achieving social justice? It has been criticised by post-modernists, some feminists and critical theorists. However, as philosophers like Nussbaum (2011) have pointed out, it is a very powerful discourse, which is deeply embedded in current political and legal systems and documents, for example the United Nation's conventions on human rights. Do you think that the concept of rights still has a place in educational theory and research, despite the many criticisms of rights theory?

**MA:** I think it depends on how we use it. I want to politicize rights discourse. Let's take a radicalized example, the right to an education. That is humanist discourse. The language of rights tends to be individuated. Most of us are familiar with the critiques. But the demand for rights is also a demand, through Nancy Fraser's (1997, 2003) point, about the politics of representation and recognition. When black people could be killed, literally murdered, for learning how to read, they were being denied what some people call bourgeois liberties. To deny the fact that rights discourses can be mobilised in radical ways is actually a performance of "whiteness" in public. I want to be quite cutting about that. I want to ask again – and this is Wittgenstein meets Marx – how is the language being used, by whom and in what context? How should we criticise it whilst still gaining an understanding of how different groups have mobilised it on a terrain that they don't control? So that is the way I think about rights talk and a good deal of other kinds of talk. How was it being used and what's the way in which it's being mobilised? I'm strongly influenced by Gramsci (2011) in this regard.[6] If I want to get people from A to Z – as someone who is trying to think about how we interrupt neo-conservatives – I'll admit, "Okay, I may need rights talk." Now how do I deconstruct it? I use a concept called "non-reformist reforms" (e.g., see Apple, 1995), which I've gotten from Andre Gorz (1967), a German Marxist theorist.[7] It says there are a million things we have to deal with. Choose, tactically, the ones that open other doors to further analysis and further politicization. So rights talk, when it is used carefully as a non-reformist reform, can get people from, say, A to D. It then allows other doors to be opened toward Z. I'm quite strategic about this.

**JB:** In educational policy and research, terms like "rights," "democracy" and "justice" are often used in a very rhetorical manner and with very little analysis or theorization. For example, it's often just assumed that if something is called democratic then it must be good. There may be little awareness that the notion of democracy is contentious and that it has been subject to criticisms, such as Plato's (1998) famous critique of democracy.

Do you think that if educational researchers and policy makers studied more philosophy or educational theory they would be able to use such terms in a more critical, sophisticated manner?

**MA:** It depends on what we mean by critical here. Let me give an example. In my books *Educating the Right Way* (2006) and *Can Education Change Society?* (2013), one of the things I focused on is words with emotional economies. I have been influenced by Raymond Williams (1985) and his notion of keywords. I think he is brilliant in arguing that words like "democracy" become sliding signifiers. They have no essential meaning. They have histories and the task of dominant groups, in many ways, is to take them out of that context. It is what Stuart Hall, using terms that are a bit too masculinist, calls "suturing" (1990, p. 226). So you disarticulate the word "democracy", which, when we hear it, creates this wash of warmth over us. We say, "Oh yes, it is democratic. It is a nice thing." You take it out of its historical context – of what in analytic terms you might say are thick forms, fully participatory forms and critical forms – and you make it into neo-liberal forms, thin democracy or democracy as choice in a market. Now the Right is brilliant at that. I think that it is absolutely central that we understand the ways in which these terms are mobilised, who uses them and their agenda. I really think that the Right are the only Gramscians left. What they do is say the following: "We will change common-sense." They understand that in order to win in the state and win in the economy, you must change consciousness. Words like "democracy" are strategically mobilised and in order to do that they have to disarticulate it from its previous quilt. They cut the stitches out and take it away from the thicker traditions of Marxism, feminism and anti-racist work and they stitch it into something else. They rearticulate it and then they provide new identities for people; they understand that language provides identities. That's a post-structural understanding and I think it is very important. Then as people begin to think of democracy as choice, it is a lot easier for the Prime Minister of Australia, for example, to say, "Why don't we give more money to private schools because, after all, they are in a market and they give parents a choice of schooling for their children. And let's destroy teachers' unions because teachers are not in favour of democracy because they are standing in the way of choice."

I think that the implications of philosophical forms, what we might call deconstructed forms, of looking at the history of language and how it is used are crucial. But only if we understand what is going on in the larger society. It is not random. Therefore, I want to do this in a way that looks at the relationship between dominant ideological forms, the way in which common-sense works and the way in which it is changed, and how words with political and emotional economies are used.

**JB:** It seems that governments and research funding bodies increasingly prefer quantitative research methods to examine educational problems, such as surveys of teachers or standardised testing of students. However, such quantitative methods have also been heavily criticised by academics in the field of education. I just completed a course in statistics over the summer and when I told some of my colleagues about this many of them questioned why I would want to learn about quantitative methods, given that I am a philosopher of education. I don't intend to conduct any quantitative research in the near future. However, I often use, and write about, quantitative research conducted by others (e.g., Bleazby, 2013, Chapter 7; Bleazby, 2015) and I want to be able to analyse that research in a sophisticated manner. Do you think quantitative research has any value in terms of addressing educational problems, given its limitations? If so, is it problematic if educational researchers just stick to theory and/or qualitative methods and dismiss quantitative research?

**MA:** How much time do we have? I've written a lot about this (Apple, 1996, 2004, 2006, 2014). Many people have (e.g., Berliner & Nichols, 2007; Ravitch, 2010; Pereyra, *et al.*, 2011). First of all, I think that the progressives have deskilled themselves. In the 1970s, I was one of the people who wrote against positivism. At the time, there was a whole movement against what we call positivism. I am now almost sorry I did that because I think we have actually done them a disservice, since almost all my students by and large do qualitative or conceptual work. When a government report comes out that mobilizes statistics, they are at a loss. So I am a bit Bourdieuian about this. There is a social field of power and there are conversion strategies that go on. Unfortunately, high status knowledge is seen as numbers. Audre Lorde (1983) has this lovely slogan that says you can't destroy the master's house using the master's tools. But sometimes those master's tools need to be used for deconstructive purposes. When dominant groups lie through their teeth – when mobilized empirical results say that, for instance, voucher schools in the United States do just as well as traditional public schools – I want to look at the data and show that they are wrong, because I think they are wrong.[8] Now the danger here is that these quantitative forms are re-emerging and they are engaged in an epistemological war. These tools then attack those of us who do theory. They attack qualitative stuff as being not real evidence. So I understand that people are critical of quantitative methods. But I think that we have deskilled ourselves. That worries me.

Quantitative methods are used in an interesting way in policy with words like "accountability." The word accountability, in Spanish and in English, has residual forms in our ordinary language. Here is the analytic side of me coming out again. In ordinary language, when I ask people about accounting, it can be in the same way a certified public accountant would: "Show me your numbers." But if you and I were talking about a school and we were both observing a teacher doing good stuff, I'd say, "Can you give me an account of what you saw?" That's a narrative. That is ordinary language already cemented in a notion that the epistemological war has been successful. That narrative, a story, has epistemological weight. But such fuller "accounts" are indeed under threat.

So I'm sort of caught again between wanting us to be more skilled in advanced statistics. My doctoral work required that I had two years of advanced statistics at Columbia. I hated it. But I needed it. At the same time, I also think we need to be highly skilled in qualitative forms of various kinds.

**JB:** In your writing you have drawn on many feminist theorists, as have I. It seems to me that some people, including researchers, are wary of feminism and of being labelled a feminist. There seems to be a lot of people who say, "I agree with a lot of what feminists say, but I am not a feminist," as if they are scared to use the term because of its perceived connotations. What do you think about the status and value of feminist theory today and how important it is within the field of education?

**MA:** I have been strongly influenced by feminist theory. However, I think people stereotype me. They don't realise how I have been influenced by the work of different feminists. My wife is a professor of women's studies and does her work on the history of the medicalization of women's bodies. So even if I wasn't interested in it, which I am, I am taught about it. That is actually very important. I want to give credit where credit is deserved. I come to these things not simply because I'm reading, but because of the materiality of my existence. It is important that we see concepts as having grounding within real life.

I have been influenced strongly by socialist feminists. I have often drawn on the work of people like Linda Gordon and Nancy Fraser (Fraser & Gordon 1997; Fraser 2013). I think Fraser is one of the clearest writers on these issues. Judith Butler's (1988, 2006) analyses of the performance of gender, as identities and performativities, is crucial for the kind of work I want to do in showing how identities get transformed discursively and how that fits into a neo-liberal and neo-conservative agenda. As you know, I write a lot about that.

This raises a conceptual dilemma, especially in my latest work, about decentred unities. How can we build alliances across our differences? I have learned from the Right that they have formed a hegemonic alliance, where they are willing to compromise. The Left is not so willing to compromise. I spent a lot of time in Brazil unable to figure out where to eat because the person who owned the best pizzeria was a member of the Maoist Party and we couldn't go there, and we also couldn't go to that other place owned by a member of the Stalinist Party. I don't ever want to recapitulate that. So here is the dilemma: how do we simultaneously keep current with the immensely productive debates about identity – about class, gender, sexuality, race and racializing practices – but also think about intersections and alliances across such differences? I can't fully answer that, in part because such politics are in constant motion. All I can do is say I tried. But it seems to me that there are self-correcting debates within feminist theory. How do any of us – you, me

**46** Jennifer Bleazby and Michael Apple

and anyone who is critical – know the debates, let them influence us, and at the same time use the material without subjecting ourselves to criticisms that we were misusing it? That constitutes a dilemma to me. All I can say is that is the task. That is a fulltime job. It requires no sleep. Knowledge of these debates can't just be gained from books, although books are crucial. We must also look for ways in which one can be in those communities because the epistemological form that you and I avow, which is the crucible of practice, is also where theory is formed. But this is a dilemma and these dilemmas are constitutive. There is no way around them. I prefer to say it is a dilemma and to work my way through it, knowing that it will never be satisfactory.

**JB:** How important do you think it is to use theories from non-Western traditions? Most of the theorists we have talked about so far are Westerners. Do you think educational researchers should make more effort to look at perspectives from the Asia-Pacific, Africa, and Middle East?

**MA:** I actually think it is very important. I spend a lot of time in Brazil with Indigenous activists and with unscheduled castes in India, and I am a professor at two universities in China. There are people using Chinese philosophical and political traditions to raise issues, even though much of this material has not been translated into English yet. Melbourne University, for example, has a good opportunity to engage with such Eastern traditions, since it is sometimes joked that it is the Chinese University of Australia. I take that as a compliment. However, for all too many universities throughout the world, "diasporic people" are seen as cash cows, which is what many universities treat them as. This is exactly the opposite of what is necessary to learn from those we too often see as "the other."

Raewyn Connell's (2007) work on Southern theories provides an interesting opening to this issue, as does Linda Tuhiwai Smith (2012) in her writings on decolonising methodology. But this too requires a caution. No white person would say of Smith's work – I would hope – that it is *the* voice of Maoridom. It is *a* voice from Maoridom. It is like asking, "What is *the* Indigenous voice in Australia?" Say what? *The* Indigenous voice? I think that we have to be aware of that being a danger.

If we're using predominantly Northern scholars then we should also look for dissident voices within the North. An example would be to look at the voices of Indigenous scholars and the voices of black and brown people in the United States. I took that as a task in my latest book *Can Education Change Society?* (2013). For one-third of the book, I decided that I was not going to look at dominant "white" voices; I not only looked at the most famous philosophers in the United States, which would be Dewey and George Counts (1932), but also at Carter Woodson (1998) and W. E. B. Du Bois (1961, 1998) – that is, black scholars who are a voice of the oppressed. Du Bois wound up living in Africa, because he could not take the marginalisation of Indigenous and black voices in the United States. I think there are ways to put ourselves in a position to try and solve

Michael Apple on praxis **47**

that. Certainly my students raise this issue with me. It's one of the topics of conversation in my classes and in the Friday Seminar where I meet with the folks who are working with me. They are from all over the world and they are continually my teachers. When my ego gets in the way, they make certain that it is rigorously criticized, which I value.

**JB:** Can you say anything about the current status of educational philosophy or theory? I'm the only dedicated philosopher of education in the Faculty of Education where I work [at Monash University], although other researchers in the faculty do conduct philosophical research on occasion. There are not many philosophers of education with tenured positions in Australian universities anymore. There are also not many teacher education courses that contain a lot of educational philosophy, or even educational theory. There seems to be a common belief that we should not be teaching theory to pre-service teachers because we have got to teach them "practical skills" for the classroom. Strangely, this belief presumes the problematic theory/practice dualism so vehemently rejected by educational theorists like Dewey and Freire. Is this also the case in the United States?

**MA:** Exactly the same, and it is also not just in the United States. It is going on in Brazil and Argentina. I spend a lot of time at the University of Manchester and the Institute of Education in London. Exactly the same thing is happening. For example, one of the departments here at the University of Wisconsin is Educational Policy Studies. It's my favourite department. My closest friends are there. I do a lot of work with it. I am one of the only philosophers, which is interesting. While I have a master's degree in philosophy, if someone were to ask me if I have read everything I should in philosophy recently, the answer would be "no." This is because I tend to try and read across disciplines. I shouldn't be the one who is teaching philosophy of education. We need someone who is specifically trained in philosophy and for whom philosophy is their life's work. The other philosopher of education at Wisconsin is Harry Brighouse (2000, 2006; Brighouse and Robeyns, 2010), who is a very fine political philosopher. But he will teach one course every other year. Increasingly, however, this material is seen as unimportant by all too many people.

In fact, in very many universities almost all the so-called foundational subjects [e.g., philosophy of education, sociology of education, history of education] are being dropped. That is a political decision and an economic decision, as well as an epistemological decision. We will not fund someone in philosophy of education, but we will fund someone who teaches management skills, test preparation or assertive discipline. The effect of this is the deskilling of researchers and teachers. Like you, I think it is a disaster. This is part of what I meant by an epistemological war. These educational theories are important resources. They enable researchers and educators to see themselves as building on traditions around analytic work and critical work (see Soltis 1990). They form part of the collective memory, which is destroyed when it is not valued and passed on to future generations. By destroying this collective memory and making people feel isolated, the battle is partly won. Forgive the militaristic metaphors, but I think it is a war.

I think that every practice has a theory embedded in it. I'm tired of making that argument. But we have to continue to make that argument. An example would be something like this: an argument is made that we have to teach real knowledge to students that will help them in the economy. Let's deconstruct that. What counts as real knowledge? Who is making the decision? These are really profound questions. If teachers don't have the skills and dispositions to raise those questions, then neo-liberalism wins and it is packaged curriculum – for profit. It is a skill, as well as a disposition, to say, "Wait a minute, why am I doing this? In whose interest is this? What's the purpose of doing this?"

**JB:** I am concerned that it will it get to a point where there are so few people with expertise in educational philosophy and theory that we will never be able to reverse this trend – that the knowledge and skills may be lost forever.

**MA:** Well, that is a real worry. I think people are philosophers in their own ways and I think that we do a disservice to teachers, administrators, curriculum workers and activists to assume that they are not thinking about their lives. I think they are. Let me tell a story. Like many of us who started out as school teachers, when things go bad you begin to doubt whether it is worthwhile doing all this theoretical and political work. When I was teaching sixth grade in the slums and a kid learnt something, I knew immediately that it was an interaction between me and her. There is something powerful about having an effect on a real person's life. So I said to my father (Harry is his name), "I'm not certain I should do any of this theoretical and political work. What's the value of this?" My father, after he retired from printing, taught printing at a vocational high school, even though he didn't have a university degree. He looked at me and said, "That is the most disrespectful thing you have ever said in your life. Your mother and I struggled for years to get you to night school to become a teacher, and to support you we had to make sacrifices. Your task is to take what you learnt and bring it back. Never say these things again." My father was a very smart guy about this. People are intellectuals in their own lives. Disadvantaged people are not mystified. They know what is going on. As Freire argued, there are traditions in political economy that are useful, that can be taught in ways that enable them to understand their own lives. Are there traditions of thinking about concepts like democracy, concepts about women's lives, about what it means to be racialized that we should have studied? Of course. And they need to be taught. How do we speak in different registers so that we continue to have dialogues with real people who can also be my teachers? So again, that is the epistemological and political form that you and I avow – philosophy and theory embedded in real life and everyday experiences.

## Conclusion

In this dialogue, Michael Apple has discussed key theories and concepts that have framed his research. One of the overarching concepts is that of praxis, an idea central to the various philosophical traditions that have influenced him. As explained, a commitment to an epistemology of praxis goes hand in hand with the notion of scholar-activists. Apple follows in a long line of educational researchers who are activists, working with diverse communities beyond academia so as to develop and apply theories that aim to transform unjust structures and systems and improve people's lives. The ideas of praxis and activism that Apple avows seem particularly pertinent now. As I was writing this chapter, Donald Trump was elected president of the United States. Although Trump's ideals and policies are often vague, confusing and contradictory, it is evident that his presidency will likely further the neo-liberal/neo-conservative agenda that Apple has spent his career challenging. Even Trump's contradictions reflect the often-contradictory nature of the Right's ideologies, as Apple (2006) describes them. It seems the power of the Right is only increasing, which should be a reminder that educational researchers and other scholars need to produce research that is more than mere rhetoric. They need to be devising and applying strategic, practical theories that can respond to these challenges.

## Notes

1 Note that different theorists may define the concept in different ways. Also, some theorists propose an idea of praxis without actually using the term "praxis."
2 For example, see Apple's critique of critical pedagogy in *Educating the "Right" Way* (2006, Chapter 3).
3 See Smith (2011) for a brief history of the concept "praxis."
4 Du Bois, who was a student of William James, is sometimes also considered to be a classical pragmatist. For a discussion of Du Bois' contribution to pragmatism see West (1989), Taylor (2004), and Glaude (2007).
5 These philosophers and sociologists are all members, or associates, of the Frankfurt School, a group of neo-Marxist scholars connected to the Frankfurt Institute for Social Research at Goethe University. Critical theory aims to criticize and reconstruct society, rather than merely explain it. Much of their critique focused on capitalism, industrialization and fascism, including the rise of Nazism.
6 For example, see Apple's use of Gramsci's notion of hegemony (1995, 2004).
7 Gorz (1967) described non-reformist reforms as anti-capitalist reforms that aim to meet human needs through structural and systemic changes. In contrast, reformist reforms aim to make improvements within the existing systems or structures. Thus, reformist reforms actually sustain existing, unjust systems and structures, such as capitalism, whereas non-reformist reforms involve a reconstruction of existing power structures.
8 Apple himself sometimes draws on quantitative research for this purpose (e.g., Apple 1996, chapter 4).

## References

Adorno, T. W., Frenkel-Brunswik, E., Levinson, D. & Sanford, N. (1950). *The authoritarian man*. New York: Harper & Row.

Apple, M. W. (1995) *Education and power* (2nd ed.). New York and London: Routledge.

Apple, M. W. (1996). *Cultural politics and education*. New York and London: Teachers College Press.

Apple, M. W. (2004). *Ideology and the curriculum* (3rd ed.). New York and London: Routledge Farmer.

Apple, M. W. (2006). *Educating the "Right" way: Markets, standards, God, and inequality* (2nd ed.). New York and London: Routledge.

Apple, M. W. (2013). *Can education change society?* New York and London: Routledge.

Apple, M. W. (2014). *Official knowledge: Democratic education in a conservative age* (3rd ed.). New York and London: Routledge.

Arendt, H. (1967). *The origins of totalitarianism* (3rd ed.). London: Allen & Unwin.

Arendt, H. (1998). *The human condition* (2nd ed.). Chicago, IL: University of Chicago Press. (Original work published 1958).

Austin, J. L. (1962). *How to do things with words*. Cambridge, MA: Harvard University Press.

Benjamin, W. (2008). *The work of art in the age of mechanical reproduction* (J.A. Underwood, Trans.). London: Penguin. (Original work published 1936).

Berliner, D. C. & Nichols, S. L. (2007). *Collateral damage: How high stakes testing corrupts America's schools*. Cambridge, MA: Harvard Education Press.

Bleazby, J. (2013). *Social reconstruction learning: Dualism, Dewey and philosophy in schools*. New York and London: Routledge.

Bleazby, J. (2015). Why some school subjects have a higher status than others: The epistemology of the traditional curriculum hierarchy. *Oxford Review of Education, 41*(5), 671–689. doi:10.1080/03054985.2015.1090966.

Brighouse, H. (2000). *School choice and social justice*. New York: Oxford University Press.

Brighouse, H. (2006). *On education*. New York and London: Routledge.

Brighouse, H. & Robeyns, I. (2010). *Measuring justice: Primary goods and capabilities*. Cambridge, UK: Cambridge University Press.

Butler, J. (1988). Performative acts and gender constitution: An essay in phenomenology and feminist theory. *Theatre Journal, 40*(4), pp. 519– 531.

Butler, J. (2006). *Gender trouble: Feminism and the subversion of identity*. New York: Routledge.

Connell, R. (2007). *Southern theory: The global dynamics of knowledge in social science*. Cambridge, UK: Polity.

Counts, G. (1932). *Dare the school build a new social order?* New York: Arno Press.

Dewey, J. (1969–1991). *The collected works of John Dewey, 1882–1953* (J. A. Boydston, Ed.). Carbondale, IL and Edwardsville, IL: Southern Illinois University Press.

Du Bois, W. E. B. (1961). *The souls of black folk: Essays and sketches*. Greenwich, CT: Fawcett. (Original work published 1903).

Du Bois, W. E. B. (1998). *Black reconstruction in America*. New York: Free Press. (Original work published 1935).

Feinberg, W. & Soltis, J. F. (2004). *School and society* (4th ed.). New York and London: Teachers College Record.

Fenstermacher, G. D. & Soltis, J. F. (2004). *Approaches to teaching* (5th ed.). New York: Teachers College Press.

Foucault, M. (1980). *Power/knowledge: Selected interviews and other writings, 1972–1977*. New York: Pantheon Books.

Foucault, M. (1995). *Discipline and punish: The birth of the prison* (2nd ed.). New York: Vintage Books.

Fraser, N. (1990). Rethinking the public sphere: A contribution to the critique of actually existing democracy. *Social Text, 25/26*, 56–80. doi:10.2307/466240.

Fraser, N. (1997). *Justice interruptus: Critical reflections on the 'postsocialist' condition*. New York and London: Routledge.

Fraser, N. (2003). Social justice in the age of identity politics: Redistribution, recognition and participation. In N. Fraser & A. Honneth (Eds.). *Redistribution or recognition? A political-philosophical exchange* (pp. 7–109). New York and London: Verso Books.

Fraser, N. (2013). *Fortunes of feminism: From state-managed capitalism to neoliberal crisis.* Brooklyn, NY: Verso Books.

Fraser, N. & Gordon, L. (1997). Decoding 'dependency': Inscriptions of power in a keyword of the US welfare state. In U. Narayan & M. L. Shanley (Eds.). *Reconstructing political theory: Feminist perspectives* (pp. 25–47). Cambridge, UK: Polity.

Freire, P. (1970). *Pedagogy of the oppressed.* New York: Continuum.

Glaude, E. S. (2007). *In a shade of blue: Pragmatism and the politics of black America.* Chicago, IL: University of Chicago Press.

Gorz, A. (1967). *Strategy for labour: A radical proposal.* Boston, MA: Beacon Press.

Gramsci, A. (2011). *Prison notebooks, volumes I-III* (J.A. Buttigieg, Trans). New York: Columbia University Press. (Original work published 1948).

Greene, M. (1986). In search of a critical pedagogy. *Harvard Educational Review, 56*(4), 427–442. doi:10.17763/haer.56.4.010756lh36u16213.

Greene, M. (1988). *The dialectic of freedom.* New York: Teachers College Press.

Greene, M. (1995). *Releasing the imagination: Essays on education, the arts and social change.* San Francisco, CA: Jossey-Bass Publishers.

Habermas, J. (1987). *Knowledge and human interests.* Cambridge, UK: Polity.

Habermas, J. (1989a). *The structural transformation of the public sphere.* Cambridge, MA: MIT Press.

Habermas, J. (1989b). *The theory of communicative action.* Cambridge, UK: Polity.

Habermas, J. (1996). *Between facts and norms: Contributions to a discourse theory of law and democracy.* Cambridge, MA: MIT Press.

Hall, S. (1990) Cultural identity and diaspora. In J. Rutherford (Ed.). *Identity: Community, culture, difference* (pp. 222–237). London: Lawrence & Wishart.

Horkheimer, M. & Adorno, T. W. (1973). *Dialectic of enlightenment.* London: Allen Lane.

Huebner, D. E. (1999). *The lure of the transcendent: Collected essays by Dwayne E. Huebner.* Mahwah, N.J and London, UK: Lawrence Erlbaum Associates, Publishers.

Lorde, A. (1983). The master's tools will never dismantle the master's house. In C. Moraga & G. Anzaldua (Eds.). *This bridge called my back: Writings by radical women of colour.* (pp. 94–101). New York: Kitchen Table Press.

Marcuse, H. (1964). *One-dimensional man: Studies in the ideology of advanced industrial society.* New York and London: Routledge & Kegan Paul.

Marx, K. (1974). *Capital: A critique of political economy.* London: Lawrence & Wishart.

Nussbaum, M. (2011). *Creating capabilities.* Cambridge, MA: Harvard University Press.

Peirce, C. S. (1905). What pragmatism is. *The Monist, 15,* 161–181.

Peirce, C. S. (1932–1958). *Collected papers of Charles Sanders Peirce, volumes I-VIII* (C. Hartshorne, P. Weiss & A. W. Burks, Eds.). Cambridge, MA: Belknap Press of Harvard University Press.

Pereyra, M.A., Kotthoff, H. & Cowen, R. (2011). *PISA under examination: Changing knowledge, changing tests, and changing schools.* Rotterdam, Netherlands: Sense Publishers.

Plato. (1998). *The republic* (R. Waterfield, Trans.). Oxford, UK: Oxford University Press.

Ravitch, D. (2010). *The death and life of the great American school system: How testing and choice are undermining education.* New York: Basic Books.

Scheffler, I. (1960). *The language of education.* Springfield, IL: Charles C. Thomas.

Scheffler, I. (1965). *Conditions of knowledge: An introduction to epistemology and education.* Glenview, IL: Scott, Foresman & Company.

Scheffler, I. (1973). *Reason and teaching.* London and New York: Routledge & Kegan Paul.

Scheffler, I. (1974). *Four pragmatists: A critical introduction to Peirce, James, Mead, and Dewey.* New York and London: Routledge & Kegan Paul.

Scheffler, I. (1985). *Of human potential: An essay in the philosophy of education.* New York and London: Routledge & Kegan Paul.

Scheffler, I. (1991). *In praise of cognitive emotions and other essays in philosophy of education.* New York and London: Routledge.

Smith, L. T. (2012). *Decolonizing methodologies: Research and indigenous peoples* (2nd ed.). New York and London: Zed Books.

Smith, M. K. (2011). What is praxis? In *The encyclopedia of informal education.* Available at: http://infed.org/mobi/what-is-praxis/.

Soltis, J. F. (1984). On the nature of educational research. *Educational Researcher, 13*(10), 5–10. doi:10.3102/0013189X013010005.

Soltis, J. F. (1990). A reconceptualization of educational foundations. *Teachers College Record, 91*(3), 311–321. doi:10.1177/002248718904000103.

Strike, K. A. & Soltis, J. F. (2009). *The ethics of teaching* (5th ed.). New York and London: Teachers College Press.

Taylor, P. C. (2004). What's the use of calling Du Bois a pragmatist? *Metaphilosophy, 35*(1–2), 99–114. doi:10.1111/j.1467-9973.2004.00308.x.

Walker, D. F. & Soltis, J. F. (2009). *Curriculum and aims* (5th ed.). New York and London: Teachers College Press.

West, C. (1989). *The American evasion of philosophy: A genealogy of pragmatism.* Madison, WI: University of Wisconsin Press.

Williams, R. (1985). *Keywords: A vocabulary of culture and society* (Rev. ed.). New York: Oxford University Press.

Wittgenstein, L. (1922). *Tractatus logico-philosophicus* (C. K. Ogden, Trans.). London: Routledge & Kegan Paul. (Original work published 1921).

Wittgenstein, L. (2010). *Philosophical investigations* (G. E. M. Anscombe, P. M. S. Hacker & J. Schulte, Trans.) (Rev. 4th ed.). Oxford, UK: Wiley Blackwell. (Original work published 1953).

Woodson, C. G. (1998). *The mis-education of the Negro.* Trenton, NJ: Africa World Press.

# 4

## GERT BIESTA ON THINKING PHILOSOPHICALLY ABOUT EDUCATION; THINKING EDUCATIONALLY ABOUT PHILOSOPHY IN EDUCATION AND EDUCATIONAL RESEARCH

In dialogue with Steven A. Stolz

*Steven A. Stolz and Gert Biesta*

### Introduction

In this chapter, Gert Biesta discusses his approach to the study of education and educational research. A useful starting point to understanding his work revolves around the meaning of the phrase "thinking philosophically about education; thinking educationally about philosophy" (see Biesta, 2015). In order to contextualise his central thesis, Biesta starts out by demonstrating how the Anglo-American tradition of educational research and scholarship has appealed to the findings of the dominant social sciences of the time, like psychology, sociology, and so on, as a means of studying education and participating in educational research deemed to be relevant to the "construction" of the field. Conversely, the Continental tradition originating in Europe – particularly the German-speaking world – is employed as an exemplar of how education as a field was not parasitic on "other" discipline areas, but has always been considered a discipline in its own right.[1] Indeed, Biesta makes it clear from his response to the initial question posed in the following dialogue that his method of educational theorising closely aligns with the Continental tradition. This is made evident when he argues that one of his aims is to provide an "alternative theoretical framework" of citizenship education that is *not* focused on identifying the kind of knowledge, dispositions, skills, and so on that need to be replicated in order to "be and become" good citizens. Rather, his method is to shift the focus from the identification of an external phenomenon to an internal, existential understanding of what it means to be and become "a democratic subject", with a particular emphasis on the role education plays in the formation of this subject. Here we have the genesis of Biesta's methodology that seeks to problematise the Anglo-American construction of education and educational research, which positions education as a "thing" to be studied from a philosophical point of view.

This then leads to the engagement with various philosophical traditions as a means to make sense of this "thing" called "education", which often results in rational impasses between rival and competing traditions, and even within the same tradition regarding contested concepts, disputes concerning the correct interpretation of a philosopher, and so on. In one sense, the former part of Biesta's key phrase used in the title of this chapter ("thinking philosophically about education") is a cautionary tale about the potential threat of being infected with myopic views about what counts as "doing" philosophy of education that does not necessarily have an educational interest. Likewise, the discipline area of philosophy in "thinking philosophically about education" acts both as a type of variable and a representation of an *interdisciplinary* approach towards the study of education that applies a diverse array of disciplines, like psychology, sociology, and so on, as if "education" is a phenomenon with *a priori* subject matter that is objectively and independently identifiable. Indeed, "thinking philosophically about education" has contributed to a perception, particularly within the English-speaking world, that education lacks academic status as a stand-alone discipline because it calls on a range of other discipline areas. In another sense, Biesta is challenging those who may reside within the Anglo-American tradition, and/or approach the study of education and educational research from an interdisciplinary point of view to (*re*)*conceptualise* and (*re*)*consider* what it means to "think educationally about philosophy". Just as the interviewer in this chapter found the latter part of the phrase initially nonsensical to understand, Biesta's insights on being prepared to be open-minded about what it may mean to approach the study of education and educational research from a Continental viewpoint are thought-provoking, particularly his central thesis that there is a distinct educational way of thinking. In Biesta's words, the Continental approach:

> is organised around a common *interest,* which … [is best viewed] … as a distinctly *educational* interest. It is an interest, roughly, in ways in which children and young people can become individuals who can act and think for themselves.

The kind of educator and education signified by the words *Erzieher, Lehrer* and *lehren* in which the educator is an instructor and transmitter of a body of knowledge is not what Biesta has in mind. Instead, the kind of educating Biesta refers to is intimately connected to conceptions of *Erziehung* that are concerned with an interest in the child or student as a subject (see e.g. Biesta, 2016a). So when Biesta states that we should "think educationally about philosophy", in a sense he is arguing that philosophy does not necessarily come with an interest in education, and hence distorts and restricts the emergence of a distinct understanding of education. Just as philosophy has the potential to liberate, cultivate, and stimulate those who are engaged in philosophy as a way of life (e.g. Hadot, 1995), so too can *Erziehung* or "educative teaching" interrupt the "tension between power and authority, aiming at the (mysterious) transformation of power into authority" (Biesta, 2016a, p. 842).

In order to reveal Biesta's use of theory and philosophy in education and educational research, this chapter identified four themes in the dialogue. These four themes are as follows: (1) empirical research; (2) thinking philosophically about education; thinking educationally about philosophy; (3) the beautiful risk of education; and (4) teaching ("learning from" and/or being "taught by"). Each theme has been purposely incorporated into the dialogue as a sub-heading to act as a guide for the reader as they progress through the chapter.[2]

## The dialogue

### Empirical research

**Steven Stolz (SS):** When educational researchers engage with philosophies, and in particular philosophies of education, it is usually to support investigations into specific research questions by (1) outlining a theoretical framework which situates a problem, and then (2) sketching out a methodology which clarifies the methods that are applied to either solving or analysing that problem. Can you share some examples of how you have used theories and/or philosophies in your educational research?

**Gert Biesta (GB):** Perhaps the best example is my own research on citizenship education and civic learning (see e.g. Biesta, 2011a; Biesta, Lawy, & Kelly, 2009; Biesta, Lawy, McDonnell, & Lawy, 2008; Biesta, De Bie, & Wildemeersch, 2013). When I started work in this field, I soon found out that a significant amount of research – probably about 95 per cent of all the research being conducted – focused on the question of how children and young people could acquire the knowledge, skills and dispositions needed to be and become good citizens. On the one hand, there was research that explored how this worked in classroom settings, investigating the relationships between the teaching of citizenship and the subsequent acquisition of the desired knowledge, skills and dispositions by students. On the other hand, there was research that explored how children and young people would acquire citizenship knowledge, skills and dispositions outside of school contexts, for example in organised leisure activities or through informal learning. While there is value in this kind of work, the thing that struck me was that all the research started from the assumption that it is possible to identify what a good citizen is, and what kind of knowledge, skills and dispositions children and young people need, therefore, to be and become good citizens. One could say that the prevailing approach saw citizenship education as a matter of *socialisation*: getting the "right" knowledge, skills and dispositions "into" children and young people.

To me this already didn't make sense at an intuitive level, as I would assume that a democratic society is one in which citizens raise their voice and think and act critically, rather than simply acting on the bias of a "template" given to them. But there is also a significant body of literature in political philosophy – such as the work of Hannah Arendt, Chantal Mouffe and Jacques Rancière, to name the authors that have been influential for my own thinking – that highlights that democracy is a much more open, undetermined and contested process. Here the question as to what it means to be democratic and act democratically is part of what is "at stake" in the process of democracy, and not something that can simply be pinned down and then handed down through education. This led me to the development of what in my own work I have referred to as a "subjectification" conception of citizenship education and civic learning; one that focuses explicitly on what it means to exist as a democratic subject, and what learning and education have to do in relation to this (see e.g. Biesta, 2011b, 2011c). Such an approach not only looks very differently at what citizenship itself means, but also places questions of education and learning somewhere "else" – not as what has to be acquired in order to become a "good citizen", but rather as that which can help to deepen one's attempts at existing as a democratic subject. This shows that a "subjectification" approach not only provides an alternative theoretical framework for understanding citizenship education and civic learning, but also raises quite different questions for research. It asks empirical researchers to look elsewhere and look differently – something I have also tried to do in my own research in this field (Biesta & Cowell, 2012).

**SS:** In terms of your background – please correct me if I'm wrong – it was my understanding that you were a physicist?

**GB:** I taught physics for about ten years, though I wouldn't describe myself as a physicist, rather as a teacher of physics!

**SS:** What, then, led you to engage with philosophy, particularly philosophy of education?

**GB:** During my time as a teacher I got interested in wider questions about teaching, curriculum, education, and so on, so I decided to go to university in the evening to study education. In the Netherlands it is possible to study this as an academic subject in its own right, not related to teacher education. Initially I thought that I would specialise in the more "technical" side of education – what in North America is sometimes referred to as the field of curriculum and instruction – but I found what was happening in that area a little boring and I was much more excited by the courses that had a significant theoretical and historical dimension. I therefore decided to specialise in the theory and history of education. I also had an opportunity to study some philosophy and eventually decided to take a degree in philosophy as well, focusing on the philosophy of the social sciences.

**SS:** Since completing your degrees in education and philosophy, what made you engage in educational philosophy and theory, as opposed to philosophy of social science?

**GB:** I actually never had the ambition to become a philosopher, but saw, and have always seen, myself as firmly rooted in the field of education. Studying philosophy was mainly because I wanted to deepen and expand my understanding of some of the underlying philosophical assumptions, ideas and theories in the field of education, and for me philosophy has always remained a resource for my educational scholarship. In the Netherlands, at least at the time when I was a student, this was still a possibility. Since then empirical research, particularly research of a quantitative nature, has become even more dominant and has significantly marginalised the more theoretical and philosophical engagement with educational questions. This, by the way, was in the Netherlands where it was never really conceived as "philosophy of education", but rather as educational scholarship informed by a range of intellectual resources, including philosophy.

## Thinking philosophically about education; thinking educationally about philosophy

**SS:**    That leads me to my next question. Recently you wrote a chapter in an edited book entitled "Thinking philosophically about education; thinking educationally about philosophy" (Biesta, 2015). I can understand the first part ["thinking philosophically about education"], but the second part ["thinking educationally about philosophy"] I am having trouble understanding. For instance, how can you "think educationally about philosophy"? If you look at some of the earlier work of P.H. Hirst and R.S. Peters (see e.g. Hirst, 1963; Peters, 1966; Hirst & Peters, 1970) they talk about philosophy being utilised as a second order activity in education. In this case, can you help me understand what you mean?

**GB:**    This is indeed quite an important issue, at least from my perspective. It has a lot to do with two very different ways in which the academic study of education has developed. One of these ways came to fruition in the English-speaking world, whereas the other has its origins in the German-speaking world – and both approaches have impacted on developments in other countries (Biesta, 2011d). I would say that in the English-speaking world the academic study of education has established itself in the twentieth century as a multi-disciplinary endeavour that focuses on the study of educational processes, practices and institutions. In its structure it is similar to such fields as business studies and communication and media studies which are organised around a particular phenomenon, and use a range of academic disciplines to study the phenomenon. This is why, in this constellation, we find such things as philosophy of education, psychology of education, sociology of education and history of education – all indicating that education, as a phenomenon, is being studied from a particular disciplinary angle. In the German-speaking world, however, the academic study of education established itself as a discipline in its own right, next to philosophy, psychology, sociology and history, and hence with its own forms of theory and theorising, its own vocabulary, its own social infrastructure – journals, academic departments, professorships, scholarly organisations, and so on.

There are two issues that are important here. One is the question of identity; the other is the question of resources. With regard to the question of identity, one could, of course, argue that both the Anglo-American construction, as I call it in some of my writings (Biesta, 2011d), and the German or Continental construction give the academic study of education a particular identity. In the Anglo-American approach, the identity is organised around a common object of study – "education" – whereas in the German approach the identity of the discipline is not a matter of *what* is being studied, but to put it briefly, of *how* this is being studied. I use the word "this" here deliberately, because this is where the difference actually lies. Again briefly: whereas the Anglo-American approach is organised around a common object of study, the German approach is organised around a common *interest,* which, in that approach, is identified as a distinctly *educational* interest. It is an interest, roughly, in ways in which children and young people can be and become individuals who can act and think for themselves.

Whereas in the Anglo-American approach it is quite "normal" to say that one can ask philosophical questions about education (after all, education there appears as an object of study and one can use philosophy to study this object), in the German approach one cannot just ask philosophical questions about education (or psychological, sociological or historical questions for that matter). There is also the idea that one can ask educational questions about education, because "the educational", if we can use that notion, stands for a particular perspective that is different from, say, a philosophical perspective. And it is in that context that it becomes possible to not just ask philosophical questions about education, but also ask educational questions about quite a lot of things, including philosophy itself. That's what I'm after with this title.

**SS:** To me it seems nonsensical. How can education contribute to philosophy?

**GB:** It's interesting that you use the word "nonsensical" because in an earlier version of a paper I wrote about these two different traditions, I received feedback along similar lines from a reviewer of the journal to which I submitted it. The idea that I would ask educational questions about education was, as the reviewer put it, as nonsensical as the suggestion that one can ask cookery questions about cooking. To me this comment actually proves the point I was making in the paper, namely that the Anglo-American and the Continental constructions are so different, not just in their social organisation, but also in intellectual and conceptual infrastructure, so to speak, that what makes perfect sense within one construction appears meaningless – literally nonsensical – in another.

Educational questions, that is, questions that take an educational perspective, are actually rather important in the field of educational research and scholarship. The main reason for this has to do with the fact that if we do not have some kind of criterion for what would "count" as education, it would be impossible to conduct any research on education. Education is, after all, not a natural phenomenon, like trees or stars, but a social phenomenon and therefore something we can only identify if we have some notion of what education "is". Empirical researchers who want to study education can, of course, walk into a school or a classroom, but they can only start doing research – more technically: they only have an object for investigation – if they have some criterion to judge what, from all the things happening in and around the school, actually constitutes a case of "education", and not, for example, training or indoctrination. That is why it is important, not just for theoretical work but first and foremost for educational work, that we are able to generate educational questions which are very different questions from, say, philosophical or sociological questions.

By suggesting that it could also be relevant to ask educational questions about philosophy itself, that is, to explore philosophy from an educational angle or interest, I am trying to show that, just as it is legitimate to ask philosophical questions about education, it is also legitimate (and interesting and important) to ask educational questions about philosophy. One area where I have done this in my own work, for example, is in relation to philosophy for children which, in my view, often remains just a matter of doing philosophy in schools rather than those engaged in philosophy for children asking what the educational significance of engaging with philosophy might be (Biesta, 2011e).

**SS:** David Carr (1999, 2003a, 2003b, 2010a, 2010b), as you would know, makes it very clear that we blur and misunderstand the distinction between schooling and education. We see schooling as education and education as schooling, but we need to understand the difference between the two. Clearly what happens within school is not educational all the time, and this blurring of the boundaries is most noticeable in undergraduate students, and, dare I say it, some postgraduate students I have taught over the years, who think that everything they do as a teacher is educational.

**GB:** Yes, this is quite helpful here, because it indicates that not everything that happens in schools is automatically educational. But more importantly, at least for the topic of our conversation, it also shows that the use of the word "education" in this context is not descriptive but evaluative: it is a judgement of what we would see as worthwhile education.

**SS:** As someone who's a native English speaker, I'm obviously biased because I think in one kind of paradigm, or one particular way. I have never seriously thought about both speaking and thinking in other languages concurrently. Since language is intimately tied to culture, I can see how this could affect your way of thinking.

**GB:** It does, although it is more than just a matter of speaking and understanding different languages – it also has to do with quite different ways in which

**60** Steven A. Stolz and Gert Biesta

the academic study of education has developed in the English-speaking and German-speaking worlds.

SS: Earlier, when you were talking about empirical research, I was wondering how such research can inform educational philosophy and theory, or philosophies in general? The reason I ask this question is in part due to the humanities often not being associated with empirical-type work, or sustained engagement with empirical scientific method, particularly in the collection of empirical data as evidence.

GB: I agree that there is indeed quite a distance between philosophical scholarship, especially if it sees itself first and foremost located within the field of philosophy, and empirical educational research which, at least in some forms, would be located in the social and behavioural sciences and not in the humanities. Particularly when notions like "the scientific method" or "evidence" are being brought in, it looks like philosophy and empirical research have nothing to do with each other and empirical research is not very relevant for philosophical work. This is what I see happening a lot, but it is not how things necessarily have to be. There are, for example, forms of empirical research – such as those stemming from phenomenology – that are much closer to the humanities and hence also much closer to philosophy. And I do think that good phenomenological research, also in education, can contribute to philosophical work as well, for example by sharpening up questions, getting a better sense of problems, and so on. In the other direction, that is "from" philosophy "to" educational research, I encounter a lot of empirical research that, in my view, is theoretically underdeveloped. Often it's methodologically sophisticated, but either focusing on very trivial questions or on questions that are plainly misguided. One significant example of this – and in my opinion this is one of the bigger, and perhaps even the biggest, problems of contemporary educational research – is the assumption that the relationship between teaching and learning is a causal relationship, and hence one that, through research, can be made more effective (that is, more geared towards the production of certain outcomes). This, from my perspective, is based on a fundamental misunderstanding of how education "works" and I think that it remains important for people doing philosophical and theoretical work in education not just to point this out, but also to develop viable alternatives – which is another thing I've been trying to do in my work (Biesta, 2016b).

### The beautiful risk of education

SS: In the prologue section of one of your latest works, *The Beautiful Risk of Education* (Biesta, 2014), you quite rightly bring to our attention how certain contemporary educational systems are trying to take the risk out of education.

GB: Indeed, and, as I just mentioned, there is also a significant research effort that tries to make education more "effective", which means that it starts from the assumption that, if there is no gap between teaching and learning, no openness, and hence no risk, education has become perfect. But that perfection, in my view, turns education into something else, something *un*-educational: a matter of production and control.

**SS:** That's right.

**GB:** And that holds an important message for empirical researchers about what kind of underlying feel they have about not only the dynamics of education, but also the purposes of education.

**SS:** I have a problem with a lot of the empirical work that takes place in the name of education that is reducible to generalisations which are never used, and/or not useful within a classroom context. It's great for academics, but as a former teacher who taught for ten years in a secondary school, I know many of my former colleagues would be thinking: "Well, what use is this to me?", "How can this help me in the classroom?", and so on. In a sense, it becomes useless for teachers and only useful to academics.

**GB:** The problem is that one way in which you can make this kind of research work within educational settings is if you change education so that it fits the logic of research. This is, of course, a very curious and problematic reversal of what the relationship should be, but nonetheless it's happening – a good example is what is called 'data-driven teaching', which has little to do with teaching and everything to do with producing data. Policy is also playing a role here, partly because some policy makers tend to like this view of education – that the main job is generating test scores and then making adjustments in order to generate better test scores, and so on. But policy makers, at least in the UK, are also trying to steer research in this direction, for example, by only providing funding for randomised controlled trials.

**SS:** Some may argue that it's a good thing that policy is trying to engage with research, particularly if the research can be used within a classroom context.

**GB:** At one level, one could say that the interest of policy makers in research should be welcomed because there may well be valuable insights for practice and for policy itself. But my concern is that the interest is quite biased, both with regard to the kind of research they want to listen to and fund to begin with, but also in terms of how such research is supposed to promote a particular "kind" of education – a particular way of enacting education according to what I sometimes refer to as "the logic of pig farming" rather than the logic of education (see e.g. Biesta, 2016b).

**SS:** Can you tell me a bit more about what you mean by "pig farming" in this context?

**GB:** For me, pig farming is a nice image for a particular way to think about education, namely in terms of an input-output logic. In such a view, which is actually quite common, teaching is seen as an intervention that needs to bring about some kind of result on the side of the student – the language of "learning outcomes" fits well in this way of talking about education. For me, however, this view doesn't fit – teaching is not an intervention, and learning is not an outcome or production – because the dynamics of education take place in the domain of meaning. Hence the way in which education works – if the word 'works' is appropriate here – is not in terms of causes and effects, which would basically be a materialistic way of thinking about education, but in terms of meaning and interpretation. Education is a matter of communication, where teachers "present" sense, so to speak, and students try to "make" sense. When you miss that, for example, by talking about intervention and learning outcomes, you've already created quite a distorted starting point.

Conceiving of education in terms of the production of learning outcomes also implies that the "right" learning outcomes are already specified in advance, which, if you take that as a template for education, actually means that you have already identified the future for the student; you have already defined what the student needs to "produce" in order to be "successful". Rather, I am inclined to think that the job of education is to open futures for children and young people – which is a far more uncertain and risky business. That doesn't mean that students should just do what they like, but if we organise education in such a way that we already know what the outcome should be at the other end, there's little future for the next generation left.

**SS:** In *The Beautiful Risk of Education* (Biesta, 2014) you talk about how engagement in education, both by educators and by those being educated, always entails a risk. Can you say how you came to this, and then why you think it's "beautiful"?

**GB:** A major motivation for my exploration of the risky dimensions of education came from many examples in policy, research and practice that try to take all the risk, all the openness, all the unpredictability away from education on the assumption that less risk, less openness, less unpredictability will always make education better. That is fine if you think that education is only about control and production, but if it is about opening up a future for children and young people – if it is about lighting a fire, rather than filling a vessel, as I say in the opening sentence – then risk is actually quite essential for education. So that's one of the main points of the book: if we take all the risk away from education we eventually have taken education itself away from education.

The idea to refer to such a risk as "beautiful" was partly in order to have a different adjective from those that are being used in the drive to make education more effective, which would not have been the case if I had spoken about the "useful" risk of education, for example. I also didn't want to call it the "good" risk of education, mainly in order to stay away from morality and ethics. What the word "beautiful" allowed me to do was to refer to a particular "gesture"; that is, when we call something beautiful we express an appreciation for the fact that it exists, that it is there. For me, that gesture is a fundamental educational gesture – if we do not start with trust in our students, with an appreciation that they are there, that they exist,

Gert Biesta on thinking philosophically **63**

there's probably little of educational significance that can happen. So this lies behind the use of the word "beautiful". What I also like is that it is a bit uncommon; I always hope that such words make people hesitate a little and perhaps think.

SS: Well it certainly does. One thing I find interesting about your use of the word "risk" concerns the connection you make with teaching as a "gift" of giving. You make an excellent point that this "risk" is due in part to not everyone being prepared to receive this gift (see e.g. Biesta, 2013a, 2013b).

## Teaching ("learning from" and/or "being taught by")

GB: This is quite a complicated argument, so let me try to see if I can shed some light on it. The context is a discussion in which I ask how we might describe the relationship between teachers and students. I suggest that it is quite common, particularly nowadays, to capture this in terms of learning and say that when teachers teach students, students learn from their teachers. My concern with this description of teaching and the teacher is that the teacher cannot really be a teacher. If all that happens is that students learn from their teachers, you could say that the teacher is, in a sense, similar to a book, or the internet, or anything else students can learn from. The teacher ends up as a resource.

This is a way of looking at the relationship between teachers and students that is "driven" from the perspective of the student, and has become quite common in contemporary education where, as I have discussed in detail in earlier writings (Biesta, 2006, 2010), almost everything that is being said in and about education is articulated in terms of learning. What begins to disappear in such a description of the relationship between teachers and students is a very different quality of teaching, namely that teaching is a process where teachers give something to their students. Sometimes they give what students want, but teaching also has to do with giving something to students that they don't want or didn't know they could want or would want. From this angle, then, there begins to emerge a rather fundamental difference between students who learn from their teachers – where it is their learning, their sense-making – and students who are being taught by their teachers – where something actually comes to them, whether they wanted it or not. This experience of "being taught" is, in my view, a very different one from the experience of "learning from", and this is what I try to highlight and explore in the chapter on "teaching" in *The Beautiful Risk of Education* (Biesta, 2014).

I would like to add that the difference between "learning from" and "being taught by" stretches further than just the classroom, and the interaction between teachers and students. For me, "learning from" and "being taught by" also depict very different ways in which we can think of our way of being in the world. Learning "from" is what in recent work I refer to as a hermeneutical gesture, where everything starts from my desire to understand, make sense, comprehend.

Being taught "by" goes in the opposite direction and is about those situations and experiences where something comes to me – whether I want it or not, whether it makes sense or not – and where, so we might say, it's for me to figure out how to respond to what, or for that matter who, comes to me.

For me, this is also an important dimension of education, because rather than confirming the student as the centre of meaning-making and comprehension, it sort of decentres the student, or puts the student differently in relation to the world. For me, this is an important reason to look again at teaching and its significance, and not to think that teaching is an outdated idea and that we only need learning (Biesta, 2017).

There is, however, one proviso here – and this shows why the argument is quite complicated – because I am not suggesting that the teacher is the one who can "produce" the experience of being taught. If that is the conclusion one would draw from what I have just said, there is a risk that before we know it we are back with the teacher as the control figure and with teaching as a matter of production. So whereas the difference between "learning from" and "being taught by" opens up a space in which we can recover and rediscover the importance of teaching, we have to bear in mind that teaching remains a risky business itself. Probably the most we can do as teachers is to be aware of the difference between "learning from" and "being taught by", and work with this difference in our teaching, but not on the assumption that we can control what it is that students will encounter as the experience of being taught. In more philosophical language one might say – and that's how I explore it in *The Beautiful Risk of Education* (Biesta, 2014) as well – that teaching is a gift, but it's not the teacher who can give the gift of teaching. The encounter with the experience of being taught is, in other words, neither in the hands of the students nor in the hands of the teachers. Does that make sense?

**SS:**    Yes, it does. There's almost a theological element to your argument. In particular, I am thinking about the Christian theology of grace. For instance, just as the grace of Jesus Christ is always constant and unconditional to all those who want to receive it, it can also be rejected, denied, ignored, and so on. In a similar way, a teacher's gift is an unconditional commitment to teach his or her students, but this gift needs to be received by students.

**GB:**    I have to confess that I studied theology for two years before I ended up as a physics teacher.

**SS:**    That makes a lot of sense in this case.

**GB:**    In conversations with a good colleague of mine, we have come up with the phrase "teaching for the possibility of being taught" and I think this nicely captures the predicament of, on the one hand, making a case for teaching, but on the other hand, not wanting to return to the teacher as this omnipotent figure who can produce and control the "arrival" of the experience of being taught. So the teacher ends up with a kind of "powerless power", and in exercising this power the teacher risks themselves as well.

**SS:** To use your theological concept of omnipotence, in a way the teacher is set up as the all-powerful, all-knowing deity. So I agree with what you're saying that it's not the best way to approach our teaching. I guess it's a way of saying we need to reconsider our understanding of what it means to teach.

**GB:** Your criticism of that position of the teacher is a valid criticism. But I don't think that the critique of "teaching as control" means that we should get rid of the teacher and just turn education towards learning. The real challenge is to think again about what the teacher is, what it means to exist as a teacher, and how teaching can be progressive rather than conservative.

**SS:** As soon as you take the teacher out of the equation you remove all the opportunities for that dialogue that you clearly talk about. In a sense, that's the essence of education, which can be traced all the way back to the sophists.

**GB:** I see a lot of developments where we're turning towards learning, or the teacher as the facilitator of learning. To me, this just misses the point of why the teacher is important.

## Conclusion

This chapter has examined Gert Biesta's approach to the study of education and educational research. As a means to expand on Biesta's method and methodology, four themes were identified in the dialogue: (1) empirical research; (2) thinking philosophically about education; thinking educationally about philosophy; (3) the beautiful risk of education; and, (4) teaching ("learning from" and/or being "taught by"). It was found that a useful starting point to understanding Biesta's work revolved around his phrase "thinking philosophically about education; thinking educationally about philosophy". Here, Biesta sets out to challenge those who may reside in the Anglo-American tradition of education to (re)conceptualise and (re)consider what it may mean to "think educationally about philosophy". Not only is such an approach thought-provoking, but more importantly the radically different alternative provided by the Continental approach to the study of education and educational research shifts the focus from the identification of an *external* phenomenon to an *internal*, existential understanding.

## Notes

1 For more detail on this account, see Biesta's (2011d) article entitled "Disciplines and theory in the academic study of education: A comparative analysis of the Anglo-American and Continental construction of the field".

2 It is also important to point out that some revisions have been made to the original interview dialogue recorded, ranging from adding, removing, or correcting obvious errors from the transcription process, through to providing greater clarity and coherence on a number of crucial concepts discussed. In most instances, we have retained the dialectical discussion that occurred between two people surrounding a common question posed so it is both engaging to the reader and generates further discussion.

## References

Biesta, G. J. J. (2006). *Beyond Learning: Democratic Education for a Human Future.* Boulder, CO: Paradigm Publishers.

Biesta, G. J. J. (2010). *Good Education in an Age of Measurement: Ethics, Politics, Democracy.* Boulder, CO: Paradigm Publishers.

Biesta, G. J. J. (2011a). *Learning Democracy in School and Society: Education, Lifelong Learning and the Politics of Citizenship.* Rotterdam, Netherlands: Sense Publishers.

Biesta, G. J. J. (2011b). The ignorant citizen: Mouffe, Rancière, and the subject of democratic education. *Studies in Philosophy and Education, 30*(2), 141–153.

Biesta, G. J. J. (2011c). Citizenship education reconsidered: Socialisation, subjectification, and the desire for democracy. *Bildungsgeschichte: International Journal for the Historiography of Education, 1*(1), 58–67.

Biesta, G. J. J. (2011d). Disciplines and theory in the academic study of education: A comparative analysis of the Anglo-American and Continental construction of the field. *Pedagogy, Culture and Society, 19*(2), 175–192.

Biesta, G. J. J. (2011e). Philosophy, exposure and children: How to resist the instrumentalisation of philosophy in education. *Journal of Philosophy of Education, 45*(2), 305–319.

Biesta, G. J. J. (2013a). *The Beautiful Risk of Education.* Boulder, CO.: Paradigm Publishers.

Biesta, G. J. J. (2013b). Receiving the gift of teaching: From "learning from" to "being taught by". *Studies in Philosophy and Education, 32*, 449–461.

Biesta, G. J. J. (2015). Thinking philosophically about education; thinking educationally about philosophy. In D. Matheson (Ed.). *An Introduction to the Study of Education* (4th edn.). pp. 64–82. London and New York: Routledge.

Biesta, G. J. J. (2016a). Who's afraid of teaching? Heidegger and the question of education ('Bildung/Erziehung'). *Educational Philosophy and Theory, 48*(8), 832–845.

Biesta, G. J. J. (2016b). Improving education through research? From effectiveness, causality and technology, to purpose, complexity and culture. *Policy Futures in Education, 14*(2), 194–210.

Biesta, G. J. J. (2017). *The Rediscovery of Teaching.* London and New York: Routledge.

Biesta, G. J. J. & Cowell, G. (2012). How is community done? Understanding civic learning through psychogeographic mapping. *International Journal of Lifelong Education, 31*(1), 47–61.

Biesta, G. J. J., De Bie, M. & Wildemeersch, D. (Eds.). (2013). *Civic Learning, Democratic Citizenship and the Public Sphere.* Dordrecht, Netherlands and Boston, MA: Springer.

Biesta, G. J. J., Lawy, R. & Kelly, N. (2009). Understanding young people's citizenship learning in everyday life: The role of contexts, relationships and dispositions. *Education, Citizenship and Social Justice, 4*(1), 5–24.

Biesta, G. J. J., Lawy, R., McDonnell, J. & Lawy, H. (2008). The art of democracy: Gallery education and young people's democratic learning. In B. Taylor (Ed.), *Inspiring Learning in Galleries: Research Reports* (pp. 242–265). London: Engage.

Carr, D. (1999). The dichotomy of liberal versus vocational education: Some basic conceptual geography. In S. Toxer (Ed.), *Philosophy and Education* (pp. 53–63). Urbana, IL: Philosophy of Education Society.

Carr, D. (2003a). *Making Sense of Education: An Introduction to the Philosophy and Theory of Education and Teaching.* London and New York: Routledge.

Carr, D. (2003b). Philosophy and the meaning of 'education'. *Theory and Research in Education, 1*(2), 195–212.

Carr, D. (2010a). The goals of education. In J. Arthur & I. Davies (Eds.), *The Routledge Education Studies Textbook* (pp. 9–18). London and New York: Routledge.

Carr, D. (2010b). The philosophy of education and educational theory. In R. Bailey, R. Barrow, D. Carr & C. McCarthy (Eds.), *The SAGE Handbook of Philosophy of Education* (pp. 37–53). London: SAGE.

Hadot, P. (1995). *Philosophy as a Way of Life: Spiritual Exercises from Socrates to Foucault* (M. Chase, Trans.). Oxford, UK: Blackwell Publishing.

Hirst, P. H. (1963). Philosophy and educational theory. *British Journal of Educational Studies*, *12*(1), 51–64.

Hirst, P. H., & Peters, R. S. (1970). *The Logic of Education*. London: Routledge & Kegan Paul.

Peters, R. S. (1966). *Ethics and Education*. London: Allen & Unwin.

# 5

## PENNY ENSLIN ON LIBERAL FEMINISM, JUSTICE AND EDUCATION

### In dialogue with Jennifer Bleazby

*Jennifer Bleazby and Penny Enslin*

### Introduction

Penny Enslin is an analytic philosopher of education and politics. Her research examines a range of contemporary educational problems, especially through the lens of liberal feminism. She has also drawn on other theoretical perspectives, such as Marxism, post-colonialism, African philosophies of education, and cosmopolitanism. As a liberal feminist, much of Enslin's research examines how different educational theories, policies and practices foster or inhibit autonomy and social justice. An overview of the key tenets of liberal feminism provides a useful framework for understanding the aspects of Enslin's work that are discussed in the following dialogue.[1]

Liberal feminism evolved out of liberalism, a political theory that emerged during the enlightenment as a response to authoritarianism. According to liberalism, individuals should be free to choose and pursue their own ideal of the good[2] so long as they do not interfere with the right of others to do the same. Thus, for liberals, a just society is essentially one that protects individual autonomy. A key point of disagreement amongst liberals concerns the extent to which the state should interfere in people's lives in order to protect individual autonomy. Classical liberals argue that the state should be limited to protecting civil liberties (e.g., the right to vote, own property, free speech, etc.) and should refrain from interfering in the economy and the private, domestic sphere. However, this can result in an unequal society because some individuals are better able to acquire resources and exercise their autonomy. For this reason, social or welfare liberals argue that the state must do more than protect basic civil liberties. It must intervene to create a more equal society. Common interventions include redistributing wealth through taxation, public schooling and health care, and support services for the disabled, marginalised and disadvantaged. Thus, social liberals place as much emphasis on equality as they do on liberty. Contemporary liberal feminists, including Enslin, Susan Moller Okin (1989a, 1989b, 1994), and Martha Nussbaum (1999, 2000), are typically social liberals. This is somewhat inevitable given their commitment to defending the rights of marginalised groups, especially women and girls, who need more than basic civil rights in order to fully develop and exercise autonomy. Like many liberal feminists, Enslin has also examined social justice issues affecting other marginalised groups, such as apartheid in South Africa and global justice for people living in developing countries.

Liberal philosophers have written much about the aims and nature of education because they recognise that schooling can play an important role in fostering (or inhibiting) autonomy. While there are competing notions of liberal education, liberals commonly argue that students should be exposed to a wide range of knowledge, skills, vocations and conceptions of the good, so as to maximise the options available to them. Education should also foster the child's capacity for independent thought and decision making so they can freely choose between these options. Thus, liberals typically oppose schooling that aims to indoctrinate or inculcate students into accepting one particular worldview or vocation. For example, many liberal feminists, including Enslin (2003), reject schooling that prepares women to fulfil only traditionally feminine roles. In addition, many liberals argue that education should teach students about their rights and responsibilities in a democracy (e.g., civics and citizenship education, human rights education, and social justice and global education, like the Scotland-Malawi Partnership program that Enslin discusses below). Equal access to quality education is also a concern of many liberal theorists. As discussed below, Enslin defends the notion of a universal right to quality education and she has examined the extent to which different groups have equal access to quality education in a globalised world (e.g., Enslin & Tjiattas, 2004b, 2006, 2009, 2015a).

Liberalism has been quite widely criticised, especially by communitarians, post-modernists and other types of feminists. For example, one common criticism is that it promotes rugged individualism and an adversarial notion of rights, which discourages community, altruism and care. Some feminists have argued that this individualistic notion of self and society is masculine and is opposed to a more 'feminine', relational notion of self. Another criticism is that liberalism is incompatible with multiculturalism because it is intolerant of cultures that prioritise community, group rights or hierarchal structures over individual autonomy. On a similar note, some feminists have argued that liberal feminism ignores differences amongst women and universalises from the perspective of white, heterosexual, middle-class women.[3]

Enslin has often defended liberal ideals against such criticisms. For example, she argues that liberalism is actually compatible with valuing cultural diversity and community (e.g., Enslin, 2003; Enslin & Tjiattas, 2004a). Although, she maintains that we should not necessarily tolerate all aspects of cultures that unjustifiably suppress autonomy, such as patriarchal cultures. Like most liberal feminists, Enslin has also reconstructed liberalism so as to avoid some of its pitfalls. For example, she rejects the private/public dualism inherent in John Rawls' theory of justice (Enslin, 2003). While Rawls argues that the state should refrain from interfering in the private, domestic sphere, many feminists have pointed out that the domestic sphere is often a site of oppression for women and girls. For example, the unpaid labour women do in the home often leaves them materially dependent on men, vulnerable to exploitation and violence, and unable to pursue other valuable activities, such as schooling and paid employment. As such, most liberal feminists want to extend the sort of rights and laws that exist in the public realm to the private realm. As we see in the dialogue below, Enslin uses liberal feminism and numerous other theories in a critical, pragmatic way, adapting them so as to effectively respond to the social and educational problems she is examining.

## The dialogue

**Jennifer Bleazby (JB):**    When educational researchers make use of philosophies it is usually for one of two purposes: (1) to outline a theoretical framework, and (2) to outline a particular research methodology in order to investigate specific educational research questions. Can you share any examples from your own research of how you use philosophy to address educational research questions and, if so, which philosophers or philosophies you have used?

**Penny Enslin (PE):**    My own research is philosophical, so I have done very little research in which I use a philosophical theory to frame, and then conduct, a piece of empirical research. But I would not want to make too big a distinction between those two complementary approaches to research. I have worked across a number of different philosophical frameworks or philosophies, depending on the kinds of issues and questions I want to explore, though mainly with a liberal feminist orientation. These have included – and it might sound a bit crazy at first glance, but I can explain it if you are sceptical – liberal feminism (e.g., Enslin, 2003; Enslin & Tjiattis, 2004a; Enslin & Tjiattis, 2006) but also a Marxist, specifically Althusserian, framework when writing about ideology in teacher education (e.g., Enslin, 1984). In another piece of research I drew on Foucault's work (Enslin, 1990), because it was the most obviously applicable to a problem I was trying to address about power in teacher education. Most recently, I have been particularly interested in post-colonial theories (e.g., Enslin, 2016).[4] Thus, it depends on what one wants to explore. I don't think it is particularly promiscuous to be drawing on a number of different philosophical approaches. They are not, as I am sure you would agree, doctrines. That is, we are not trying to restate our faith in any particular position.

Let me mention the sorts of things that I think we can do by working within those philosophical frameworks on a chosen problem. Several decades ago, there would have been an assumption that one takes different 'isms' from philosophical traditions and applies them to particular issues.

Penny Enslin on liberal feminism **71**

However, I think the practice of philosophy of education is much more fluid and imaginatively useful now than it used to be. The most important action that one is undertaking when working philosophically is to develop arguments about a particular problem. In order to do that, one needs to work with some key concepts. Two concepts that I have been particularly interested in are "democracy" and "justice". These complement each other and have been at the heart of much of what I have worked on in relation to education in the last few years. I would also say that what we want to do is analyse the arguments and assumptions of those who influence what goes on in education. Philosophers are particularly well equipped to closely examine the claims made by people in powerful positions – in educational hierarchies and government, and by policy makers – and to probe their assumptions and the kinds of arguments they make. But most importantly, I think that what philosophers do – and it is a very practical activity – is argue a substantive position on what we should be doing.

**JB:** A lot of educational policies, including school curricula, uncritically use terms like "democracy" and "justice" and "civics and citizenship", as if these are not contested concepts. It seems that many educational researchers and policy developers fail to perform a thorough analysis of these complex concepts. In philosophy these terms have long been subject to critical analysis and theorisation. As a lot of your work looks specifically at such concepts, can you give any examples of how philosophy has enabled you to analyse some of these concepts in order to respond to educational problems?

**PE:** In my early work the critical targets were easy to identify. I was critiquing ideologies and policies about education under apartheid in South Africa (e.g., Enslin, 1984, 1986, 1990, 1992). The officially sanctioned philosophy of education known as Fundamental Pedagogics provided apologies and bogus justifications for segregation and for privileging one worldview over another – dressed up as a science. I developed that body of critique working within the mainstream approaches to philosophy of education of the time. The critical tools put forward by philosophers like Althusser or Foucault offered illuminating ways to discredit those ideologies. Liberal theory also provided tools for contesting authoritarian conceptions of childhood and for defending autonomy as an aim of education in their place (Enslin, 1992).

Now that I am working in Europe, which has quite a sophisticated policy context, one of the targets of my critique is the assumption that developing a competitive national economy is a good thing (e.g., Enslin & Tjiattas, 2004b, 2015a). Perhaps an associated assumption, but one which is now much more problematic because of the global financial crisis of 2007–8 and the Brexit Referendum of 2016, is the idea that a powerful Europe is a self-evidently desirable policy goal and that education has a role to play in making European countries (whether collectively or individually) competitive against other parts of the world. Those assumptions are often unspoken, but they creep into policy, rendering it immoral. One issue that

**72** Jennifer Bleazby and Penny Enslin

philosophers of education need to point out is that if you make privileged regions of the globe more competitive, including through their education systems, that will make it much more difficult for other parts of the world that are disadvantaged by post-colonial inequality to function adequately in favour of their citizens.

JB: What are some other specific examples of educational issues that you are working on now and how are you using philosophy to examine these issues?

PE: Let me describe the context and then I will explain the issue. In Scotland, we have programs that aim to encourage Scottish children to engage with children in schools in Malawi (see Scotland-Malawi Partnership, 2009; Scottish Government, 2005). This is largely because of the historical relationship between Scotland and Malawi and the idea that these countries are meant to have a "special relationship". Philosophers teach us to be attuned to terms like this and whenever a special relationship is mentioned, one needs to be alert and critical. But I think it is largely a benevolent project and it brings in a set of activities to do with collaboration between two fairly small countries around education, health and various other spheres. I am interested in what is happening in such projects and what our assumptions are when we encourage Scottish children to write letters to children in Malawi and, in particular, to collect funds to send to schools in Malawi for feeding programs and to build classrooms and so on (Divala & Enslin, 2008; Enslin, 2011; Enslin & Hedge, 2010; MacKenzie, Enslin & Hedge, 2016). There is a potential politics of benevolence there that troubles me, but I also think it is far too easy to just condemn that kind of project and sneer at it. That is a cheap way out of reflecting on a problem. I prefer to resist insistence on political correctness in relation to a whole host of educational issues. Rather, I am interested in asking whether there is charity involved in that sort of collaboration and, if so, does that morally discredit it or is there a way that we could frame such relationships so that they are not examples of charity? Charity has a long and, I assume, respected tradition in Western Christian thought about our relationships with others. Does it need to be abandoned as a useful concept or can it be reinterpreted? Incidentally, I do need to acknowledge that on many of these issues I work with colleagues and friends who influence how I think. A lot of this work is not purely about my own ideas. While not always explicit in such reflection, an underlying liberal framework prompts questions about whether and how partnerships might foster or hinder autonomy.

Related to that issue, – and in trying to think about issues of justice and democracy between countries – I am also working on how we relate post-colonialism, as a framework, to cosmopolitanism (Enslin, 2011, 2016). They are both useful ways of trying to frame those kinds of projects between children in two different countries. I am looking at the strengths and possible weaknesses of both these theoretical perspectives. They are different. Cosmopolitanism is quite obviously sceptical about nationalism

Penny Enslin on liberal feminism **73**

as a framework for thinking about politics and about ethics. Whereas, historically, nationalism has been a necessary tool in the process of decolonisation. For example, nationalism played a role in countries in Africa and Asia in the process of freeing themselves of their colonial masters, in mobilising resistance. Nationalism does seem to be at odds with the more universalist assumptions that cosmopolitanism tries to embrace. At the moment, I am trying to work between those two theories and to see which of them might be the most useful in understanding educational engagements between countries.

**JB:** I have also examined some of these issues, especially in relation to community service learning, focusing on the concepts of charity, service, democracy and citizenship assumed by this educational practice (Bleazby, 2013, chapter 8). I think it is another educational practice where people can be quite uncritical. They just assume it is good to send students out into disadvantaged communities to do community service work, whether these be local or international communities. This is seen as an example of active citizenship education but there is often no examination of the notions of charity, service or citizenship that have been assumed. The person providing charity or service is generally in a superior position to the recipient of the charity. They are a giver to someone else who may be rendered dependent on the charity. This can reinforce existing inequalities. There are some really problematic aspects to it. However, as you say, we don't just want to say that it is bad as there are potential benefits to such practices. I just read a news article about schools sending their students over to developing countries to do things like visit orphanages or help build schools, but the work performed is often not really very useful to the community. The assumed benefit of the project seems to be that the kids doing the charity work feel good about themselves or become more altruistic. It supposedly makes them nicer people, but no one is doing any sort of critical examination into the benefits for the community that receives their charity.[5]

**PE:** I suppose at its worst it is a kind of aid-tourism. This is where I think philosophy is so practically useful because we should not dismiss those kinds of activities, but we do need to probe the underlying assumptions and the way we talk about them: the terms on which we encourage people to engage in service learning. By doing that, we can actually improve those practices by better understanding them. I was on a plane to Ethiopia for a conference a couple of years ago and there was a crowd of English teenagers who were en route, as it turns out, to build a school in Malawi. They kept the whole plane awake because they were so exuberant and they were very keen to talk about what they were going to do when they got to Malawi. Then, just as the plane was about to land, one of them shouted to the others, "Hey, what language do they speak in Malawi?". It was a very revealing moment because she perhaps should have thought about that before getting on the plane. But we need to learn from those moments and think about how we

**JB:** could remove the tourism element, so that they are, educationally, more defensible and useful.

**JB:** Earlier you mentioned liberal feminism. In Australia, there has been quite a bit of public debate about feminism in recent years, partly because we had our first female Prime Minister, Julia Gillard, who described herself as a feminist. During her prime ministership, there were many issues relating to her gender and she gave a very powerful, quite famous speech about misogyny in modern-day Australia (Gillard, 2012; Channel 10, 2012). This gave rise to quite a bit of discussion about the relevance of feminism today and what it means to be a feminist. A lot of people seem to think there is just one type of feminism and that all feminists agree and have the same opinion. Many people seem to assume quite a superficial, stereotypical notion of feminism. Can you explain liberal feminism specifically and how it differs from other types of feminism?

**PE:** Yes, we watched Gillard's famous speech here. I agree with you that there is considerable diversity, and often hostility, among feminists about which 'brand of feminism' is the best. Liberal feminists would start from the basic position that some form of autonomy is desirable for everybody, regardless of gender. I favour the view expressed by Susan Moller Okin of aiming for a just world without gender (see Okin, 1989a, 1989b; Enslin & Tjiattis, 2006). What that means of course is open to discussion. But gender should not determine people's life chances or the many ways in which we can live fulfilling lives. So feminism is also about men and liberating all of us from stereotyped gender roles. An important feature of liberal feminism for me is that it invites us to be sceptical about claims for culture and for privilege that defend unjust practices (see Enslin, 2003; Enslin & Tjiattis, 2004). I also like the way that liberal feminism helps us to overcome the assumption that there is a private sphere that should not be subject to critique and discussion of any kind (see Enslin & Tjiattis, 2006). That supposedly private sphere should also be open to criticism.

**JB:** As a liberal feminist, what other liberal theorists would you use? Do you use people like Rawls (1971) and, if so, how compatible is his theory with feminist objectives?

**PE:** I've used Rawls' work quite a lot, but with reservations (e.g., Enslin, 2003; Enslin & Tjiattas, 2006; Enslin & Tjiattas, 2015b). His basic theory of justice was ground-breaking in that it set much of the agenda for political philosophy and ethics for the second half of the twentieth century. What I don't agree with in Rawls' work is that he steps back from critically examining the private sphere, so he leaves the domestic alone. Also, he largely insisted that his theory of justice was for one society. He was talking about the United States and I think that Rawls was too reluctant to be critical of illiberal cultures and their practices. So to a considerable degree he was not a friend of feminists or of cosmopolitan conceptions of justice, although the

Penny Enslin on liberal feminism **75**

JB: best feminist interpretations of liberal theory have built on some of his basic ideas while amending some others.

JB: You also mentioned that you have used Marxism, and you mentioned that this combination of theories might sound crazy. Liberalism and Marxism are often considered to be opposing theories. How do you use them together? How can they be complementary?

PE: Well, I am not sure if I have succeeded in making them complementary! [Laughs.] I have worked in separate pockets with the two, in regard to different problems. There are interesting questions we can all ask of ourselves as researchers: "How coherent must our body of work to be?; "Does coherence require a consistent and unified theoretical stance?" I haven't got a neat answer for you because I have applied those different theories to different problems. I found Althusser very helpful in setting up the idea of an ideological state apparatus, in order to understand the ideology that was used in teacher education under apartheid and, quite crudely, to thus justify educational as well as other forms of segregation. I have never explicitly tried to put that together with liberalism to work on some other problems. However, I increasingly go back to Marx and his relevance; I find him more relevant as the years go by. In particular, one of my biggest worries about what is happening to education, and to the world in general, is how global capital is out of control. It is beyond the regulation of citizens, national governments and of international bodies. Neo-liberal influences now dominate the ways in which policy is cast, the way in which schools and universities are organised, managed and understood. I think that the Marxist tradition of analysis of capitalism is useful for examining this issue, although Marx would have seen capitalism as a necessary stage in history, with something to follow after. What is going to come after should be worrying to all of us. So it is indeed strange to become more and more of a Marxist the older one gets. Although, I am not saying that there is any one doctrine that I would want to say is mine. Theory is not like a religion. So your question is a very good one, but I cannot give you a conclusive and definitive answer.

JB: I guess what you are saying is that whatever the problem is that you are trying to examine, you would draw on any theoretical resources you can that are going to be useful.

PE: Well, yes. I suppose there are some theories that I have not drawn on. Although I have used Foucault's analysis of power in relation to teacher education in South Africa, I think the position or the framework that I am least attracted to would be post-structuralism or post-modernism. They are interesting but, constitutionally, I have not found myself able to draw on them.

JB: There are aspects of liberalism that are quite unfashionable amongst educational researchers at the moment, especially because liberalism is assumed to be incompatible with post-modernism or multiculturalism, but probably also because it is associated with neo-liberalism. I suspect a lot of research

**76** Jennifer Bleazby and Penny Enslin

students and early career researchers just think that certain theories are completely off limits. Do you find this problematic?

PE: There is too much of a tendency in philosophy of education for positions and frameworks and what you might want to call methodologies to be in vogue, dominant and required of other people, and you are right in questioning the tendency to conflate liberalism and neo-liberalism. I would prefer for there to be more diversity in the ways that we allow people to do philosophy of education. I worry about what happens when philosophy and philosophy of education become a matter of policing each other for political correctness so that there are certain ways we are not allowed to think or certain sins of which we need to be persuaded to repent.

One of the themes that I am interested in is universalism – and it probably relates to my interest in liberalism. I am defiantly a universalist, of a kind. Universalism became one of the no-go areas in philosophy of education. However, I think that in some respects it is an important position to take (e.g., Enslin & Tjiattas, 2006, 2009). For example, I am insistent that every child on the globe has a right to quality education. Not some underfunded, really poor imitation of schooling, but a right to the best that should be available. We should spend more, equally, on the education of all children. That is a stance that I want to defend.

That does raise tricky questions around cultural difference. I have been inclined to argue that we have been too willing to endorse, in the name of multiculturalism, cultural practices which are anti-educational and bad for women, and, in some ways, probably bad for men as well (e.g., Enslin, 2003; Enslin & Tjiattas, 2006). One of the features that worries me about what has happened in philosophy of education is that there is too much of a tendency to pay attention to the principle of justice as recognition, and as recognition of difference. I am not saying that we should not recognise in that way, but there needs to be more focus on redistribution of resources (Enslin & Tjiattas, 2009). In my view, philosophers who have argued around that sort of distinction are very important. I think here of somebody like Nancy Fraser (1997, 2003, 2005, 2007).

JB: I did my PhD in a School of Philosophy in Australia and, at the time, there was this increasing tension between analytic philosophy and continental philosophy, to such an extent that it was rumoured that in some schools of philosophy major factions emerged. Have you ever found this to be an issue?

PE: Yes. I think the situation has improved in some ways but what you are describing does sound familiar. I would want to mention two contexts, though this is not about my current workplace, where I do not think this kind of issue exists. In my early career in philosophy of education I was attracted to liberalism and liberal philosophy. That was a deeply uncool way to be doing philosophy of education at the time and it was expected that one should take a more Marxist line. I understand why, given the circumstances in South Africa (see Enslin, 1997). It was the height of the struggle against apartheid, there was a lot of violence, and it was a deeply divided society. I can see why people would have been pushed into competing camps, but it was regrettable. At the same time, we all move on and Marxism came to be rather sidelined by the increasing dominance of post-structuralism. I find it ironic that I would really like more Marxist theory to be done now. Those kinds of ideological wars are very destructive and very unfortunate.

My own education was in the analytical tradition and I did find myself analysing concepts. There was a period in which each key concept in philosophy of education was almost routinely subjected to careful conceptual analysis. I think quite a lot of the work done on indoctrination was in Australasia, wasn't it (e.g., Snook, 1972a, 1972b)? We worked on all of those concepts and that was quite useful, but things are much better now that philosophy of education is far more normative. So there is much more argument about what we *should* be doing. In that sense, it is very much more practical. The fact that in the more recent context of philosophy of education there is much more of a presence for continental philosophy of education, which has contributed to opening up possibilities for a wider range of ways of doing philosophy of education, has been a good thing.

**JB:** Do you think there are other problems or issues with the way philosophy of education is typically done today? Are there challenges that philosophers of education should be aware of and to which we should be responding?

**PE:** One of the big challenges for philosophers of education, and it is significant that this conversation involves one person in Australia and one person in the United Kingdom, is that there is still a dominance of philosophy of education as done in the West, or what is often called the North; although the "global North" is an odd term to use if we are including Australia, but you know what I mean. We have most, if not all, of the resources. We have jobs in which philosophers of education are given time to write, to do research and to publish. The dominant journals are based in our countries and in North America. And although Australian and New Zealand philosophers of education have probably made more of a concerted effort to engage with other philosophies of education,[6] particularly through the work of the journal *Educational Philosophy and Theory*, there is more work to be done; at least in terms of a more systematic engagement with philosophy of education that emerges out of traditions and practices and ways of thinking in other parts of the world.

Some of the work that I am doing, and have been doing over a number of years, is a critical engagement with African philosophy of education (e.g., Enslin & Horsthemke, 2016). It is important that voices from that quarter be heard. I wonder whether we do enough to bring to the fore philosophy of education from, in particular, China and India. The teaching where I currently do the most concerted work in philosophy of education is in a course called Modern Educational Thought, which is a master's level course where we consider a range of different approaches to understanding what education is. Most of my class consists of students from China. I feel some regret that we do not have more about philosophy from outside the West. We need to do more to foster engagement and research which draws on non-Western frameworks. Although I think that Western theories are very useful, too much of the research that we frame for all students in leading universities, like yours and mine, automatically opts for some kind of a standard Western framework. Even when you correctly asked me about how I reconcile that rather odd cluster of frameworks that I use, I concede that I am not going very far beyond them. I am not saying everybody should, but I think that there is work to be done in that kind of engagement.

JB: In philosophy, academics tend to work by themselves a lot – at least they predominantly publish by themselves. There is not as much joint authorship as there is in the field of education, where publications with multiple authors are common, often because many people are involved in the data collection for empirical projects. Do you engage in much collaborative research as a philosopher of education and, if so, can you describe the nature of the collaboration?

PE: I do write with several colleagues, and in different parts of the world. In my experience, what we do is to start by articulating a problem, and then we might talk about it a bit and work out what we want to say. Then we work separately on preparing different parts of the paper and go through many drafts and many Skype conversations to refine the argument. My guess is that this is probably quite different from how it would be on an empirical research project. It works quite well. I think you have to know each other fairly well and I can see that it could be a disaster if you are not able to negotiate disagreement, say around what is relevant and what should be in a paper. I did not do collaborative research for a long time and then was persuaded to co-author with a colleague, and it has worked sometimes. I can see that it might not work under some circumstances. But the whole product would, in the end, be both people's writing.

JB: Do you think that empirical research in education could make better use of philosophical theories and methods? Have you ever collaborated on any empirical research projects?

PE: I have on one project here in Scotland (MacKenzie, Enslin, & Hedge, 2016). It does seem to me that collaborating on empirical projects is more complicated. My assumption is that all educational research has got some kind of a philosophical framework. Sometimes they are not acknowledged but the best empirical research has got a well worked out framework. To give you an example, I have worked with a student who recently completed a research project on how music teachers in post-apartheid South Africa have adjusted to teaching both Western and African music in their classrooms (Drummond, 2015). She interviewed 12 teachers. The interviews worked up some wonderful data through her engagement with them about their

Penny Enslin on liberal feminism **79**

practices, their own autobiographies and how they learnt music and became teachers. Her data is lovely, but she needed to frame it in order to set up her questions and analyse the data that resulted from her interviews. So she draws on post-colonial theory to explore how, traditionally, Western music othered indigenous music in different parts of the world. She also considered ethnomusicology and studies in which researchers set out to understand and explain indigenous music in Africa, how it is constructed and how it has a different social purpose. We would not have the fine study that she produced without setting up that theoretical framework.

JB: Part of the reason we are doing this project is that we are concerned that many educational researchers, and especially research students, do not have a strong background in educational philosophy or theory. This concern is not just about a lack of students writing purely theoretical or philosophical theses. As you have explained, we think that students doing empirical studies can only conduct sophisticated data analyses and set up their projects well if they have a good grounding in educational theory. Do you find this to be an issue with the research students you supervise?

PE: At the University of Glasgow, I would mostly supervise research students who are doing what we would call a conceptual project. We deliberately use that language because many people do not like the word "philosophy" and I find myself avoiding using it. Otherwise, I would co-supervise with a colleague if the student's project is an empirical one. I really do agree that the best projects have got a suitable theoretical framing that enables one to ask the right questions and then, of course, to do an analysis of the data that is really illuminating. In our doctoral training, we encounter a fairly dominant view that most research is empirical and I think that is a pity. But one has got to respect the kind of research that students want to do and if that is the way most people want to go, then it is our role to support it. I feel sad that I have to avoid using "philosophy" and I don't teach any courses that have got the word "philosophy" in their name.

JB: That is the same here. I mostly teach courses about curriculum, pedagogy and assessment, with various philosophical theories worked into the courses where they are relevant. However, the word "philosophy" is rarely used in course materials or by teaching staff. Why do you think people are wary of philosophy? I have found this wariness of philosophy to be even more apparent in education than in other fields or disciplines.

PE: I suppose people think it is very difficult and very abstract.[7] For me it is highly practical. There is nothing more useful than a good theory that you can use to illuminate educational issues. Researching education in post-colonial contexts on issues like educational aid, for example, needs to frame research questions and to understand the significance of a project by engaging with theories of development and underdevelopment to see a particular country in a post-colonial context. Such projects benefit from theory, even if we don't call it philosophy. I suppose philosophers increasingly do draw on sociology

**80** Jennifer Bleazby and Penny Enslin

and sociological theories. Although they are different in some significant ways, they can also be very useful in creating a theoretical frame for research.

**JB:** The United Nations has a long history of fostering the practice and teaching of philosophy.[8] UNESCO's[9] Paris Declaration for Philosophy (Droit, 1995) stated that philosophy should be taught at every level of education and when it is taught it should explicitly be called "philosophy".[10] The document is adamant that people use the word "philosophy", presumably so that teachers and students are familiar with the texts and methods of the discipline of philosophy, recognising it as a distinct academic discipline with a long and important history. However, as you indicated, philosophers of education often use other terms, like "educational theory", because so many people seem averse to philosophy. I am often tempted to be defiant and say we should call it philosophy because that is what it is and so that, as a discipline, it doesn't just die out and become indistinguishable from other related, but distinct disciplines, like sociology.

**PE:** That is a hard one. I applaud the stance taken in the UNESCO Declaration, but I am not sure which one is the right approach to take. I would like to be defiant about it and insist on using the word "philosophy" but I would rather give priority to persuading people to see the usefulness of what the discipline has to offer, by drawing them into the activity without necessarily describing it as philosophy, at least to begin with.

## Conclusion

Enslin's body of work challenges some common misconceptions about educational research and philosophical methods. For example, she rejects the assumption that philosophy is merely abstract or conceptual and makes little contribution to 'real' educational problems. She has used philosophical methods and theories to explore pressing social justice and educational problems and to outline and defend practical solutions to those problems. Enslin's work also demonstrates why educational researchers should avoid the uncritical adoption of theoretical or methodological fads. This following of fads can result in useful ideas (e.g., rights, autonomy, etc.) and methods (e.g., analytic philosophy) being avoided, while fashionable ideas are uncritically adopted and applied, sometimes in problematic or even harmful ways. For example, Enslin's research does much to demonstrate the enduring value of liberalism, despite the many criticisms levelled at this theory from different quarters. Enslin demonstrates how the liberal ideas of individual autonomy, social justice and universal human rights can be used to critique unjust educational and social practices and construct more democratic alternatives. These liberal ideas are not necessarily incompatible with valuing diversity and community. Rather, the recognition and protection of universal human rights, including the right to pursue one's own conception of the good, has often been used to defend cultural diversity and equality. Liberal feminism provides conceptual tools that may help all researchers respond to a wide range of pressing social justice issues, such as the refugee crisis, climate change, developing world poverty and the dangers posed by the spread of neo-conservative and neo-liberal ideologies.

## Notes

1 It must be noted that there are many different variations of liberalism and liberal feminism, and there is often considerable disagreement amongst liberal philosophers. This is only a very rudimentary overview. For a more detailed account of liberalism and its different types see Gaus, *et al.* (2015). For a more detailed account of liberal feminism see Tong (2009).
2 For example, people have the right to choose their own lifestyles, occupations, hobbies, associate with who they please, etc., so long as they don't infringe on the rights of others to make similar choices.
3 For some critical analyses of this debate see Kiss (1997), Brennan (1999), Schwartzman (2002), Tong (2009), Bleazby (2013, Chapter 6).
4 For examples of post-colonial theory see Said (1993) and Gandhi (1998).
5 As Enslin and Hedge (2010, 2011) point out, policies relating to the Scotland–Malawi Partnership do show a critical awareness of these potential problems. For example, relevant policies state that the partnerships should be based on collaborative projects that are mutually beneficial rather than on a relationship of charity where wealthy Scottish schools provide material resources to schools in developing countries.
6 The journal *Educational Philosophy and Theory* is the journal of the Philosophy of Education Society of Australasia (PESA). While the society has always been dominated by Australian and New Zealand philosophers, in recent years the society has focused on increasing the participation and influence of philosophers from other parts of the Asia-Pacific, as well as from Africa. There has also been more effort to foster research in indigenous philosophy within the society. For example, an indigenous philosophy group has been established, the annual conference has been held in Hong Kong, Hawaii, Taiwan and Fiji, the journal has published two special issues on Asian philosophy in 2014 and 2016, including one with abstracts in Chinese, and a 2012 special issue of the journal was devoted to African philosophy of education.
7 See Conroy, Davis and Enslin (2008) for a defence of a philosophical approach to educational policy development and educational practice. This paper includes some discussion of the "widespread resistance" to the use of philosophy within the educational policy community and the privileging of empirical methods (both qualitative and quantitative).
8 For an overview of this history see UNESCO (2006, 2007).
9 The United Nations Education Scientific and Cultural Organisation
10 The exact quotation from the Paris Declaration is: "All individuals everywhere should be entitled to engage in the free pursuit of philosophy in all its forms and in all places where it may be practiced. Philosophy teaching should be maintained or expanded where it exists, introduced where it does not yet exist, and designated explicitly as "philosophy". The complete Declaration is reproduced in Droit's *Philosophy and Democracy in the World: A UNESCO Survey* (1995, pp. 15–16). It was signed by the participants of UNESCO's International Study Days on "Philosophy and Democracy in the World", held in Paris on 15–16 February 1995.

## References

Bleazby, J. (2013). Social reconstruction learning: Dualism, Dewey and philosophy in schools. New York and London: Routledge.

Brennan, S. (1999). Reconciling feminist politics and ethics on the issue of rights. *Journal of Social Philosophy, 30*(2), 260–275. doi:10.1111/0047-2786.00017.

Channel Ten. (2012, October 10). *Julia Gillard's misogyny speech* [video file]. Retrieved from: www.youtube.com/watch?v=SOPsxpMzYw4.

Conroy, J., Davis, R. & Enslin, P. (2008). Philosophy as a basis for policy and practice: What confidence can we have in philosophical analysis and argument? *Journal of Philosophy of Education, 42*(S1), 165–182. doi:10.1111/j.1467-9752.2008.00631.x.

Divala, J. & Enslin, P. (2008). Citizenship education in Malawi: Prospects for global citizenship. In J. Arthur, I. Davies & C. Hahn (Eds.). *Handbook of education for citizenship and democracy.* (pp. 215–222). London: Sage.

Droit, R. (1995). *Philosophy and democracy in the world: A UNESCO survey.* Paris: UNESCO Publishing. Retrieved from: http://unesdoc.unesco.org/images/0010/001041/104173 eo.pdf

Drummond, U. (2015). Music education in South African Schools after apartheid: teacher perceptions of Western and African Music. Ed.D dissertation, University of Glasgow. Retrieved from: http://theses.gla.ac.uk/6298/

Enslin, P. (1984). The role of fundamental pedagogics in the formulation of educational policy in South Africa. In P. Kallaway (Ed.), *Apartheid and education: The education of black South Africans.* (pp. 139–147). Johannesburg, South Africa: Ravan Press.

Enslin, P. (1986). Apartheid ideology in South African education. *Philosophical Forum, 18,* 105–14.

Enslin, P. (1990). Science and doctrine: Theoretical discourse in South African teacher education. In M. Nkomo (Ed.), *Pedagogy of domination: Toward a democratic education in South Africa* (pp. 77–92). Trenton, NJ: Africa World Press.

Enslin, P. (1992). The political mythology of childhood in South African teacher education. *Discourse, 13*(1), 36–48.

Enslin, P. (1997). Contemporary liberalism and civic education in South Africa. *Current Writing, 9*(2), 77–90. doi:10.1080/1013929X.1997.9678023.

Enslin, P. (2003). Liberal feminism, diversity and education. *Theory and Research in Education, 1*(1), 73–87. doi:10.1177/1477878503001001005.

Enslin, P. (2011). Education for global citizenship: The cosmopolitan and the patriotic. *Citizenship, Social and Economics Education, 10* (2–3), 91–100. doi:10.2304/csee.2011. 10.2.91.

Enslin, P. (2016). Europe and the post colony: Possibilities for cosmopolitanism. In M. Papastephanou (Ed.). *Cosmopolitanism: Educational, philosophical and historical perspectives.* (pp. 151–162). Dordrecht, Netherlands: Springer.

Enslin, P. & Tjiattas, M. (2004a). Liberal feminism, cultural diversity and comparative education. *Comparative Education, 40*(4), 503–516. doi:10.1080/0305006042000284501.

Enslin, P. & Tjiattas, M. (2004b). Cosmopolitan justice: Education and global citizenship. *Theoria, 104,* 150–168. doi:10.3167/004058104782267097.

Enslin, P. & Tjiattas, M. (2006). Educating for a just world without gender. *Theory and Research in Education, 4*(1), 41–68. doi:10.1177/1477878506060682.

Enslin, P. & Tjiattas, M. (2009). Philosophy of education and the gigantic affront of universalism. *Journal of Philosophy of Education, 43*(1), 2–17. doi:10.1111/j.1467-9752.2009.00664.x.

Enslin, P. & Hedge, N. (2010). A good global neighbour: Scotland, Malawi and global citizenship. *Citizenship Teaching and Learning, 6*(1), 91–105. doi:10.2304/csee.2011.10.2.91.

Enslin, P. & Tjiattas, M. (2015a). Getting the measure of measurement: Global educational opportunity. *Educational Philosophy and Theory* (early online publication). Retrieved from: www.tandfonline.com/doi/abs/10.1080/00131857.2015.1048667?journalCode=rept20

Enslin, P. & Tjiattas, M. (2015b). Philosophical approaches to educational research: Justice, democracy and education. In P. Smeyers, D. Bridges, N. Burbules & M. Griffiths (Eds.), *International handbook of interpretation in educational research methods*. (pp. 1143–1164). Dordrecht, Netherlands: Springer.

Enslin, P. & Horsthemke, K. (2016). Philosophy of education: Becoming less Western, more African? *Journal of Philosophy of Education, 50*(2), 177–190. doi:10.1111/1467-9752.12199.

Fraser, N. (1997). *Justice interruptus: Critical reflections on the 'postsocialist' condition*. London and New York: Routledge.

Fraser, N. (2003). Social justice in the age of identity politics: Redistribution, recognition and participation. In N. Fraser & A. Honneth (Eds.). *Redistribution or recognition? A political-philosophical exchange* (pp. 7–109). London and New York: Verso.

Fraser, N. (2005). Reframing justice in a globalizing world. *New Left Review, 36*, 69–88.

Fraser, N. (2007). Mapping the feminist imagination: From redistribution to recognition to representation. In J. Browne (Ed.), *The future of gender* (pp. 17–34). Cambridge, UK: Cambridge University Press.

Gandhi, L. (1998). *Postcolonial theory: An introduction*. New York: Columbia University Press.

Gaus, G., Courtland, S. D. & Schmidtz, D. (2015). Liberalism. In E. N. Zalta (Ed.). *The Stanford Encyclopaedia of Philosophy* (Spring ed.). Retrieved from: https://plato.stanford.edu/archives/spr2015/entries/liberalism/

Gillard, J. (2012). Transcript of Julia Gillard's speech [transcript]. *Sydney Morning Herald*, October 10. Sydney: Fairfax. Retrieved from: www.smh.com.au/federal-politics/politi cal-news/transcript-of-julia-gillards-speech-20121009-27c36.html

Kiss, E. (1997). Alchemy or fool's gold? Assessing feminist doubts about rights. In U. Narayan & M. L. Shanley (Eds.), *Reconstructing political theory: Feminist perspectives*. Cambridge, UK: Polity Press.

MacKenzie, A., Enslin, P., & Hedge, N. (2016). Education for global citizenship in Scotland: Reciprocal partnership or politics of benevolence? *International Journal of Educational Research, 77*, 128–135. doi.org/10.1016/j.ijer.2016.03.007.

Nussbaum, M. (1999). *Sex and social justice*. New York: Oxford University Press.

Nussbaum, M. (2000). *Women and human development: The capabilities approach*. Cambridge, UK: Cambridge University Press.

Okin, S. M. (1989a). *Justice, gender, and the family*. New York: Basic Books.

Okin, S. M. (1989b). Humanist liberalism. In N.L. Rosenblum (Ed.), *Liberalism and the moral life* (pp. 39–53). Cambridge, MA: Harvard University Press.

Okin, S. M. (1994). Political liberalism, justice, and gender. *Ethics, 105*, 23–43.

Rawls, J. (1971). *A theory of justice*. Cambridge, MA: Harvard University Press.

Said, E. (1993). *Culture and imperialism*. London: Vintage.

Schwartzman, L. H. (2002). Feminist analyses of oppression and the discourse of "rights": A response to Wendy Brown. *Social Theory and Practice, 28*(3), 465–480. doi:10.5840/socth eorpract200228319.

Scotland-Malawi Partnership. (2009). *Practical guide to school partnerships*. Edinburgh, UK: Scotland Malawi Partnership. Retrieved from: www.scotland-malawipartnership.org/files/5514/3999/1136/Practical_Guide_to_School_Partnerships_FINAL_DRAFT_JF_edit_v4.pdf

Scottish Government. (2005). *Co-operation agreement between Scotland and Malawi*. Edinburgh, UK: Scottish Government. Retrieved from:http://www.scotland.gov.uk/Publications/2005/11/scotland-malawi-agreement

Snook, I. A. (1972a). *Indoctrination and education*. Boston, MA: Routledge & Kegan Paul.

Snook, I. A. (Ed.) (1972b). *Concepts of indoctrination: Philosophical essays*. Boston, MA: Routledge & Kegan Paul.

Tong, R. (2009). *Feminist thought: A more comprehensive introduction* (3rd ed.). Boulder, CO: Westview Press.

UNESCO. (2006). UNESCO Intersectoral Strategy on Philosophy. Paris: UNESCO Publishing. Retrieved from: http://unesdoc.unesco.org/images/0014/001452/145270e.pdf

UNESCO. (2007). *Philosophy: A school of freedom*. Paris: UNESCO Publishing. Retrieved from: http://unesdoc.unesco.org/images/0015/001541/154173e.pdf

# 6

# JOHN HATTIE ON INTERPRETATION, THE STORY OF RESEARCH AND THE NECESSITY OF FALSIFIABILITY

## In dialogue with Maurizio Toscano

*Maurizio Toscano and John Hattie*

## Introduction

Questioning how philosophy may inform educational research is fraught with difficulties because these two domains of inquiry are always and already seamlessly entwined. A convincing response to this issue of philosophically informed research may take the form of a personal account in which these fields find themselves merged in the practices, thoughts, influences and experiences of the researcher. The following dialogue with John Hattie offers such a personal narrative about the connections between educational research and the philosophies and theories that inform it.

Hattie's narrative offers exposition and argument, for sure, however along with his willingness to profess he also brings a keenness to confess. A confession in this sense – unlike an argument or thesis – emerges out of an awareness of how one's actions, words and thoughts have been shaped by forces so intimate and proximal that they ordinarily escape our capacity to articulate them publicly. A confession is about that which suddenly dawns upon us as a kind of self-evident self-motivation that needs to be made public – for the sake of others as much as the confessor. Thus, while an argument about research might offer something quite independent of one's deepest commitments, Hattie's confessions bring to light his own commitments as a researcher and reaffirm them publicly.

Hattie's principal confession here encapsulates the idea that research is a form of thinking, and that some modes of thinking provide a more robust orientation towards the world and its proper articulation. For Hattie, research-as-thinking goes beyond a thin type of scientific realism; that is, beyond one that merely asks us to match our thoughts and theories to the things and happenings in a world as if the latter were independent of us. What Hattie proposes as a way of thinking-about-thinking is a much more active sense of scientific realism in which one explores the world by seeing how it responds to our actions and how our actions move in response to the world. It is a model of research built upon the principles of reciprocity and sensitivity: reciprocity describing how research sets up a feedback loop with the world, and sensitivity establishing the strength of that dynamic feedback. That is, how much we are willing to move and be moved by others. Stripped of technical language, the claim is that research is synonymous with acting (searching) and re-acting (re-searching) within a world shared with others, and this searching-researching is done in the service of finding some mutual assurance of stability and security against the capriciousness of life. Research then, as a fruitful mode of thinking, is not just scientific thinking of a brute mechanical or abstracted kind, but a human activity that embodies our entanglement and interdependence with others.

The idea that research engages strongly with the activity of thinking as a productive synthesis of the scientific and the psychological finds its clearest expression in Hattie's confession about the importance – and contemporary neglect – of the powerful stories that good research must tell. Again, we see an emphasis on research needing to offer an account of the world that is more than just a claim, and certainly more than directing our attention towards evidence and data. Hattie underscores the importance of stories as the primary means of holding and exchanging both personally and collectively derived, action-orientated meaning. So, when the story provided by the researcher resonates with the stories of teachers, then one can be confident there is something meaningful, solid, and reliable in both. In other words, one has found a mutual basis for meaningful action.

One might say of a story – the story that arises from research – that it conveys the strength of one's conviction as a researcher. That is, the story is a signal to others of the moral and logical force of the actions and reasons promoted in the story. It is for this reason that Hattie couples conviction (what he later refers to in the dialogue as "the boldness of research") with the impact it promises to make on others. Researching is thus a risky and courageous activity, because the story must speak truthfully and authentically to the experiences of the researcher and the subject of the research.

This risk brings us to the philosophical question – and final confession – regarding the nature of the conviction of the researcher, her story, and its mutual acceptance or rejection in the field of public action. It is precisely the potential to be wrong – to be shown by others that we may be wrong – that sets research of the kind advocated by Hattie apart from research that is impelled by the drive to confirm positive claims. Hattie confesses to the pivotal influence of Karl Popper[1] who turned science on its head by making the falsifiability[2] a condition for scientific theory making. In the spirit of Popper, then, Hattie asks that the boldness of the researcher be taken as an invitation to the world and to others to find something wanting in her story. For the figure of truth appears only once we have diligently and courageously traced out the ground of our own errors.

## The dialogue

**Maurizio Toscano (MT):**   I have heard that you refer to yourself as a psychometrician? I want to start by asking about the trajectory that leads a person to becoming a psychometrician.

**John Hattie (JH):**   But you misheard it. I'm a psycho-magician. My background, as an undergraduate, was as a teacher in the study of education. I did history and philosophy of science. When I was an undergraduate you had to do a language to get a degree. I was pretty hopeless at languages. I did French; failed it miserably. The second year they changed the rules; they introduced another language – statistics. I did the statistics course and then continued on in that area. So I always had statistics and some mathematics in my background, as well as education. In the 1960s and 1970s the quantitative paradigm was dominant. Qualitative was virtually non-existent.

I was quite good at it. Then I had an instructor, Tom Maguire, who taught us the whole notion of statistics, measurement, and its application in education and he's the one that encouraged me to go on into the statistics and measurement area. So that's how it happened.

**MT:**   The statistics course; what undergraduate degree was that part of?

**JH:**   It was a Bachelor of Arts, because you had to do a language, and statistics was treated as a language.

**MT:**   Did you think of it as a language?

**JH:**   You've got to worry about who on earth would ever think that! But I was very grateful for it. I'm sure if I'd done the French I would never have used it again, but statistics; obviously I have.

**MT:**   In what way was the application of statistics thought about? You said the dominant paradigm was measurement. Did they consider measurement as applied to the humanities, the social sciences or just the sciences?

**JH:**   Well, certainly in the social sciences in terms of doing experimental designs; the Campbell and Stanley (1963) book was the gospel that everyone learned regardless. In the degree I did you had five compulsory subjects. You had to do – can I remember them? – philosophy, history, sociology, psychology and counselling. I'm very grateful for this breadth, and that I did the philosophy right through my degree. I would probably have dropped it early on if it was not compulsory and I'm very pleased that I didn't. In psychology, even in sociology, the quantitative approach was dominant. Today, if you trained in this area, quantitative work would be absolutely in the minority.

**MT:**   Did you have a sense of some of the connections between all those subjects? It must have been quite a broad mix.

**JH:**   It was, but the message which came through all the time was: "It's about the story. What is the story you're telling?" I'm very pleased I have that background because I could have easily been one of those measurement people

## 88 Maurizio Toscano and John Hattie

who set up experimental designs, random control studies, and hypothesis testing and believed that was the end of the story. It was drummed into me all the time that they were tools. They were a means to an end. The end was the story. The other fortunate thing – and it dates me considerably – is at that time, in Otago (New Zealand), we had a brand-new professor of philosophy (W. Musgrave) who was into philosophy of science. I completed his courses.

The luxury was that Karl Popper was on study leave there. He was well into his seventies at the time. He ran some classes and I was fortunate enough to go to some of those classes. Obviously I was brainwashed because I think one of his core notions, falsifiability, sticks with me about the story. It's kind of like the Visible Learning (Hattie, 2008) work I do.[3] What is the story? Who's going to falsify the story? The data aren't that important – of course it is important to get right, but it doesn't tell the story. We do. I think that's the thing that I got from those days that I'm most grateful for. Certainly, my PhD students know in every meeting, I'll say: "Well, what's the story today?"

**MT:** Having mentioned Popper and his philosophy of science, do you think that has been influential on your conceptions of measurement? Do you think you've pieced together a coherent philosophical view?

**JH:** I'd like to think I have. Certainly, I'd like to think that the kind of work we're doing is still at the edge of the field of measurement. My background and expertise is in Item Response Theory (IRT) and Structural Equation Modelling (SEM) – that's the bread and butter of everything we do. After the 1960s and 1970s, we're producing a lot of footnotes to what the measurement people did back then. But the biggest change which I think should happen, because it hasn't happened yet to a great extent, is along the lines of what we did when we started in the late 1990s in New Zealand developing their assessment scheme: we started backwards. We said, "What's the story we want to tell? What's the story we want the teachers to get, the principals to get?"

We devised the reports for those teachers first. We trialled them on teachers. We asked them: "What do you see?" If they didn't see what we wanted them to see, we got it wrong (so often many blame the teachers for not understanding the measurement language). We asked them: "What would you do next?" Wow, that was a tough question, because most teachers said: "Well, we'd print the report." Which we knew was an abject failure because they'd just put it on their shelves or in the rubbish. It didn't change their decision-making or how they thought about their own or their students' actions and learning. The first report that we created took us over 80 focus group sessions to even get close to an answer. Then after we created the reports, we back-filled them with the tests. My argument being that in a measurement community we are often focused on the technicalities of excellence, but we haven't been focused on the interpretation of data and how our users interpret the data. Particularly with the Internet, you can go and find a billion tests and as many reports. Unfortunately, what's happening is that the commercial providers are coming up with unbelievably fancier, prettier and more colourful graphs and reports. But no one is really checking to see how these data are being interpreted. There is no validation that the reports are clear and have utility for the user, and there is too much onus on the user to learn and know the details of the measurement systems. So with my focus on asking "What's the story?", I want the users of the material I produce to get the story right and to see its consequences.

In the validity era of the 1990s, Messick (1995) wrote an article in which it was said that validity wasn't intrinsic to the nature of the text. The old-fashioned view about validity amounted to: does a test measure what it's supposed to measure? Now that view went out in the 1960s and 1970s. But in the 1990s the argument that came in was validity is a function of interpretations and actions, and having a preponderance of evidence that the test does facilitate users making valid and dependable interpretations. I think that is right. So really all the work we've been doing, and are still doing, in the testing and measurement area is on the reporting side.

**MT:** Is thinking about the interpretive side still one of the major challenges for researchers?

**JH:** Totally, yes. I've been the president of the International Test Commission[4] for several years and the Commission is trying to get test developers to move more towards this new understanding of validity. But I'd be struggling to name five or six people around the world who are working in the areas of interpretation and action. That's probably an exaggeration, but so many test developers are still stuck on the psychometric side of it. Certainly, you'd look at NAPLAN[5]; it's resplendent with tests but each state develops guidance for its teachers and principals to interpret the reports – another case of not using backward design. For a while, Queensland (Australia) had 80 pages per student of printed graphs.[6] No one ever asks: are they being interpreted correctly? I have this pet hate for the notion of assessment literacy. How insulting is it that we ask teachers to learn our language? We should be learning their language. No, we've not even begun to take interpretation seriously. The world is passing on to us millions of tests, and yet reports are coming out with no attention to validity.

**MT:** Do you think there's a demand for interpretation because, to some extent, people want at least a synthesis, conclusion or a usable statement? Do you think that counts as a demand for interpretation?

**JH:** I think it does. Schools are awash with data. The trouble is every time something new comes out in testing it results in us offering even more data to the schools. I think there are probably more data sitting in back cupboards than anywhere else. But it's the interpretation that matters – and I think there's a hunger for more interpretive information in schools about these data. Take, for instance, our Assessment Tool for Teaching and Learning (asTTle)[7] that we developed in New Zealand. It's a tool that is voluntary; teachers don't have to use it, and yet well over 70 per cent of teachers and schools are still using it today, 14 years later. This demonstrates a massive hunger for interpretation because the whole of asTTle is based on the principles and practice of interpretation.

I can't imagine any test in Australia that teachers would voluntarily demand 14 years in a row, since most of the tests in Australia are like thermometers: you get numbers out of it, and yet there's no emphasis on interpretation. For most teachers, and for most of us, a number is not an interpretation. It's an indicator. So why don't we, as test developers, go that next step and say: and this is what these data indicate?

**MT:** I was thinking about the issue of this call for interpretation and I wonder – without creating a false dichotomy – whether this is, first, a call for implementation of interpretation, and second, a theoretical call to change our attitude towards what counts as the proper use of data.

**JH:** Yes.

**MT:** Perhaps there is also a third aspect, which is related to the fact that interpretation is not just restricted to the immediate purpose but a larger purpose. I wonder if you could speak to those three things: the call from practitioners, the call for a theoretical re-evaluation of the use of data, and the notion that interpretation goes beyond the immediate purpose it serves?

**JH:** Well the first thing that I would note is that if you want to really make an impact on students' learning it is very much a function of the moment-to-moment decision making and judgements of teachers. Your one-off, annual event is hardly likely to change those moment-to-moment decisions. Certainly, when you see excellence in schools, and there's plenty of it out there, teachers share a conception of what is usefully challenging for students. They understand what it means to progress. These conceptions of progress, the high but appropriate expectations, are what I want to influence.

The first thing you have to appreciate is that teachers have very strong theories about their teaching. If you meet with a teacher and as an aside say, "You're wrong, you should have my theory," then first, you're being insulting to a human, and second, you're denying the 15–20 years of evidence they have: their experience. So, how do you work with them to help them appreciate the notion of falsifiability? Is there another way they can look at how they're treating students? Can they see the effects of what they do through the students' eyes?

A lot of the teaching literature is about reflection, which I don't have a lot of time for because 80 per cent of what happens in the classroom the teacher doesn't see or hear. So why would you want a teacher to reflect on that: the 20 per cent? Like Alice in Wonderland, I want teachers to see themselves as much through the eyes of others – particularly through the eyes of their students, but also through the eyes of their peers. You want other people that can come into the classroom and effectively say to a teacher, "Well, have you thought of looking at this student this way? Can you see this student can do this, but this student can't do that and yet you think they can? Did you see what happened with these students when you did this?" How do we augment the teacher's beliefs? How do we seek ways of informing teachers about what they think happened through seeing the consequences of their actions on students? There are some teachers' beliefs that we dramatically want to change, like the deficit thinking which some teachers have – that "some kids can't learn" – by showing them what kids can do.

I think that's the kind of interpretive model I want to get to; gently, gently, but relentlessly pursuing the notion that there are other ways that teachers can see the impact they have. Unlike a lot of professional development, which starts from the premise that teachers have a deficit and that this deficit can be fixed by this professional development, all I do, via the Visible Learning message, is give permission to teachers who already demonstrate excellence to continue what they are doing. The major message is: how can you help teachers understand their impact and know what impact means? I think that's where the interpretation part comes in. I've drifted off your question.

**MT:** You have, but it's come full circle in some sense because it's pointing back to that notion that you've got to go beyond the data – that you've got to include much more. I was speaking with Paul Smeyers in another dialogue for this series (see Chapter 10), and he was saying that one thing unique about education research is you've got to take in the bigger picture and go beyond the minutiae and technical application.

**JH:** Yes. It's about judgments. My favourite philosophy quote is by Nietzsche: "there's no such thing as immaculate perception" (Nietzsche, 2006). How can you have teachers look at students (and themselves) in other ways? It is about falsifiability. I'm saying there are other ways of looking at teaching. I think that's very powerful. You adopt the view that you're walking alongside and helping the teacher see themselves as others see them.

**MT:** What I'm piecing together from what you're saying is an evolving picture of what you see educational research as being about. Do you want to elaborate on what you think the purpose of educational research is, or what the purpose of research is, given measurement is always directed at something?

**JH:** I think the word is pretty important; re-search – we're re-looking and re-searching. Again, it's that Popperian notion of building theories that are bold and contestable. I think that is our fundamental job: to interpret the evidence and make bold conjectures, and then see how further evidence might falsify these claims. The evidence gathered over 150 years on how teachers teach hasn't changed dramatically. Of course, it's changed, but not as dramatically as it did after the industrial revolution. I think it's a matter of coming up with better interpretations, and these have certainly changed and helped the profession see itself through a different lens.

**92** Maurizio Toscano and John Hattie

I firmly believe there is a practice of teaching. There are things we know. There are things we know that we shouldn't do. The current thinking is that the essence of most teachers' being is that they have the autonomy to teach as they want. I contest that. If how they teach is *not* having the appropriate levels of impact on students, then they have no right to continue to teach that way!

I think it's unfortunate that we don't have more academics who are prepared to come up with bold theories. Many don't want to make bold conjectures, because they could be chopped off. They could be wrong. But that's the point. Unfortunately, many of them think that their job is to report what they've found. I think that's a misuse of the luxury that we in academia have. Our job is to help better interpret the world.

**MT:** One of my favourite philosophies of science comes from Niels Bohr who spoke of a world-apparatus complex (Bohr, 1962) – the idea that if you create a particular instrument, it is connected with the world and reveals something about it which differs with each instrument. So I imagine that if you create new tools there is not simply new data, but also new ways of interpreting.

**JH:** It does, but take structural modelling, which is a particular way of analysing data, as an example. It's a tool that came out in the mid-1970s and is dominant in the quantitative field. For many users now, it's relatively easy to use. However, I would argue it's put psychology education back 30 or 40 years, because while people are now applying the tool – it looks fancy, it looks sophisticated, and it *is* sophisticated – the majority of structural models are not interpreted, do not test theories, and often merely compete with the "null case." They're not part of the theory of action. They're not part of the theory of reason. They're just a tool.

So in that sense I would argue that some of our tools have put us backwards. I'm not a great fan of taking a set of data or going to observe a class and reporting this. You walk into a classroom with a massive lens. The philosopher that I'm intrigued with at the moment is Charles Sanders Peirce and his theory of abduction (Peirce, 1974).[8] I struggle with this theory; I'm a deductivist. I have no qualms about that, but in my weak moments I think it's not quite as simple as that. Maybe there is a place for abduction.

I have a colleague, Brian Haig from New Zealand, who has written a lot on abduction in the area of measurement (Haig, 2008). It's pretty convincing – you do go in with a theory but maybe it can be modified by the evidence. You do put together ideas. I think it's a massive obligation of ours to be more upfront about our own lenses. So when you use the notion of tools, they are a means to an end. Whilst obviously I do a lot of research using those tools, the potential misuse of them is enormous.

**MT:** The notion of abduction is interesting because in practical, everyday reasoning we use it all the time.

**JH:** Yes, exactly.

**MT:** Sometimes there's a gap between what researchers say they're doing, what they're claiming their research is all about and what they actually do. Do you think that in fact researchers are much more eclectic in their approach to research and maybe in practice much less committed to what they suggest they're doing?

**JH:** You're possibly right, but I'm not a fan of eclecticism. Eclecticism is what you do when you don't think. I think that there is an obligation to have a world view and test it. I think the question with abduction is how it gets you around the causal problem – what comes first. It is an interplay between the inductive and the deductive, and that's probably why I like it. But there's no question, even in abduction, that you are still responsible for checking your interpretations. I think that comes back full circle; it is about making bold statements.

We're building a model at the moment on learning strategies. The team keep saying, "Oh, but we haven't got the data to test that yet," and I'll say, "But that's the beauty of the model." Other people (and our own future studies) can now help explore these conjectures from the model. Like the Visible Learning model, there are some bold speculations in our learning model.

What stuns me is that I've been writing about the theory underlying Visible Learning since 1989 (the first publication), but no one since that time has ever really come up with a different explanation of the data. People quibble with the data, but the data was the easy part. It may sound a lot, a quarter of a billion students, but it's not. It's an Excel spreadsheet; anyone can see it, I've published all the data. I'm just stunned at times when people say: "The data are off here, it's a decimal point out here." I think, "Look, you missed the point." No one has contested the explanation, the interpretative Visible Learning theory. That's when it's going to be exciting: when someone presents a different explanation.

Take Howard Gardner – he stood out with a very strong theory and changed how a lot of people saw the notion of multiple ways of becoming excellent; Carl Rogers had a strong theory, so did B.F. Skinner and Chomsky. I think they're the kind of people we should be aiming towards. Now, whether they are right or wrong isn't really the question; just look at their incredible contribution to the way in which we as academics look at our world. I think that's our job. Just one last thing – it's that question of evidence. I think Gert Biesta was here (in Australia) last year?

**MT:** Yes.

**JH:** He wrote a superb article which impressed me (see Biesta, 2007, 2010) where he argued that evidence was the most – or should be the most – contested term in our business. I think he's absolutely right. When people state "we have evidence" or "we have research," I quiver. Everybody has research. Everyone has evidence. The core question, however, is: what is your interpretation of it?

**MT:** You've mentioned some influential theorists. Of course, people who are beginning in research ask questions like: "Where does theory and philosophy of education fit in to my project? What it is that I'm doing in research?" I wonder whether many researchers in education are looking towards theorists and asking what does the theorist say about this, or which theorist should I choose, rather than developing their own theory? Do you see that as a kind of shortfall in research training, that one is often looking to someone else to set things up for you theoretically?

**JH:** Yes, even when you start off it's not as if you don't have a theory or interpretation of the world. You do. I think the fundamental question, again, is the Popperian question: what evidence would it take for you to accept that you're wrong? I think that's the most powerful thing we need to teach right through our careers, particularly early on. We all know what the opposite of that is: what evidence would you accept that you're right? This is confirmation bias; I think that's what drives me mad. In this business we're constantly looking for the evidence that confirms our current belief. We're not contesting it. It's about that way of thinking. It's not about having a particular theory, it is about contesting our own theories.

If you look around, in virtually every discipline there are people on whose shoulders we should be standing. It's not as if you're going to come along and suddenly reinvent the wheel. What have others done? What other good theories do people have out there? I think the obligation to re-search what has happened in theory development is critical. Otherwise your chance of making a difference and giving back to your profession is miniscule, if you can't anchor it in what's happened before. The naivety of believing that you can come along and change the world is absurd – we've had centuries of people trying to do that. One part of me thinks people should know theories, like in my own area of psychology at the moment.

I struggle when I ask most people in this building and out at schools to name two contemporary theories of learning; most people can't. And Vygotsky is not one of them by the way. Different theories of learning are a very, very contestable area.

**MT:** There's a question about the distinction between theory and philosophy because there's philosophy of science and then there are theories developed through empirical research. Often they are entangled so it's very hard to distinguish where a theory begins and the philosophy ends.

**JH:** Yes.

**MT:** But, of course, in a lot of educational research – which involves empirical work but also operates in the psychological space – philosophy can be very useful in determining what counts as psychology, or the subjective and the objective. Can you speak to your philosophical approach to psychology, especially since you are looking at how the field of measurement brings new insights and allows you to make psychological claims?

John Hattie on interpretation **95**

**JH:** I think humans want to make sense of the world and they want the world to make sense for them as a person. Sometimes those two things are inconsistent. There is a sense that we want to have some predictability when we put ourselves in situations, so we're seeking evidence for that. Or sometimes we don't put ourselves in situations because we don't want to have the unpredictability. There is also a kind of "terror management"; there are some things we want to manage so that we don't get terrified with extreme circumstances. So we protect ourselves from things and sometimes we invent or believe explanations that have no foundation. Like if I was to say I believe the sun goes around the earth – I can remain very happy with that belief about my world and continue forth, regardless that we know this is false. Scientifically it's nonsense. But it doesn't matter that science says it is nonsense; it doesn't affect my day-to-day living. In this way we live with many inconsistent ideas and thoughts. But sometimes you do have to suspend your stories and consider that maybe there's a different interpretation. If that's all we do, we're a pretty healthy set of humans.

It's that biblical argument: "do unto others as you would have them do to you";[9] which is powerful. But if you have a particular view of the world and you want to insist on others thinking the same way, that's where it gets nasty. Rather it's that constant inquiry of what's that person thinking at the moment? What's going on in his or her mind? That respect of the other I think is a pretty powerful notion. Surely it's the essence of all interactions, particularly in the world of teaching we're in. But I think you've encountered them. I've encountered them. Teachers who will tell you their world view, insist on their world view, trot out confirming evidence to support this world view (usually very selective evidence), and ask you to parrot their world view back to them. It's not a very healthy state. I have completely and utterly gone off your question.

**MT:** But maybe I'll raise another issue. Of course, with the rise of neuroscience there's much more interplay between psychology and the sciences, particularly the science of measuring phenomena associated with the brain. That may create a tension with an ethical response to others, trying to put yourself in someone else's position. It's a moral craft, as education is.

**JH:** Yes.

**MT:** Today we have this mechanistic view of behaviour. I wonder what you think about that shift?

**JH:** Well certainly – since we got the Science of Learning Research Centre[10] a few years ago, I went back to school in the psychology department and did courses in neuropsychology to be able to talk to these people. Mechanistic it certainly is not! The variation in brain patterning is dramatic. We have a kind of guiding rule in our team that we're not ever going to talk about "neuromyths"[11] or "neuro-trash."[12] There is so much out there that it would make you go mad at the end of the day. We want the opposite. A lot of the brain science stuff at the moment is very reductionist. I can assure you that when you ask me a question, the thinking does not occur in your foot. Yes, I can see patterns in your brain. Yes, the faculty psychologists of the nineteenth century were kind of right: the brain is mapped. (Although they were wrong in that there are no bumps to help in the detection of thinking!) But the brain is mapped exactly now and it's relatively easy to see where certain elements fire. It is chemical; it is electrical. A lot of the findings that neuroscientists are discovering are exactly what was discovered in psychology in the 1940s. The brain reacts to stimuli; we can make, and see, the brain fire when certain stimuli and thinking is evoked. That's not a criticism. That's just where it is.

What we're trying to do is come up with a better narrative of our knowledge of the brain and education. In fact, only this week we were looking at this intriguing question: if you look at surface and deep knowledge, when is the right moment for me as a teacher to tell you to stop learning more and start relating and extending? I'm asking my colleagues in the neuroscience area if they can reverse engineer that for me. You can see differences in the brain when processing surface thinking compared with deep thinking because the different functions of the brain spike when you learn more, compared with the functions of relating and extending. Can we reverse engineer this to help teachers better understand when someone has sufficient knowledge? Then they could stop, and get the student to relate and extend. I think that's where the excitement is. However, it's probably a good 10 years off before we can take neuroscientific findings and use them in the classroom.

There are some things that we have known since the 1960s and 1970s, for instance that working memory is a very powerful notion. A lot of teachers wouldn't have much understanding of students' working memory and how to reduce load on the memory. The level of working memory varies dramatically across different children and occasions. The concepts of rehearsal and consolidation; there are important differences between what you should do when you first introduce something and then what you should do when you want to consolidate this knowing. Take memorisation – if you memorise something soon after first encountering the ideas the long-term benefits are close to zero. But if you use memorisation to consolidate after you first learn and explore something, then it's very, very powerful. You can see the science is changing and the translation from the classroom to neuroscience and back again is beginning to build a (at the moment very shaky) bridge. I think there is a lot to learn in the interplay of education, psychology and neuroscience. At the moment it's pretty early days, but it's fun.

**MT:** It's reassuring that as a researcher who exercises judgment you can take advantage of all the exciting things that are going on without being bogged down by the kind of research that is just making claims that can't be tied back to it.

John Hattie on interpretation  **97**

I just wanted to finish off our conversation with a question concerning general advice about using philosophies in the theoretical framing of educational research. You've offered some amazing insights into how you've used philosophical theories in your own research and said much about your field of research in general. I was wondering if you had any advice to someone who is starting off in research or is still developing their research? Do you have some advice about how they should orient themselves towards theory and philosophy in the service of research?

**JH:** I know it's simplistic, but there are two sides to it. One side is knowing how others have come up with stories about the world. The other side is having a sense of how you make decisions about evidence and about information – the methodology of the sciences. I think those are the two things that I'd want people to question and learn about. I would encourage every new researcher to discover a different way of looking at things and trying that methodology. I tried induction, I tried deduction, I tried abduction. Just try them to see what affect each has on the way you view the world.

Learning those skills is dramatic because they cut across everything we do, from reading a novel to doing a mathematics equation. It's how you go about your thinking. Probably the theme throughout my career has been that notion of how we go about thinking. I always see myself as a measurement person and now see the world through this lens. But the notion of learning is pretty powerful. Ironically, I'm coming back to "learning" at the end of my career, which is great. To go through the limited experience I had from Plato right through to Pestalozzi, they had ways not only of creating a story but also a methodology for doing it. At the time I probably didn't see it that way, I just thought they were interesting ways of looking at the world. It's had a dramatic impact on me – that my world view may be wrong, whereas a lot of academics would like to argue their world view is right, particularly in education, and therefore they say you shall do it this way. It is humbling to continually remind yourself that you may be wrong, but I think it's what makes the difference.

**MT:** From the perspective of research – as someone involved in research training – can you imagine a model or paradigm for how we should teach the next generation of researchers?

**JH:** Yes, I despair at the lack of research training. Most research training is learning tools, or worse: thinking ethics is filling out ethics approval forms. I have been involved for many years to try to get research methods away from tools use. Now there's nothing wrong with tools. You need them. We've got some pretty sophisticated tools both in the qualitative and quantitative area. Yes, they do take time to learn. But they are but tools to help in the process of falsifiability.

The other despair I have is that we don't pay careful attention to giving students different perspectives on the use of these tools. I'm a

**98** Maurizio Toscano and John Hattie

quantitative researcher. I've dabbled in qualitative research, but I don't have the patience. I don't have the world view in order to see the data through a qualitative lens. In qualitative research you have to suspend your story. I'm not very good at that given I'm a deductionist. I want to test my story. I wish I'd been given much more training in the early days of seeing this in different ways. Sometimes you do have to stop, wait and suspend your story. So, my impatience sometimes gets in the way of me seeing things differently.

I also have little time for the concept of "mixed methods," which usually means using tools from the quantitative and qualitative research toolboxes. Instead, I would rather have a new researcher develop the underlying thinking of quantitative and qualitative approaches. In my own work, I never pretend to be a qualitative researcher. Instead, I find people who can think this way and have them join as part of the team. I mostly want to hear how they interpret and see the same data, the same classroom through their qualitative, interpretative lens. I cannot pretend to see the same data in these, often diametrically different, ways – it is their thinking, their interpretations, their processing that I value – and thus "mixing" them misses the power of the ways of approaching and using these methods.

**MT:** Could it be that that needs to start earlier in one's education?

**JH:** Yes, there's no question. In my area of quantitative research, I think the reason we are losing the battle is you can't easily pick it up in one course. It requires gestation. It is a whole set of skills and knowledge. It is much more horizontal in the sense that you can't just pick up a narrow set of specialised skills. You do need a base of knowledge. You need to know about probability, basic algebra, t-tests and regression before you can even begin to know about structural modelling and IRT theories. But that takes time, and time is scarce.

## Conclusion

This dialogue concerning the place of theory and philosophy in educational research brings to the foreground a number of crucial but often neglected aspects of what it means to do meaningful research. Hattie has drawn on his own extensive experience in research to reveal insights about the philosophical influences on his practice. The first of these insights emphasises the importance of interpretation. Interpretation in research is for Hattie far from an afterthought to data collection and collation; rather it is the means by which the researcher actively tests her own thinking against the world she wishes to understand and influence. Moreover, Hattie encourages us to see interpretation in light of Popper's call for intellectual boldness and courage; for interpretation in this Popperian sense deliberately invites the informed criticism of others so that one's thinking can come to better resonate with the world as it is rather than the world as one wants it to be. Finally, Hattie shows that mastering the art of conveying the story of the research is a powerful means of connecting courageous thinking with the concomitant risk of finding oneself in error.

## Notes

1 Karl Popper (born 1902 – died 1994) was an Austrian-British Philosopher of Science best known for his criticism of both inductivist methods of science and the justificationist approach to knowledge, which he countered with his theories of empirical falsification and critical rationalism, respectively. For a more detailed introduction to Popper's biography and philosophical works see https://plato.stanford.edu/entries/popper/
2 Falsifiability refers to the principle that one cannot confirm a scientific theory through the accumulation of evidence that is positively correlated with that theory. Rather, according to Popper, what makes a theory scientific is that we can set up an experiment, the results of which could show the theory false. See Popper (1959, 1963) and Keuth (2005).
3 Visible Learning (Hattie, 2008) refers to Hattie's seminal meta-study by the same name.
4 https://www.intestcom.org/
5 NAPLAN, or National Assessment Program – Literacy and Numeracy, is a standardised test administered to students across Australia. See https://www.nap.edu.au/naplan
6 See for example: https://www.qcaa.qld.edu.au/p-10/naplan/test-reporting-analysis
7 asTTle, or Assessment Tool for Teaching and Learning, is a tool developed to assess New Zealand students' achievement and progress across a number of curriculum areas including reading, writing and mathematics. It is online at https://e-asttle.tki.org.nz
8 Charles Sanders Peirce (1839–1914) was an American philosopher and mathematician associated with the early development of pragmatism as well as the field of semiotics. Peirce took abduction as a mode of inference alongside deduction and induction. He describes the distinction famously thus: "Deduction proves that something must be; Induction shows that something actually is operative; Abduction merely suggests that something may be" (Peirce, 1974).
9 Luke 6:31 and Matthew 7:12.
10 https://www.slrc.org.au/
11 See https://www.oecd.org/edu/ceri/neuromyths.htm
12 See Tallis (2011).

## References

Biesta, G. (2007). Why "what works" won't work: from evidence-based education and the democratic deficit in educational research. *Educational Theory*, 57(1), 1–22.
Biesta, G. (2010). Why "what works" still won't work: from evidence-based education to value-based education. *Studies in Philosophy of Education*, 29(5), 491–503.
Bohr, N. (1962). *Atomic theory and the description of nature*. New York: The Macmillan Company.
Campbell, D.T. and Stanley, J. C. (1963). *Experimental and quasi-experimental designs for research*. Boston, MA: Houghton Mifflin Company.
Haig, B. D. (2008). Scientific method, abduction and clinical reasoning. *Journal of Clinical Psychology*, 64(9), 1013–1018.
Hattie, J. (2008). *Visible learning: A synthesis of over 800 meta-analyses relating to achievement*. New York: Routledge.
Keuth, H. (2005). *The philosophy of Karl Popper*. Cambridge, UK: Cambridge University Press.
Messick, S. (1995). Validity of psychological assessment: Validation of inferences from persons' responses and performances as scientific inquiry into score meaning. *American Psychologist*, 50(9), pp.741–749.

Nietzsche, F. (2006). *Thus spoke Zarathustra*. (A. del Caro, Trans. R. Pippin, Ed.). Cambridge, UK: Cambridge University Press.

Peirce, C. S. (1974). *Collected papers of Charles Sanders Peirce*. C. Hartshorne and P. Weiss (Eds.). Cambridge, MA: Harvard University Press.

Popper, K. (1963). *Conjectures and refutations: The growth of scientific knowledge*. London: Routledge.

Popper, K. (1959). The logic of scientific discovery (English edn.). London: Hutchinson.

Tallis, R. (2011). Neurotrash. *Prospect Magazine*, 2011.

# 7

# NEL NODDINGS ON CARE THEORY AND CARING PRACTICE

## In dialogue with John Quay

*John Quay and Nel Noddings*

## Introduction

Nel Noddings is renowned internationally for her work in care theory, with good reason. Care theory embraces what Noddings describes as "a fundamental human need": "to care for and be cared for" (1992, p. xi). Hence caring is not a mere detail which is read onto human persons but rather is a fundamental aspect of the human condition. Noddings explains that, "The only universals recognized by care theorists are those describing the human condition: the commonalities of birth, death, physical and emotional needs, and the longing to be cared for" (1995, p. 188). Noddings' claim also highlights the nub of her philosophical contribution: that caring is relational. Thus "'carer' and 'cared-for' are not permanent labels attached in stable and distinct ways to two different sets of people. They are labels for parties in an encounter or in a series of encounters in a continuing relationship" (1995, p. 189). Whilst it is possible to identify the carer and the cared-for, these are not categories that can be understood in isolation of each other. Both parties are held in an ongoing dance of care. According to Noddings, "Both parties, not just one of them, are constrained by the ethic to care" (1995, p. 189).

Such integration builds on the methodological access to caring enabled through phenomenology. Indeed, Noddings states, "In my work, I have attempted a phenomenology of *caring*" (1995, p. 66). Noddings' investigations highlight the experience of caring, which cannot be described without reference to relation:

> The one-caring, in caring, is *present* in her acts of caring. Even in physical absence, acts at a distance bear the signs of presence: engrossment in the other, regard, desire for the other's well-being. The one cared-for sees the concern, delight, or interest in the eyes of the one-caring and feels her warmth in both verbal and body language.
>
> *(1984, p. 19)*

**102** John Quay and Nel Noddings

An important corollary of this phenomenological conceptualisation of care as relational is that it cannot be codified. In her own words, Noddings declares that her "insistence on including the cared-for as an active contributor to the caring relation makes it impossible to codify caring" (1995, p. 188). This creates a dilemma for the application of care theory in some forms of empirical research. In this dialogue Noddings questions the efficacy of research that attempts to measure caring. She is interested in these studies but tries to steer researchers away from such methodologies. In taking this position, she highlights the importance of understanding the methodological roots of concepts one is drawing on to theoretically frame an investigation, both in terms of data collection methods and techniques of analysis.

These methodological roots often reach deeper into the lives of researchers than we would initially assume, suggesting that biography cannot be discounted in understanding the origins of theorisation. This, in itself, exposes the situatedness of theories in practices. For Noddings, family life was central to the development of care theory, as she explains in this dialogue. At least three broad aspects of her life come together in care theory: being a mother, being a mathematics teacher, and being an educational philosopher.

As a fundamental human need, caring is expressed through family and also through education. Hence Noddings' claim that "caring is the very bedrock of all successful education" (1992, p. 27). Caring is also visible in various philosophical works that aim to comprehend the fundamentals of human beings. Martin Buber's assertion that "in the beginning is relation" (1937, p. 18) played a key role in Nodding's thinking, philosophically legitimising her rich family life through an emphasis on the "human need for response," as she explains in this dialogue. Others, such as Carol Gilligan, Simone Weil and Virginia Woolf, reinforced these ideas by drawing on the experiences of women, enabling Noddings to refine and further develop care theory.

In the following dialogue, Noddings illuminates various aspects of her pathway to care theory, its application in empirical research, and her hopes for education and educational research. The insights she provides showcase a career of thinking that help inform the endeavours of others working in this field.

## The dialogue

**John Quay (JQ):**    My first encounter with your work was through care theory, which was exceedingly important as it put "care" on the map as a legitimate conceptual focus for research. By positioning caring as an ethical relation you also provided an expansion on more traditional notions of caring, which enabled application in empirical work.

**Nel Noddings (NN):**    Yes, the very first thing that arises in my work, and the main part of my work that is widely used right now – it's very gratifying – is care theory of course (Noddings, 1984, 1992, 2010). Empirical researchers using it will often want to come up with some sort of measurement, some sort of numerical approach to caring and I think that's a mistake. Some of the [quantitative] studies are pretty good, but when people talk to me ahead of time – and this happens a lot with doctoral students and young research-ers – I try to guide them away from lists and scales and so forth because I really don't think you can measure something like caring with num-bers. That's the first thing that arises, the conflict between using numerical approaches, lists and scales and so forth; in other words, trying to quantify care. Instead, I try to guide people into some sort of qualitative research and that usually takes the form of narrative or biographical case studies. These fit nicely with care theory.

**JQ:** Could you elaborate further on this fit between caring and qualita-tive methods?

**NN:** Well, because you can't reduce caring to numbers. I wish people would listen to what Einstein is reputed to have said: that some things can't be measured, implying that there are some things that are just not best han-dled with numbers. What happens is that the empirical researcher who wants to get, let's say, a 20-item scale on caring, is looking at possible behaviours that could be called caring. But in care theory, you can't label them caring unless you see what happens to the other, unless you see the relation filled out, unless you see not only what the teacher did but also what the student did as a result. That's not captured in a list of 10 or 15 items that the researcher is identifying as 'caring'. An act performed by a teacher might be a caring act, or might not be. If you're looking at things through the lens of care theory, it would depend in part on whether the teacher is responding to an expressed need of the student or an assumed need that maybe has nothing to do with what the student really wants. You see what I'm getting at there?

**JQ:** Yes, I do. Knowing your own background as a mathematics teacher, I was wondering how you bring the notion of caring and the notion of math-ematics teaching together.

**NN:** I think they go together beautifully myself. As a mathematics teacher I'd be dealing with numbers every day and in many ways. But in dealing with my students, hopefully I would not be attaching numbers to the ways in which we were interacting. See, it's a different world.

**JQ:** You theorise caring as a relation between the person caring and the per-son being cared for. How did this theorisation initially develop? How did it unfold?

**NN:** You know, you're one of the very few people who has ever asked that ques-tion and it really is such a good one. It happens that I can answer it, too, because I remember going through this. My first few years as a professor, I produced a lot of pretty good analytical papers because that was the going thing at the time. If you wanted to make it as a philosopher of education and get tenure and all the rest of it, then you had to show that you were get-ting analytical papers published in the best journals and so forth. I was doing that and things were going along just fine. Then I actually stopped one

## 104 John Quay and Nel Noddings

day – this was while I was still in California, I can even remember the spot in the house where I sat down – and I asked myself this question: how can I bring the two parts of my life together? Those two parts are my academic work and my family life. You may or may not know, but my husband and I had five of our own biological children and then we adopted five more.

JQ: Wow.

NN: Yes. And in addition to that, we had other kids in and out of the house for as long as a year at a time. That was an extremely, extremely important part of my life. So, there was that big part of my life and here is this other part, philosophy. So I asked myself: how could I bring the two parts of my life together? The answer: well, let's look philosophically at caring – and that's how it started.

JQ: Do you remember the pathway that you followed? It began with this insight, and then there was a journey that you went on in exploring it philosophically?

NN: Oh yes. The first influential writer for me on this was Martin Buber (1937) and I may have read something by Buber before I asked myself this question; I don't know the chronology on that. But, to many people, this is interesting because care theory has become substantially well-known within feminist philosophy.[1] Yet that's not where it started for me. It really started with the work of Martin Buber on relations. I can still pull out some of the basic quotes: when he says that "in the beginning is relation" (1937, p. 18); it's the beginning of one of his chapters. Then everything he describes after that is a filling out of the notion of relation. I was enormously impressed with that. And then I began to read other materials that contributed to it. Right from the start, of course, John Dewey was an important influence. He didn't specifically use the language of relation in the way Buber had done, but everything Dewey described about the best schools and classrooms reflected that notion.

JQ: What led you to Buber in the first place? How did you find Buber and his work? I ask because I know one of the things that you find yourself doing when investigating theoretically is acting like a detective and trying to find some work that gels with where your thinking lies.

NN: I was teaching a course in affective education and so I was reading on a whole set of related topics, including religion. I also read Paul Tillich's book on being (Tillich, 1952). That's when I first used Buber, but I can't say exactly who or what put me on to him but it was in connection to teaching affective education.

JQ: How did your interpretation of Buber evolve, in particular in regard to the specific aspects that stood out for you in his work?

NN: It evolved rather rapidly because his discussion of relation and the human need for response just connected with me and that whole part of my life that I was trying to bring together with my analytic philosophy. So it fitted just perfectly.

## Nel Noddings on care theory  **105**

**JQ:** There's a move that you made from Buber's work to your work. Could you give us some more details regarding how this happened?

**NN:** This is a product of my own life, and thinking and reflecting on this: to look at the concepts that are central to care theory defined relationally – and that's different from just saying, here is a person who cares and here is what that person does. I wouldn't be able to affirm or disconfirm any claim along those lines unless I heard the story, unless I knew what the cared-for needed, expressed as a need, and how the cared-for responded to the care. So that made the relational connection fundamental. I still think even now that that is probably the single most important contribution of care theory: its emphasis on relation. I was reading a lot of political philosophy at the time too, and noticed over and over again the emphasis on the individual. If you look at virtue ethics, again you've got this emphasis on the individual: the virtuous person does such-and-such. And there are times when you read such accounts and you say, "What was the result? What happened to the person on the other side of it? Does that matter or doesn't it?" If you're studying philosophy at a place like Stanford, then you're reading Immanuel Kant. Kant is, in many ways, an absolutist, as can been seen, for example, in his famous statement "never tell a lie." Care theory said to me, "that's crazy," because of course we should tell lies sometimes. We tell lies to spare another person hurt. We tell lies to save another from harm and so forth. Then that leads to all kinds of questions about where you draw the line, et cetera. But the most important feature is that when you're looking at it from the perspective of care theory, you're always looking at the relation; you're not just looking at this person who is a simple or good or spectacular carer. You can't say anything about the quality of that caring unless you look at both parties.

**JQ:** Were there other significant influences, theoretically, in the development of care theory for you?

**NN:** Oh sure. Carol Gilligan was influential. Not in that first writing of *Caring* (1984), because I finished writing that book at just about the time when her book, *In a Different Voice* (1982), came out. It came out in 1982 and that's when I was finishing up the writing of *Caring* and then it was in process for a couple of years because it was a new sort of thing and I was a new author and you know how those things sometimes take a lot of time. But there was some feminist philosophy appearing in journals and that certainly influenced what I was doing. It isn't where the basic theory came from, but it certainly was an important influence. Then I presented a paper at a conference. I don't remember what the conference was, but I remember it was in New Orleans. A colleague there said, "What you're presenting is a strong, feminist theory," and I hadn't even thought of that before. That's how odd this was, that I didn't come to it from feminist theory. Of course, after he said that, I began to read more in feminist theory. Then I brought those two things together; they should have been together right from the start. But

**106** John Quay and Nel Noddings

we're talking about how things came about and I'm telling you honestly how they came about.

**JQ:**  I understand. I was wondering what you think feminist theory added to the relational theory of Buber (1937) in the development of care theory?

**NN:**  It helped to add a lot of specificity in particular, and this is something I'm still working on now. Much feminist work concentrates on trying to achieve equality for women, but equality for women in a male-defined world. So if you're asking how a particular woman is doing in this world, whatever she's doing is compared with what the most successful men are doing in the public world. I'm not saying that is a bad thing; I'm glad that I wound up with a good position and made a good salary and all that. The more fundamental problem is to change that world so it isn't a male-defined world but a male and female, a human-defined world, and we still have a long way to go on that. I became very interested in the work of Jane Addams (Addams & Lagemann, 1985), for example, and Pearl Buck, who was held in semi-contempt by a lot of my colleagues because they didn't think she should ever have received the Nobel Prize [for literature] in the first place. But the biographies of her parents (Buck, 1936a, 1936b) are just so powerful on the very topic we're talking about now, the difference in lives of men and women. And her work was influential in our adopting three Korean/American children. Also, Virginia Woolf has been a very, very important influence in my life, and she was trying to point out the same thing. In *Three Guineas* (1938), when she's talking about ways to achieve peace, she tells her male questioner that women can't do it by using the same language and procedures that men use. She's trying to get across to him that it isn't just a matter of women being accepted as equals in the male-defined public world, it's a matter of changing that whole world. To me, that's enormously powerful.

**JQ:**  Thank you. How much time did it take, do you think, to evolve care theory to a point where you were happy with it?

**NN:**  Well, I'm still working on it of course. I think I was happy with it and excited by it right from the start, but here's a place where empirical researchers not only use philosophical theories but contribute to them. Two of the things I talked about in *Caring* are "engrossment and motivational displacement" (1984, p. 16). I don't remember why I first used the word engrossment, but now when I'm writing about it I instead use receptive attention[2] and so I've spent quite a bit of time in describing the difference between the kind of attention students use in the classroom where a good part of their mind is on "what the teacher is going to ask me about and that's what I should learn," and receptive attention, which is a totally open, vulnerable position in which you really are listening to the other. There I've drawn on the work of Simone Weil, for example, who talks about that (1977).[3] Now, when I'm writing about the thing I initially called engrossment, I remind people that it means sustained, receptive attention: when we put our own projects and objectives aside, not forever but temporarily, and we really listen, we open ourselves to the other. There are many writers who have had something to say on this, but for me, the two most powerful are Simone Weil and Virginia Woolf; two very different people.

Just last week I had a graduate student write to me, asking questions, trying to sort through things, and she described an incident that she observed in her research. And she said, "But I don't know what to do with this? What do I do with engrossment and motivational displacement?" She asked this because she was so stuck on the list of vocabulary words that she wasn't really thinking about what those words were pointing to. I had to spend time with her, saying, "You've got it sitting right in front of you in this incident; you're looking at it." Then I switched to the words sustained, receptive attention. The teacher in her data was listening to the student. She was not imposing her own views or desired outcomes. She was genuinely listening to the student. Then she [the teacher] did something; she quit what she was initially trying to do and she did something else. And that's motivational displacement. So it was right there, but because it wasn't defined in one, two, three, four, you know, this particular researcher just couldn't come to grips with it. I think she's okay now, but this is just one example and it's so recent that I thought it might be useful for you to hear it.

**JQ:**   That is very useful because it makes me think about the evolution of concepts: how "engrossment," which you used earlier on, has developed into "receptive attention", and the subtly different meaning that the new way of trying to express that concept conveys. I was wondering if you could say more about the importance of concepts in communicating your work in a way that other people might understand?

**NN:**   Right, for me, questions of that sort come mainly from students, and sometimes students in parts of the world who have difficulty with some of the concepts simply because they're expressed in English. I communicate quite a lot now with students in China and Japan and we often have to talk for a while in order for them to be able to translate what I'm saying into something that's useful for them and still is as faithful as possible to what I've said in the first place.

I think the connection between empirical researchers and theoretical or philosophical researchers should be more interactional than it is. For me it has been, and that interaction has been enormously valuable because, as I said, this really important concept of "engrossment" was misunderstood by a lot of people. When they explained to me why, I was led to try to find something better and I think "sustained receptive attention" is better; it meant that I had to say what the difference between receptive attention and classroom attention is.

That sent me to a lot of psychological literature, which was enormously useful on that concept of "attention" right away. For example, the book *Moral Questions in the Classroom* by Katherine Simon (2001) offers a beautiful

**108** John Quay and Nel Noddings

examination of high school classrooms in which we can see caring happening or not happening. It's a collection of small narrative studies and I've got a whole bunch of those. There's Katherine's work, and the work done by the Developmental Studies Center[4] with Marilyn Watson. Again, what you usually find in those studies is at least a collection of short stories that describe caring quite beautifully, where teachers try one thing and they don't quite make a connection and then they try another thing. But the fundamental idea is the establishment of relations of care and trust. In fact, Marilyn Watson's book has this in the title, *Learning to Trust* (2003), and that is enormously powerful.

JQ: With those works, do they use some of the more specific concepts from care theory that you have introduced?

NN: Yes. Many of them actually use the words that I initially used but more of them now use "attention," "response," and "expressed needs."

JQ: Do any of those works use quantitative measures to attempt to show caring in action?

NN: Some of them do, and I'm always interested, but mostly I'm a bit put off by them because I think they get off the main point when that happens.

JQ: Are there aspects of your journey through developing care theory, that you think might help researchers on their own journey in dealing with theory and trying to piece together some form of framework that helps them to understand what's going on in their data, be it quantitative or qualitative?

NN: Yes. I think by and large lots of interaction and discussion. I have colleagues at Stanford who can't be bothered answering emails from students at other universities and I can see why they don't; they're up to their ears in work and these are not their students. But I think that kind of interaction is enormously valuable because it isn't a one-way thing. Again, the power of relation is underscored. I have learned so much from young people doing empirical research, and struggling with it. So I know some of the difficulties that they're having and it has been helpful to me. As I've already described, it enables changes in language, and elaboration of what I meant in the first place, to help make it clearer and I think we need more of that.

One of the things – I hesitate to say it – that is sadly missing in philosophy of education these days is usefulness. You hardly ever see a philosopher of education quoted and really used. I'm delighted that a lot of my work seems to have connected with people, but part of that is because I believe so firmly in the whole idea of connection.

JQ: I was wondering what you thought care theory might contribute to qualitative methodologies?

NN: I think a lot, because it draws attention to the details of observation; you're looking at something happening and you've got to be able to describe the overall environment, and then you've got to describe what you see happening, and then, hopefully, how the people involved in it would describe that. So, in some cases, you wind up with something like *Rashomon*.[5]

Nel Noddings on care theory **109**

**JQ:** I don't know *Rashomon*.

**NN:** I think it came out of Japan; that wonderful story in which some incident occurs and a whole set of people are asked to describe it and they're all asked separately. You get this wonderful set of stories that don't agree with each other at all. It makes for a wonderful drama. So when we talk about *Rashomon*, we mean that here is an incident and here are seven different descriptions of that incident with very little agreement.

**JQ:** I was wondering if you had any general advice for research students, who may be grappling with an empirical task or with a more theoretical task or philosophical study, as to how they may go about it? Or perhaps some likely hurdles they may confront and ways that these might be overcome? Things that you experienced yourself and had to push through in order to develop the ideas that have shaped your career.

**NN:** I think probably the most important thing is to have a relation of care and trust with a mentor. For graduate work, that continuing relationship can be so, so important. And of course, at its best it grows into a lifelong friendship, which is not the least result of graduate studies; I'd put it right up there at the top. You can always advise someone to get that kind of mentor, but they can't always get that kind of mentor because it doesn't always happen. The other thing is to listen to competing positions. Don't just latch onto a supposed panacea, but look at the whole range of the possibilities, weigh them, see if they can be brought together somehow.

**JQ:** Do you recall your mentors? Who supported you in those more formative years?

**NN:** Larry Thomas was my advisor at Stanford.[6] He had a very good formal reputation, but he didn't produce a whole lot of original work in philosophy; he was pretty much devoted to his teaching. But he certainly grabbed my interest in philosophy of education, encouraged me and was extremely important in my development as a professional.

**JQ:** Can you recall anything more specific about Larry's influence on your work, any specific examples?

**NN:** I can't in the sense of any influence on the development of care theory for me, it was just his introducing me to philosophy to begin with and directing me to the work of John Dewey. I was telling some students the other day that after I did my masters in math and we moved to California and I started at Stanford, I decided to take two courses in philosophy of education to get them out of the way. Of the whole period of the doctorate, we were required to have two courses in philosophy of education and I thought, "Well, I've got to do these, I might as well do them now."

During that term, the whole house started filling up with philosophy books; I was just so grabbed by it. So if you want the influence of a mentor, there's the first influence: there were philosophy books all over the house. Then I started taking courses not only in the school of education, but in the philosophy department, which was quite different from what I

**110** John Quay and Nel Noddings

was getting in philosophy of education, but that wasn't a problem for me because of my background in math. This was a highly analytic department and so I had no trouble whatever in following the arguments, following the logic. But the problem for me was, why are they arguing about this? On some matters, I still wonder. That's why I had to spend a lot of time reading and talking and so forth. People will often ask about the transitions from math to philosophy, and on one hand it was an enormous transition, and on the other hand it was a very easy transition because of the background in logic.

JQ: Do you recall some driving questions from that time when you were beginning to dip your toe, if you like, into the water of philosophy of education?

NN: I don't know what I can say about that, because on the one hand I was interested in educational and moral/political issues right from the start, but on the other hand, the very first formal philosophy class I took, as I recall, was theory of knowledge. I became quite fascinated with epistemology, and that's when I started reading Piaget. I must have read everything Piaget ever wrote. Of course, it's obviously connected to education. And again, on doing the course in epistemology, there was no problem whatever in following the arguments. Maybe I was a born philosopher? But that basic question, "Why are they arguing about this?" – it kept me going, kept me reading and investigating.

JQ: You mentioned competing positions and paying attention to those rather than dismissing them by just looking for things that support your own work. Have you got any examples of those that may help communicate what you mean to graduate students and others?

NN: Oh sure. The temptation is to dismiss behaviourists. If you're captivated by Jerome Bruner, and I love Bruner's work, you're tempted to throw Skinner out entirely. But when you do that, you are missing something.[7] Some of Skinner's work is wonderful and I have several of his books here. You can find literary gems among the theorists that you're not all that fond of. I mean I would discount most of behaviourism, but I wouldn't throw it all out. And similarly, that whole attitude carries over into education. I do not like the fact that our teachers in this country are now often forced to teach a particular kind of lesson with a behavioural objective and then a specific presentation and then checking to be sure that it's taught, but I wouldn't throw it out. There are days when, as a math teacher, I'd do exactly that, so it raises the questions, "When would I do it? Why would I do it? When would I not do it?" and "Why would I not do it?" So the whole world of philosophy opens up again. That's why I would say pay attention to the controversies and look at them with an open mind. I have even recently quoted Charles Murray (2008)[8] favourably and of course he's a somewhat notorious conservative who got a terrible reputation for his work on race with Herrnstein.[9] But if you read Murray, there are some things worth reading there.

## Nel Noddings on care theory  **111**

**JQ:**  That raises the question for me: "How much effort does it take to really understand a particular author, a particular theorist, a particular philosopher?"

**NN:**  I think it takes quite a lot, but you don't have to understand everyone that you read thoroughly. If you're going to make use of it, then you've got to spend more time and understand more deeply, but otherwise I think browsing is useful in philosophy, as it is anywhere else; just becoming familiar with names and general positions and so forth. It's only when you're going to zero-in on a particular concept or idea that you've got to research really deeply.

**JQ:**  Do any particular names come to mind in terms of difficulties you've had in coming to terms with particular concepts?

**NN:**  Gosh, if I thought about it, there would be so many. I'm trying to think how and when I came across David Hume, who is certainly in the top three philosophers for me. I've quoted him in the *Caring* book because he puts an emphasis on feelings: we're not motivated by reason, we're motivated by feelings (1984, p. 79). Of course, I've had loads of very, very interesting discussions with some philosophers on that; with Harvey Siegel, for example. I mean he and I get along very well and we agree on many things, but he really feels that reason can motivate us. I think reason can direct us, and that's what Hume said too, but I don't think it can motivate us. We have to feel something, we have to want something. So that realisation led me to read more of Hume and he's not an easy read. If you've ready any of him, you know, it's not easy. But once you're motivated to do it, then you've got a reason to stick with it for a while too.

**JQ:**  Is there anything else that you might want to add, thinking about our audience of research students and academics here grappling with issues of theory and trying to connect theory with empirical work?

**NN:**  Something that I'm doing a lot of writing on now, which I think is awfully important, is interdisciplinary work. I would certainly advise young researchers, whether they were empirical researchers or philosophical researchers, to read widely and broadly and not to get stuck in one narrow little line, because there are so many wonderful things out there. I'm writing about interdisciplinary work and I'm sitting looking at the paragraphs I've just quoted in which a whole bunch of mathematicians are named, talking about the Jewish Holocaust. At the very end of it, someone asked David Hilbert, a great mathematician, whether mathematics at Gottingen had been damaged by the removal of Jewish mathematicians, whether mathematics there had suffered; Hilbert replied: "Suffered? It hasn't suffered, Minister. It doesn't exist anymore."[10]

You look over that paragraph and you see the names Hilbert, the city of Gottingen, Gauss, Riemann, Felix Klein and so forth. And when I read something like that I say to myself, "Why are these never mentioned in the math class?" The kids who take four years of academic mathematics in high school never even hear the name of a mathematician. So there's no

**112** John Quay and Nel Noddings

connection to the other parts of the world. I guess if I have any general advice that I would really try to pass on to people, it's to pay some attention to interdisciplinary work; don't get stuck in some narrow little corner.

JQ:   Fantastic. Thank you so much, Nel.

## Conclusion

Noddings has made an enormous contribution to the conjoint fields of educational practice and educational research. Her journey through theory is actually a journey through life: an ongoing attempt to comprehend the fundamentals of human being through the lens of relation, as Buber had done, which highlights for her the importance of caring. Sharing this legacy has connected her with researchers, teachers, students, parents and others across the world, challenging her to more clearly communicate the concepts she has chosen to convey her original phenomenology of caring. Her work continues to inform developments in education and associated fields, highlighting the importance of the relation between theoretical endeavours and practical enterprise.

## Notes

1   Seminal feminist texts on care theory, apart from those authored by Noddings, include: Carol Gilligan, 1982; Mary F. Belenky, Blythe M. Clinchy, Nancy R. Goldberger, and Jill M. Tarule, 1986; and Sara Ruddick, 1989.
2   See Noddings, 2010, pp. 47–48 and 2012.
3   See Noddings, 2010, p. 47 and p. 52.
4   The Developmental Studies Center is now the Center for the Collaborative Classroom. See their website for further details (Center for the Collaborative Classroom, 2017).
5   The Rashomon effect describes a situation where those people involved in an event (usually more than two) interpret it in contradictory ways. It was derived from a Japanese movie of the same name where four individuals were involved in a particular circumstance but offered conflicting accounts (Kurosawa, 1950).
6   To access further details regarding Nel Noddings' career, see Amrein-Beardsley, 2010.
7   For further discussion, see Noddings, 2015a, p. 165.
8   See Noddings, 2015b, pp. 31–32.
9   See Herrnstein and Murray, 1994.
10  See Noddings and Brookes, 2017, p. 23.

## References

Addams, J., & Lagemann, E. C. (1985). *Jane Addams on education*. New York: Teachers College Press.

Amrein-Beardsley, A. (2010). Inside the Academy: Video interviews with Nel Noddings [Video files]. Available online at http://insidetheacademy.asu.edu/nel-noddings.

Belenky, M. F., Clinchy, B. M., Goldberger, N. R., & Tarule, J. M. (1986). *Women's ways of knowing: The development of self, voice, and mind*. New York: Basic Books.

Buber, M. (1937). *I and Thou*. (R. G. Smith, Trans.). Edinburgh: T. & T. Clark. (Original work published 1923).

Buck, P. S. (1936a). *The exile: Portrait of an American mother*. New York: John Day.

Buck, P. S. (1936b). *Fighting angel: Portrait of a soul.* New York: Reynal & Hitchcock.

Center for the Collaborative Classroom. (2017). Who we are. Available online at www.collaborativeclassroom.org/who-we-are#Developmental_Studies_Center.

Gilligan, C. (1982). *In a different voice: Psychological theory and women's development.* Cambridge, MA: Harvard University Press.

Herrnstein, R. J., & Murray, C. (1994). *The bell curve: Intelligence and class structure in American life.* New York: Free Press.

Kurosawa, A. (Director). (1950). *Rashomon* [Motion picture]. Tokyo, Japan: Daiei Studios.

Murray, C. (2008). *Real education: Four simple truths for bringing America's schools back to reality.* New York: Crown Publishing.

Noddings, N. (1984) *Caring: A feminine approach to ethics and moral education.* Berkeley, CA: University of California Press.

Noddings, N. (1992). *The challenge to care in schools: An alternative approach to education.* New York: Teachers College Press.

Noddings. N. (1995). *Philosophy of education.* Boulder, CO: Westview Press.

Noddings, N. (2010). *The maternal factor: Two paths to morality.* Berkeley, CA: University of California Press.

Noddings, N. (2012). The language of care ethics. *Knowledge Quest,* 40(4), 52–56.

Noddings, N. (2015a). *A richer, brighter vision for American high schools.* New York: Cambridge University Press.

Noddings, N. (2015b). *Education and democracy in the 21st century.* New York: Teachers College Press.

Noddings, N., & Brookes, L. (2017). *Teaching controversial issues: The case for critical thinking and moral commitment in the classroom.* New York: Teachers College Press.

Ruddick, S. (1989). *Maternal thinking: Towards a politics of peace.* Boston, MA: Beacon Press.

Simon, K. G. (2001). *Moral questions in the classroom: How to get kids to think deeply about real life and their schoolwork.* New Haven, CT: Yale University Press.

Tillich, P. (1952). *The courage to be.* New Haven, CT: Yale University Press.

Weil, S., & Panchias, G. A. (1977). *The Simone Weil reader.* Mt. Kisco, NY: Moyer Bell Limited.

Watson, M. (2003). *Learning to trust: Transforming difficult elementary classrooms through developmental discipline.* New York: Jossey Bass.

Woolf, V. (1938). *Three guineas.* London: Hogarth Press.

# 8

# MICHAEL PETERS ON SCIENCE, GENEALOGY AND OPENNESS IN EDUCATIONAL RESEARCH

## In dialogue with Steven A. Stolz

*Steven A. Stolz and Michael Peters*

## Introduction

In order to make sense of Michael Peters' approach to educational research, a brief critique of what "genealogy" is and why it is often considered a "new" method to philosophy is a useful starting point. The reason for this critique is due in part to the method itself, but more to understand how Peters employs a form of genealogy and scientific method in the service of educational research. Although scientific and genealogical method are not the same, there are some similarities in the principles that underpin them both, particularly in relation to the provisional nature of knowledge, truth, language, history, value, and so on. The fame of "genealogy" or the "genealogical method" would appear to rest with Nietzsche's (1887/1998) usage in his book entitled *On the Genealogy of Morality*. That said, Foucault (1971) popularised the idea that "genealogy" represents a new historical and philosophical method in his essay entitled "Nietzsche, Genealogy, History". Foucault (1971, pp. 77–80) argues that the genealogist "refuses to extend his faith in metaphysics" and so "opposes itself to the search for 'origins'" in the search for "immobile forms that precede the external world of accident and succession". Here, we have an example of Foucault's claim that the genealogical object has no "origin" or "essence of things". In one sense, this forms the basis of his scepticism about "fact" and "objectivity", but more importantly it reveals the crucial role of *interpretation*. In another sense, this is not what Nietzsche (1887/1998, preface, §7) means by genealogy as he is only interested in what has "really existed, really been lived", and *discovering* this with a "completely new set of questions" and "new eyes". This is why Nietzsche's genealogical method is different because it is concerned with breaking the chain of value transference by showing that the value or meaning is discontinuous over time. Of course, the object of Nietzsche's genealogical critique is morality; however, this could easily be replaced with other values or meanings in the illustration of no unitary value or meaning being transferred over time. Likewise, values and meanings arise from multiple points of origin and hence why to Nietzsche it is nonsensical to speak of moral absolutes because we are bound to mistakenly attribute prior histories of morality with its present value, meaning, purpose, and so on. The fact that there is no unitary and/or single point of origin about morality renders morality unstable. As such, it is the *connection* morality has with *present* value, meaning, purpose, and so on that Nietzsche (1887/1998) desires to sever because *we are not entitled to infer about its origin* (see for example, first treatise, §1–3).

Another notable method used by Peters in the service of educational research is the employment of genealogy with science that is best described as a "genealogy of science". This is made evident in the following dialogue, where Peters' genealogical account of science is both autobiographical and historical. Here, Peters highlights how he was influenced by significant paradigm shifts in both science and philosophy, particularly those who were the catalyst for these dynamic shifts, like Popper, Kuhn, Foucault, Wittgenstein, and so on. Although scientific objectivity and historical subjectivity often leads to divergence, Peters wants us to know that there is a post-modern objectivity that can complement, rather than be antagonist towards subjectivity, which he refers to as "openness". Peters' theory of openness attempts to converge the objectivity of scientific realism with the subjectivity of anti-foundationalism that rejects absolutes and welcomes the idea that knowledge is "non-linear", "open", and "dynamic", with the realisation that the present purpose of educational research is the *latest* functional meaning imposed on it from different points of origins. It is precisely this ontological attitude towards the impermanent nature of knowledge, truth, and so on that Peters wants to embrace and champion. It is this distinguishing feature of *openness* that underpins Peters' approach to education and education research, which is reinforced by Peters' own words in the dialogue, when he states:

> By openness I mean the shift from linear to non-linear, from closed to open, from static to dynamic and also an openness in relation to questions of ontology.

Although this account neatly encapsulates the "non-linear", "open", and "dynamic" nature of Peters' account of openness, most importantly it brings to our attention the problems of *discovery* and *justification*, particularly in educational research. Indeed, Peters quite rightly reminds us about three things in relation to research: (1) discoveries are grounded in, or derive their inspiration from theory; (2) no matter how objectively research may proceed, claims, findings, and so on will always be in doubt due to the ever-present possibility of counter-evidence being provided; and (3) prior theories influence what observations are made and significance is assigned, and this is why there is no theory-neutral or epistemologically- neutral bodies of knowledge, judgement, and so on. Even though we are reminded of the limiting features of research, another distinguishing feature is the importance of the dialectical method in all research. As a result, the dialogues found in this edited book and the dialogue found in this chapter are part of this dynamic tradition in which the central method being employed is *truth through reasoned argument*.

For the purposes of this chapter, four themes were identified in the dialogue as a means to elucidate the use of theory and philosophy by Peters in educational research. These four themes are as follows: (1) analytic method; (2) genealogical analysis of discourse; (3) philosophy of "openness"; and (4) the important role of philosophy in education and educational research. Each have been intentionally inserted as a sub-heading throughout the dialogue to guide the reader as they progress through the chapter.[1]

## The dialogue

### *Analytic method*

**Steven A. Stolz (SS):** I have been reading your book *Education, Philosophy and Politics: The Selected Works of Michael A. Peters* (Peters, 2012a) in preparation for this interview and one of the core themes of this project is to understand more about how well-known educational scholars use theory to engage with philosophies in their educational research. Often, theory and/or philosophy is used to support the investigation of a specific research question or questions by either: (1) outlining a theoretical framework which situates the phenomenon, the problem and the issue; and/or, (2) outlining a methodology which clarifies the methods applied. Can you share some examples of how you have used theory and/or philosophies in your educational research?

**Michael Peters (MP):** Well, let me answer this question in an autobiographical way. When I started philosophy, I did a Philosophy of Science degree at the University of Canterbury where Karl Popper had a position from 1937 to 1943. The course began with the recent history of analytic philosophy and the analytic method. I recall starting with Frege and Russell's logical atomism and then turned to Wittgenstein's *Tractatus*. So it was very much tied up with philosophy of mathematics, pretty abstract material, and the analytic method per se. It ought to have included the failure of logicism or the program to reduce mathematics to its logical foundations and Gödel's famous Incompleteness Theorem. In the second part of the course, it went on to look at contemporary debates in philosophy of science, in particular the Kuhn-Popper debate. It started with reference to Karl Popper's (1953/1959, 1963) philosophy of falsifiability and falsification – a kind of method to adopt in science that he refers to in *The Logic of Scientific Discovery*, and later in *Conjectures and Refutations*. Falsification begins for Popper with the problem of induction, a problem that falls out of the history of philosophy as first highlighted by David Hume. Popper was talking really about a method of verification, and the logic of confirmation versus the logic of falsification. He solves the problem of induction through inverting the logical asymmetry between verification and falsification by examining the "truth" of generalisations from confirmed instances of observation. How many instances of confirmation do you need to verify a law in science? This is often referred to as the problem of the "Black Swan". The classic example is the observation of black swans. Every swan that you've seen so far is white, but it doesn't negate the possibility of seeing a black swan in the very next observation. This one negative observation is enough to invalidate the generalisation that all swans are white. So he solves that problem through the logic of falsification. Popper's falsifiability and falsification comes out of the Vienna Circle of Logical Empiricism, of which he was a member. So we're talking the turn of the twentieth century when most of the Vienna Circle philosophers escaped Nazi Germany by going to Europe or to England or to America. Hans Reichenbach, Herbert Feigl, and even Thomas Quine who was an American on the outskirts of that circle, as well as Popper and Wittgenstein were members of the Circle. The term logical positivism came to symbolise the method of science. Reichenbach talked about it in terms of the unity of sciences through the method of science that became the general method of verificationism that Moritz Schick summarised in the handy slogan: "The meaning of a sentence is its method of verification." In a sense, these are also in part the origins of analytic philosophy that Wittgenstein and Popper had an important role to play in developing. In particular, Popper developed a method of falsification which is the inversion of verification that he then thought was the ultimate knock down in terms of scientific methodology. All science, including social science and therefore education as science, was thought to progress by means of bold conjecture, as Popper put it, and falsification – the search for the negative instance.

The next debate which dealt with these issues was the Popper–Kuhn debate. In *The Structure of Scientific Revolutions*, Kuhn (1962) challenged the logical underpinnings or foundations of verification theory and how truth could be ascertained. So when Kuhn historicises that question and then begins to look empirically at the history of science as a way of proceeding he showed that scientists progressed by "normal" and "revolutionary" science. "Normal science" is puzzle-solving within the existing paradigm; "revolutionary science" led to a new paradigm. In one sense, what we have here is a philosophical history of science versus a historical methodological investigation of science itself. These two accounts came into conflict and Kuhn's historical theory seemed to contradict Popper's account of science. At the beginning of the debate Kuhn's views seemed very radical in that they contradicted Popper's logical account of science and indicated that theory-change and theory-preference was not really a rational process at all. Kuhn compared paradigm change in science to a religious conversion, with scientists acting conservatively and desperately trying to hang on to their theory by "saving" ad hoc hypotheses.

Kuhn's views became increasingly more conservative in his later writings and in line with a lot of other people operating in those days, for instance, Norwood Russell Hanson's view about theory-ladenness of observation. Hansen argued observation was theory-laden so that facts were only picked out by the theory adopted rather than the other way around (i.e.

facts confirming a theory). Later the view was broadened to the "value-ladenness" of science. In those days the cultural turn came to characterise scientific change as not a rational process, but more like Kuhn's "gestalt switch" as a term for paradigm change. Therefore, the process of paradigm change began to throw the philosophy of science world into disarray and to cast doubt on whether there was a method that guaranteed scientific truth.

This was the first line of inquiry where I came across the question that framed the narrative of the philosophy of science in the Western world, at least from the beginnings of the logical verification movement to the adoption of a kind of falsification theory and then accounts that drew lessons from history and culture: from Popper's falsificationism to Kuhn's history of science. I became very influenced by the historical and cultural accounts of science. The other strand that impressed me was represented by the way Wittgenstein had left the Vienna Circle and repudiated his earlier verificationism to adopt a "language-game" approach. In fact, when Wittgenstein (1922/1961) finished the *Tractatus*, he thought he had solved all the major problems of philosophy. In accord with that belief, he gave up philosophy and went off and actually taught in three different schools in Austria for six years after training as a teacher in Vienna in 1919. It wasn't until Frank Ramsey came along that he was persuaded to re-join the Vienna Circle, but this time he led the Circle in a very different direction. His later work embraces a cultural understanding of science and mathematics. This cultural understanding, if I can say this in philosophical shorthand, is a cultural method. In fact, the whole "cultural turn" of the twentieth century in my view is due in large part to Wittgenstein's (1953/2009) *Philosophical Investigations*. Although I spent quite a lot of time in the early days looking at Wittgenstein's (1956/1978) *Remarks on the Foundations of Mathematics*, I was so influenced by the cultural turn that he took that I did my PhD on Wittgenstein and the cultural and historical turn across philosophy, humanities, and social sciences that casts doubt on a universal method for assuring the "truth" of science. One of its effects has been to see cognition as something that is deeply embodied, extended, embedded, and enacted. This paradigm of cognition comes out of a cultural turn which I think is the current paradigm in cognitive science and has been advanced by scholars like Jerome Bruner and Rom Harre. Let's call it the paradigm of "embodied cognition". I've been very persuaded by that notion and I was very persuaded by Paul Feyerabend who, in his book entitled *Against Method*, took Wittgenstein in a different direction that could be viewed as a rejection of analytical philosophy and the idea that there is a single scientific method that can guarantee truth of science (as logically indubitable). So the cultural turn and embodied cognition do play an important role in epistemology. I think this movement is a reaction against the form of analysis that came to us in the analytic revolution of philosophy beginning with members of the Vienna Circle, and logicians like Frege, Russell, Wittgenstein, and so on.

The notion of method, under the influence of Wittgenstein, Ryle and the Oxford philosophers, gets picked-up by linguistic philosophy and the presumption inherent in ordinary language philosophy that suggests that attention to our language and words, a strategy called the "sematic ascent" can resolve first order problems. This led to the notion that there exists something called the "analytic method" that philosophers can use to analyse philosophical problems. An off-shoot of this was "conceptual analysis", a method much used by philosophers of education to clarify educational concepts. You can see why I was, and still am, hostile to this as a means of proceeding in philosophy of education.

## *Genealogical analysis of discourse*

**SS:**   In the introduction section of your *Selected Works* (Peters, 2012a) you mention that you have also been influenced by the works of Nietzsche and Foucault, and so I am interested to know more about this, given my interest in Nietzsche. As a result, if I was an undergraduate or a layperson how would you explain the central method and/or methodology that you use in your educational research?

**MP:**   Nietzsche and Foucault use the term "genealogy" and this means something different from its common usage. Nietzsche (1887/1998), in his book entitled *On the Genealogy of Morality*, talks broadly about the genealogical method. Nietzsche's background as a philologist accounts for his concern about a history of concepts. Although, Wittgenstein and Heidegger would use the term "language", the use of the term "discourse" rather than "language" provides a kind of discursive space and a concept of power relations that structures discourse – who speaks, under what conditions, with what effects? Today, some graduate students and academics would want to use the term "discourse" and adopt "discourse analysis" as the method. Wittgenstein, Nietzsche, Heidegger and Foucault suggest a philosophy of language that today features the genealogical construction of discourse, of its rules, its concepts, and the history of those concepts. In some sense, this approach works subversively as a challenge to accepted opinion and methodology.

Of course, Nietzsche is using the genealogical method in relation to the question of value. How are those values struck? Why are they important? What we understand from genealogical analysis is a set of hierarchies which are composed often from binary oppositions that privileges one concept over another. How does this come about? Well, when you give up on transcendental guarantees after the "death of God", then you have to ask yourself, historically, how did they come about and whose interest do they serve? That investigation inevitably will lead you to analyse a set of power relations. That's why I really think that there is a degree of sympathy between the work of Nietzsche, Heidegger, Wittgenstein and Foucault. At least this is the argument that I have tried to make several times during the course of my career. When you look

**120** Steven A. Stolz and Michael Peters

at the historical relationships between these thinkers, of course you know that Wittgenstein is strongly influenced by Nietzsche as is Heidegger. Heidegger's (1961/1979, 1961/1984, 1961/1987, 1961/1982), work that he started in 1936 and didn't finish until the sixties, the four volumes of Nietzsche – just called *Nietzsche* – are absolutely path-breaking. Whatever you think of him as a Nazi sympathiser, whatever you think of him as a philosopher of "being", you have to say his book on Nietzsche is penetrating and insightful. One of the problems here for philosophy is that good ideas come from "bad" people. How do we cope with that? Well, in actual fact what epistemology teaches us is it's not ad hominem arguments that we should pay attention to, and the owner of an idea does not necessarily affect the idea's value. We want to assess the importance of the idea on its own merits and be able to discuss that. Certainly, when we begin to talk about language and the function of language as we do with the revolution in analytic philosophy, or if we take a genealogical investigation of ideas, concepts, and so on, rather than an analytical one, or perhaps both together, then we can understand a lot more in philosophy of education. Conceptual analysis in and of itself is blind. To paraphrase Kant, genealogical analysis in and of itself is empty. I think they're both important and supplementary – there is an argument, methodologically speaking, for considering them together.

There is an argument to accept both the analytic method and the genealogical together because we are interested in the logic of concepts, but we're also interested in the logical construction of argument as it functions and its relations in the history of those arguments. I also think that we need to pay attention to power relations in philosophy, particularly if we take the historical and the cultural turn.

**SS:** I have been reading a fair bit of Nietzsche lately and without a doubt *On the Genealogy of Morality* is one my favourite pieces of work. Unfortunately, a lot of his work has been misunderstood, misinterpreted, and misappropriated for different ends. This is why Nietzsche unfairly gained a reputation for anti-Semitism, for being a Nazi, for being self-contradictory, plus a range of other charges. This only came about when critics quoted snippets out of context from his whole corpus. Indeed, Kaufmann's (1974) brilliant commentary, entitled *Nietzsche*, repudiates all of these false claims with scholarship of the highest order. Maybe this should serve as a warning to all of us to have a concern for the original context in which something is critiqued, but for a range of complex reasons this rarely occurs. That said, I'm sure we could talk about Nietzsche for quite a while, but I wanted to ask you about the notions of "philosophy as pedagogy" and "pedagogical philosophy" that you have sought to develop. So the logical question to ask is: What do you mean by these concepts?

**MP:** You are absolutely right to emphasise this point, Steve. I think we can learn from philosophers such as Nietzsche, Heidegger, Wittgenstein, and Foucault. I often refer to these philosophers as "philosophers of subjectivity" and

Michael Peters on science **121**

one of the things I want to say about them is that they really talk about philosophy as a way of life. I might also say that in some sense they are often committed to philosophy in terms of the Greek notion of the kind of spiritual wisdom through a series of spiritual exercises that are performed on the self – the transformation of the self through these philosophical exercises. The latter is an example of what I call "pedagogical philosophy". Or as I want to see them, in terms of the "philosophy as pedagogy". So I take the cultural turn, I take the autobiographical turn, particularly when you talk about philosophers who are clearly engaged in philosophy as a way of life, rather than an academic part-time activity, such as professional academics who come in five days a week and spend three or four hours writing clever papers that get published in philosophy journals. When you study those kinds of philosophers, then you understand something about philosophy *as a way of life*. I think that the great historian Pierre Hadot (1995), from the Collège de France, has written a very good book called *Philosophy as a Way of Life*. His main source of inspiration here is Wittgenstein, who also influences his method of "language-games". So you have somebody from the Collège de France, Pierre Hadot, who strongly influenced Foucault, who used Wittgenstein and Wittgenstein's life as an illustration of philosophy as a way of life. I think he did this very early on in the piece and Foucault knew of Wittgenstein through Hadot. They also talked about the whole question of Western aestheticism through that kind of paradigm and therefore understood Wittgenstein, although Foucault never referenced him in any paper that I'm aware of.

**SS:** Please correct me if I'm wrong, but in the introduction of your *Selected Works* (Peters, 2012a) you outline how these philosophers have influenced your work, which in turn I think has resulted in a very interesting line of thought in relation to subjectivity and objectivity. Would it be correct of me to say that you're almost, in a sense, quite critical of real objective existence or realism based on the influence of those great works and/or thinkers?

**MP:** No, I don't think so. I think that because I am as much materialist as I am a historicist. So, when I think about discourse I think about it as existent material symbols that take the historical forms of genre and writing. I have a book out with that title (Peters, 2011b), and one of the things I think that people ought to do is to trace different forms of thinking through the development of philosophical genres. For instance, when you talk about philosophy as a kind of writing, one might say that demands an analysis which is both historical and materialist because you're referring to material discourses. You're saying, look here, when we study philosophy we study its forms, its forms of writing, so we can talk about the *treatise*, the *thesis*, or more ancient forms like the *fable*. We could talk about a range of different forms that philosophy has taken as a kind of writing and written form. The form of the *dialogue* is a clear example. You can see that these forms or genre embrace a concrete material literary form and they *become* texts. Those texts

**122** Steven A. Stolz and Michael Peters

have a history. They're written at a certain point. We often try to date those texts. The people that write about them classify them as "Enlightenment" or "Renaissance" or "Modern" forms. They refer to their own historical times and that historical material is philosophically analysed as a kind of writing. Interesting enough, Richard Rorty (1984) of all people, in *Philosophy in History: Essays on the Historiography of Philosophy* and some of his other works, talks of philosophy as a kind of writing. So I'm not opposed to "realist epistemology", though I think it takes a variety of different forms. None of it is contradictory of anything that I stand for in a realist or critical realism sense. I would say, though, that in terms of philosophy of subjectivity, it does not mean that I'm uncritical of foundationist epistemology because I am anti-foundationalist and embrace the form of post-foundationalism. I embrace that form of post-foundational epistemology on the grounds of current progress in science and mathematics. The examples that I want to use for post-epistemological foundations come in the first instance from mathematics. Briefly, I want to look at Gödel's incompleteness theorems. If it's impossible in principle to provide logical foundations for arithmetic then it's impossible in other spheres of human existence, including ethics.

So we must embrace Gödel's incompleteness. Instead of incompleteness, I call it "openness". By openness I mean the shift from linear to non-linear, from closed to open, from static to dynamic, and also an openness in relation to questions of ontology. So we're talking about non-linear, dynamic *systems* that have the capacity to transform one kind of system to another with different properties. Now I think that's a mathematical model of evolutionary cosmology. Another example is Heisenberg's uncertainty principle in physics. I think that's also extremely pertinent to me as a scientific principle for non-foundational epistemology. The third one of course is Einstein's theory of relativity and the lesson that observation is relative to the observer. Those are the three principles that I would like to use in the social sciences and humanities. There's nothing in that that's not realist. I'm drawing my examples from mathematics and science, from the best mathematics and science that are available to me. But I am against the notion of realism or critical realism if it implies a correspondence theory of truth and a representative view of language as depicting reality, and also as a method that guarantees scientific truth.

## Philosophy of "openness"

**SS:** You've just led me to my next question. What do you mean by your philosophy of "openness", particularly the point you make about moving away from dialectic dialogue to dialogue that is open, intercultural conversations?

**MP:** I think this conversation that we're having at the moment on Skype is a small example of "openness" – which communication technologies facilitate. Now, we are at a very early stage of human history in terms of global interconnectivity. I think that philosophy needs to take that into account, and I call this the "philosophy of openness". It has a geopolitical dimension as well. Open education is a very strong part of it and, let me say, this philosophy that I'm trying to develop is very different from the traditional defenders of the open society, like John Dewey, Karl Popper, and Jürgen Habermas.

My view of openness is very different because I see openness as a kind of complexity that has a logical structure which we can trace back to its origin in the Boolean two-valued logic used in electronics in terms of a circuitry, packet switching, and enabling a logical operation of the truth table that Wittgenstein invented and that is the basis for humanity entering into the digital realm. This is a different conception than Rorty's notion of philosophy as a kind of conversation. To me, we're at a very early stage of this openness that permits free and transparent conversation as well as control and surveillance. When we look at indexes of global interconnectivity, we see there are more than three billion mobile phones in the world now, roughly half the world's population. This is growing rapidly, as is interconnectivity. That doesn't mean everybody's got one because some have got two or three, but it does mean that we're at a very early age of human history which I'm going to call "open globalism" and a move towards a kind of globalism which is open and characterised by a type of complexity that is non-linear, dynamic, emergent, and self-organising similar, to the World Wide Web. So when I say openness is a form of dialogue of intercultural communication, then that's really the direction in which I'm moving in terms of the development of my own philosophical thinking. Away from Dewey, Popper, and Habermas, towards an understanding of the limits of openness and the paradoxes of openness because those earlier theories were all defences of liberal modernity. What we see more recently is, for example, that incident in Sydney where people were killed by – I won't say a jihadist – somebody who believed that he belonged to a jihadist form of Islam. In talking about openness as a stage in the evolution of scientific communication and as a form of philosophical conversation – two different forms – we have to be careful not to believe the hype of social media from Facebook and Apple. But we must support these two models of openness as a bulwark against epistemic foundationalism and moral fundamentalism of all kinds. I think that these forms of openness are characterised by "peerness" – peer-to-peer interactions that are peer governed at different levels of content and maybe not yet at the level of infrastructure. These forms – like material genres and the kinds of writing I talked about earlier – are non-foundationalist and ontological in that they have the capacity to self-organise and co-construct themselves. We might even talk about creative self-organisation as an emergent feature.

You confront paradoxes here like the paradoxes of the liberal state in this way. I think that liberal epistemology faces the same thing as the digital

**124** Steven A. Stolz and Michael Peters

form of it. You see the way in which the system can be used against itself. The same with any system that develops global civil society. The asymmetries of power where one person acting against the norms of trust can wreak havoc and bring the system down. One rogue state or individual can have disproportional effects in an interconnected or "ecological" environment. The asymmetry of power characterises these global digital systems making them very fragile and open to manipulation.

SS: What are your thoughts on those individuals who don't want to be connected or don't want to be part of the global community? Does that then do away with your whole notion of openness (see for example, Peters (2013) and Peters & Roberts (2011))?

MP: Well, there is not just one notion of openness. There are many forms of openness and we have to acknowledge the limits and also the paradoxes, hence why it is contestable as an emergent form. The form of openness from Dewey to Popper to Habermas is quite different. I think the Wittgensteinian view of overlapping consensus is an interesting view and more accurate. In some views of Wittgenstein's overlapping family resemblances, people would say you get "incommensurability" at the end of the spectrum. Now, of course there will always be opposition when you go to fundamentalism. Fundamentalism, whether it be Christian or Islamic, defines itself against openness. They are, by definition, closed systems. They're closed systems of thought because the truth is something that is not discoverable or made – it is not out there. Fundamentalists know it already. They possess it. They have that truth already. It's not an evolving, evolutionary concept. Islamic and Christian fundamentalism both reject evolutionary theory, whatever form it takes, because the Priest or Iman has privileged access to the word of God and has a privileged place to interpret it for the masses because it's not interpreted by everybody and anybody in the public domain. Openness that is based on very different processes depends upon the diversity of opinion and an emerging consensus in the long term. We can call this "epistemic democracy" or "community of inquiry" after Peirce. I believe that "ecological diversity" must be preserved as it is the necessary basis for the richness of human thought out of which creativity emerges.

So if "truth" emerges out of a closed system, it is due to interpretation, and the masses have to accept that the word of God or Allah is the source. It is a process of revelation and self-evidence that seems corrupt to me. There will always be closed systems as long as there are people who literally believe in the inalterability of the word of God in that sense. So I stand opposed to all forms of fundamentalism and all forms of literalism because I believe, like Dewey, in the democratic form of life, but unlike Dewey I don't think that this form must take the American form. I believe in the experiment of freedom which is the basis for a social democracy that is a form of inquiry where truth emerges in a Peircian or Deweyan sense out of the multitude of voices and over the long term. It's not associated by authority with any one individual, but is based on evidence or argument. So of course, I would have to admit that there are and have been always closed systems of thought which have ossified and which are only concerned with one thing, which is the prosecution of the word. Well, I find that ugly and highly damaging, and I find that a strong source of anti-modernity. I think it is anti-progressive; I think it runs against equality of individuals; I think it is strongly anti-women, anti-children; I think that it is strongly "anti" the "other", that it is non-inclusive. It stands for a frozen set of values which are privileged on the basis of authority, rather than inquiry.

## The important role of philosophy in education and educational research

**SS:** I want to change topics, and finish with one last question. Some people on the outside of educational philosophy and theory argue that all the discipline or sub-discipline area does is critique like a "sniper from the side", and thereby does not contribute anything new to education and/or educational research. What role do you see philosophy playing in education and/or educational research (see e.g. Peters (2011a, 2011b, 2012a, 2012b) and Peters & Bulut (2011))?

**MP:** Well, I have two views on that. First, I think a lot of analytic philosophy is practised in places like the UK and America as though nothing's happened since the 1960s and 1970s. The world is exactly the same as it was when R. S. Peters (1966) wrote *Ethics and Education* and they are content to analyse concepts until the cows come home. My criticism is of an analytic method that is ahistorical and apolitical, which tinkers with liberal values in an unselfconscious way while the world burns around them. So they're not addressing the critical questions of multi-culturalism in society or the birth of conservative British identity values as a pedagogical value, or philosophy in the era and the epoch of the Anthropocene period when we're said to occupy a place of geological epoch for the first time with the capacity to destroy the very planet that supports us. How can philosophy of education continue to tinker and play with the clarification and analysis of concepts under those circumstances?

Second, which is more a British view of philosophy education coming out of Hegel, is a critical view which issues in critique after critique after critique. The only way you can get a positive mathematically with Hegelian dialectics is through a double negative. The famous negation of negation. That's a long way around to making some kind of constructive and positive response. So I define myself in opposition to both of those views of philosophy of education. I think we need to move very quickly indeed to those pressing problems that our planet faces. We can name some of them, such as the increasing need for viable forms of intercultural communication, education against populist nationalism and racism, the education of the

**126** Steven A. Stolz and Michael Peters

world's children, the pedagogy of the biosphere and ecological democracy, and so on.

Each of these problems requires in part an educational and pedagogical response that demands a form of openness. For example, educational inclusiveness that is about widening the circle of literacy and access in an age of "Internet rights", where rights to the Internet ought to be universal so that others can be part of the conversation. At the level of political economy, I call this the mode of educational development – although the word "development" is suspect – that I think constitutes the next paradigm to shift societies past the damaging effects of industrialism such as inequality, environmental pollution, labour alienation, and so on. This is not about the doctrine of "free trade" dressed up as openness, but really a more ontological thesis about what humankind can become in the moment of collective intelligence.

I want to end by thanking you for taking the time to arrange this conversation based on a set of astute questions. The very notion of dialogue to the Socratic form, where Socrates always comes out on top, and where the conversation is structured through a kind of dialectics is characteristically different. We have covered a lot of ground from an account of logical positivism that dominated science in the twentieth century to conceptual analysis that dominated philosophy of education in the 1960s and 1970s. We have also focused on Wittgenstein as a fulcrum in producing the cultural turn in philosophy – we might say the social and historical turns as well, especially if we think further about Nietzsche and Foucault who together legitimated a kind of genealogical analysis that admits questions of power relations in philosophy and discourse. Finally, we also traversed some ground to do with openness in both its epistemological and ontological forms as a species of evolution currently reflected in a range of technologies, as significant as the invention of writing was to the Egyptians, the Chinese, the Greeks, and eventually the world. For me these questions carry an important educational dimension where issues of pedagogy are not far behind. This would constitute my sense of a new philosophy of education that is more sensitive to questions of power, to sustaining an intercultural dimension, to attending to our habitat and impending ecological disaster, and to examining the logical and self-emergent forms of collective intelligence that grace a species-wide form of inclusiveness and openness.

## Conclusion

In this chapter we have explored Michael Peters' approach to educational research through a dialectical discussion found in the form of a dialogue. We argued that Peters employs a range of methods, but four notable themes emerged in the dialogue as a means to elucidate his use of theoretical and philosophical frameworks, and also to provide clarity around the methods employed. These four themes were as follows: (1) analytic method; (2) genealogical analysis of discourse; (3) philosophy of "openness"; and (4) the important role of philosophy in education and educational research. Based on the dialogue, it was concluded that Peters' use of genealogical and scientific method share some similarities, particularly in relation to the provisional nature of knowledge, truth, and so on. Likewise, we highlighted Peters' concept of "openness" concluded that a central thread of his research is the use of the dialectical method and the employment of *truth* as a product of a theory of enquiry and discourse.

## Note

1 The initial interview was conducted via Skype and captured by a digital recording device in February 2015. At the time of the interview, the first author was located at the University of Melbourne (Melbourne, Australia), and the second author was located at the University of Waikato (Hamilton, New Zealand). It is also prudent of us to mention at this juncture that some edits, revisions and so on have been made to the original interview dialogue captured that range from adding, removing, or correcting obvious errors from the transcription process, through to providing greater clarity and coherence on a number of crucial concepts discussed. Where possible, the dialogue has been edited to recapture the dialectical discussion that occurred between two people in a form that it is both engaging to the reader and generates further discussion and research.

## References

Feyerabend, P. (1975). *Against Method: Outline of an Anarchistic Theory of Knowledge*. London: New Left Books.

Foucault, M. (1971). Nietzsche, genealogy, history. In. P. Rabinow (Ed.), *The Foucault Reader* (pp. 76–100). New York: Pantheon.

Hadot, P. (1995). *Philosophy as a Way of Life: Spiritual Exercises from Socrates to Foucault* (Trans. M. Chase). Oxford, UK: Blackwell Publishing.

Heidegger, M. (1961/1979). *Nietzsche, Volume I: The Will to Power as Art* (Trans. D. Krell). New York: Harper & Row. (Volume I was originally published in 1961 and was translated into English in 1979.)

Heidegger, M. (1961/1984). *Nietzsche, Volume II: The Eternal Recurrence of the Same* (Trans. D. Krell). New York: Harper & Row. (Volume II was originally published in 1961 and was translated into English in 1984.)

Heidegger, M. (1961/1987). *Nietzsche, Volume III: The Will to Power as Knowledge and as Metaphysics* (Trans. D. Krell). New York: Harper & Row. (Volume III was originally published in 1961 and was translated into English in 1987)

Heidegger, M. (1961/1982). *Nietzsche, Volume IV: Nihilism* (Trans. D. Krell). New York: Harper & Row. (Volume IV was originally published in 1961 and was translated into English in 1982)

Kaufmann, W. (1974). *Nietzsche: Philosopher, Psychologist, Antichrist* (4th edn.). Princeton, NJ: Princeton University Press.

Kuhn, T. (1962). *The Structure of Scientific Revolutions*. Chicago, IL: The University of Chicago Press.

Nietzsche, F. (1887/1998). *On the Genealogy of Morality: A Polemic [Zur Genealogie der Moral. Eine Streitschrift]* (Trans. M. Clark & A. J. Swensen). Indianapolis, IN: Hackett Publishing. (Original work published 1887.)

Peters, M. (2011a). *Neoliberalism and After? Education, Social Policy and the Crisis of Western Capitalism* (2nd edn.). New York: Peter Lang.

Peters, M. (2011b). *The Last Book of Postmodernism: Apocalyptic Thinking, Philosophy and Education in the Twenty-first Century.* New York: Peter Lang.

Peters, M. (2012a). *Education, Philosophy and Politics: The Selected Works of Michael A. Peters.* London and New York: Routledge.

Peters, M. (2012b). Educational Research and the Philosophy of Context. *Educational Philosophy and Theory*, 44(8), 793–800.

Peters, M. (2013). The Concept of Radical Openness and the New Logic of the Public. *Educational Philosophy and Theory*, 45(3), 239–242.

Peters, M. & Bulut, E. (Eds.). (2011). *Cognitive Capitalism, Education and Digital Labor.* New York: Peter Lang.

Peters, M. & Roberts, P. (2011). *The Virtues of Openness: Education, Science and Scholarship in the Digital Age.* Boulder, CO: Paradigm.

Peters, R. S. (1966). *The Ethics of Education.* London: Allen & Unwin.

Popper, K. (1953/1959). *The Logic of Scientific Discovery.* London and New York: Routledge. (Original work published in 1934.)

Popper, K. (1963). *Conjectures and Refutations: The Growth of Scientific Knowledge.* London and New York: Routledge.

Rorty, R. (1984). *Philosophy in History: Essays on the Historiography of Philosophy.* Cambridge, UK: Cambridge University Press.

Wittgenstein, L. (1922/1961). *Tractatus Logico-Philosophicus* (D. F. Pears & B. F. McGuinness, Trans.). London and New York: Routledge. (Original work published in German, 1921 with an English translation published in 1922.)

Wittgenstein, L. (1953/2009). *Philosophical Investigations* (G. E. M. Anscombe, P. M. S. Hacker & J. Schulte, Trans.) (Rev. 4th edn.). Chichester, UK: Wiley-Blackwell. (Original work published 1953.)

Wittgenstein, L. (1956/1978). *Remarks on the Foundations of Mathematics* (G. E. M. Anscombe, Trans.). (Rev. edn.). Oxford, UK: Basil Blackwell. (Original work published in 1956.)

# 9

# RICHARD PRING ON MAKING RESEARCH *EDUCATIONAL* RESEARCH

## In dialogue with R. Scott Webster

*R. Scott Webster and Richard Pring*

### Introduction

Over the many years Professor Richard Pring has been working in education and in educational research, he has consistently encouraged his readers and listeners to be heedful of the very nature of education, including what makes research in this field distinctively *educational* research. Pring's philosophical focus is shared by relatively few other educators, one of whom is John Dewey (1938, p. 91), who argued that for any progress to occur in the practices of education, we must first devote "ourselves to finding out just what education is". This remains a perennial challenge. Yet in most of the current literature dealing with education the complex concept of "education" is usually absent and in its place is the narrower concept of "learning" (Biesta, 2010). This latter term lends itself more easily to managing the work of teachers, researchers and schools, mainly through a "how to" approach of required applications.

Since the time of psychologist Edward Thorndike in the early 1900s, educational practices, including educational research, have been under pressure to become more explicitly "evidence-based", which is code for "scientific" (Lagemann, 2000). However, interpretations of what counts as evidence have tended to negate the contributions made through philosophical thinking, overlooking or ignoring moral and ethical concerns and replacing these with an emphasis on empirical evidence that is apparently value-free and without need of philosophical examination. Smeyers and Smith (2014, p. 25) highlight how the pressure to adopt approaches to practice and research that are more scientific or clinical have made education "vulnerable" to losing this deeper understanding. Consequently, efforts to pursue a richer comprehension of education, with its inherent moral, ethical and political aspects, have become increasingly marginalised. Pring's work stands at the forefront of efforts to re-focus educational practice and research on these issues.

In his book *Philosophy of Educational Research* (2015), Pring promotes the importance of maintaining a philosophical approach to educational research. He justifies this partly through an appeal to the practical impact that philosophical thinking is able to offer the activities directly associated with education. Indeed, coming to understand the very nature of education itself – including what it means to be an educated person, and what makes teaching and learning experiences educational rather than *mis*educative or indoctrinatory – is largely a philosophical activity. As Pring stresses in this dialogue, being philosophical is vitally important for guiding and regulating all the activities associated with education, including how we understand knowledge and schooling (1971, 1976). It is therefore important to avoid creating a dualism between thinking and doing, and between philosophical understanding and practical activities. In this sense, Pring's (1995; 2004a) approach is reflective of the works of Dewey, addressing various "false dualisms", such as practice versus theory, thinking versus doing, qualitative versus quantitative, vocational training versus liberal education, and traditionalism versus progressivism. It is therefore not surprising to see that Pring (2007; 2016) has written extensively about the work of Dewey.

If researchers are to embark upon investigations of various phenomena associated with educational practice then Pring advises, in this dialogue, to firstly develop a deeper understanding of the nature of education itself. While research in the social sciences, particularly in psychology, sociology, cultural studies and philosophy, might offer some valuable insights for educators, Pring nevertheless guides us to focus our attention more clearly on concerns that are specifically *educational* concerns. Some key points of his work include the need for teachers and researchers to better understand the moral aspects which are inescapably involved in educational practices (1999, 2004a). Such an understanding of education involves philosophical thinking, especially with regards to the question, "What does it mean to be an educated person?" – not via attainment of academic qualifications but with regard to our understanding of what it means to *be* a more virtuous community member.

## The dialogue

### What value does philosophy of education have for educational research?

**Scott Webster (SW):**  You have argued that when educational researchers are embarking upon their research they should first gain a clearer understanding of the nature of education, which is a task specific to the philosophy of education. Engaging with philosophy, and in particular philosophies of education, is valuable in supporting our investigations of specific research questions in two ways. The first is to outline the theoretical framework which situates the phenomenon, problem or issue that is specifically of educational concern. Second, philosophy of education is valuable for outlining a particular methodology which clarifies the methods that are to be applied.

Can you please share some examples of how you have used philosophies to do these two things?

**Richard Pring (RP):**  I'd like to start by referring to the big project that I had, which was a review for the Nuffield Foundation of education and training for 14–19-year-olds,[1] which was in the process of being redeveloped. This is a big issue here in England, as more and more people are staying on in schooling until they are 19 years old. Therefore, you've got this range of interests and abilities. What are we going to do to provide a good education and at the same time preparation for life afterwards, whether it be universities or whatever? So in pursuing this we took on an enormous number of reviews from teachers in schools, universities, employers, research and so on. One of the research issues was, "How do you pull together all this diverse material in order to provide a review of what's happening with a view to the decisions which ought to be made?" We decided to ask the basic ethical question, "What counts as an educated 19-year-old?" What are those qualities, intellectual, moral, social and so on, that an education system ought to be developing in order for these people to become educated? In order to think about that ethical question, one had to acknowledge that we're not just talking about the intellectually able, the highly academic; we're talking about the whole range of abilities and interests. What are those things that make them educated persons?

Therefore, the next question is, "What counts as being a person?" What do we mean by someone being a person and therefore a fully developed person? That was the kind of philosophical question that we posed in order to bring some sort of unity to all the different kinds of data we obtained. Educational questions are really a branch of ethics, namely, "What are the sorts of values, in terms of knowledge, morality, aesthetics, intellectual and moral virtues and so on, that in different ways we need to develop in all young people?" This formed the philosophical basis for reviewing the research and thinking where we should be going.

### The ethical nature of education

**SW:**  You mention here that you were intending to use this philosophical understanding to help inform your decision-making. Can you explain how you argued for the basic framework of this research project, as an *educational* project, to be *ethical* rather than economic, especially considering the expectations of funding providers?

**RP:**  That's a very important question, because first of all, having produced our report, we involved politicians – including a very significant member of parliament of the Labour Government, as it was then – to introduce us and to react to the report, et cetera. We disseminated the report to various people, particularly politicians. So there was a sense in which we had to think about how our work was actually going to have some sort of impact. A lot came out of that in terms of the public debate.

But these ethical questions run counter to the ways in which there's a dominance of economic significance in educational research. I'm not denying that this has a place, because part of helping to develop people as persons is to enable them to be able to live satisfying, fruitful lives, lives in which they can have a sense of dignity and worth. This is inevitably tied up with economics. Nonetheless, the problems that we were confronted with, which subsequently I've thought a lot about, are characterised by the difference between the language of moral knowledge, if you like, and what I call the language of management, which now permeates and dominates much of the educational thinking as far as politicians are concerned.

Philosophically, how we see the world depends very much upon the sort of language through which we describe it. If you see the dominance of a moral language, you will see the world differently in terms of success and failure, poor standards and good standards. You will see them differently if you start off with a language which is essentially taken from the business world and a world which is concerned with efficiency in achieving particular targets which are related in the main to economic performance. So that becomes a real clash, it seems to me, of values. Therefore, the philosophical issue emerging from this is to look critically at the kind of language which now permeates educational discourse, particularly from the political point of view.

This really goes back quite a long way in terms of increasing emphasis upon targets, and those targets being highly specific and easily measured. A form of behaviourism is behind all of this. Of course, this goes back a couple of decades but now permeates and dominates educational discourse. Therefore, we witness a language of very specific targets and performance indicators. Now we are talking about pupils and their parents as consumers of education. I think that the most appalling thing is that teachers are reduced to those who *deliver* the curriculum. So there's a whole language here which needs to be taken apart and examined.

One of the problems is that the kind of values which one might say are the educational values one wants to argue for, such as people being virtuous, caring and interested in ideas, cannot be logically reduced to highly specific behavioural targets. Therefore, the philosophical critique must be one that looks at the way in which notions like standards are being understood in political discourse. To examine how the notion of the curriculum is something which teachers *deliver*; as though the ends of the curriculum, the purposes of the curriculum, are themselves defined elsewhere by politicians and their advisers, and then given to the teachers to simply "implement".

This dominant language can change the concept of a teacher from being an educator into being, increasingly, a trainer. How do you get these pupils to achieve these targets? Several people have researched how this is affecting practices in schools, where teachers are seeing their role move away from that of educator. Consequently, a lot of teachers are leaving the profession. I think two-fifths of new teachers now leave within the first five years.

Richard Pring on *educational* research  **133**

It's partly because they go in with enthusiasm to communicate their subject of English, science, etc., but find instead that their job is merely to train these youngsters to hit these targets, which themselves define the standards by which schools and teachers are judged.

So there's a need for a critique of this language. Back to that basic philosophical question, "What do you mean by standards?" There's lots of evidence now coming out – as a result of this kind of philosophical critique – of the ways in which teachers find it necessary to cheat the system, because unless they do their schools will go down the league tables. That gives rise to issues about public service and the for-profit development of education. That is a whole area in which I've been very involved and interested.

Education practices often involve a clash between different philosophical views. One of my favourite philosophers is Michael Oakeshott (1975, 2001, 2015) who talks about education as introducing young people to what he calls "the conversation between the generations of mankind" (Oakeshott, 2001; Pring, 2010, p. 28). By conversation, he means that the present state of scientific knowledge is itself the result of scientists engaged in conversation with previous scientific discoveries and theories: critiquing them, refining them and building on them. It's a kind of conversation. It is the same with history and literary criticism.

By introducing pupils very carefully to these traditions of conversation, you're getting them on the inside of what he called the voice of poetry, the voice of science, the voice of philosophy. Now getting pupils on the inside of these voices is very different to getting these pupils trained to hit particular targets. It's Oakeshott's notion of a conversation between generations which I think captures that educational enterprise better than anything else.

## The roles of values, particularly for research which is assumed to be mainly empirical

**SW:** Something struck me here when you refer to the importance of language, in particular moral language versus the language of management. We appreciate the relationship between language and thinking, and you have argued how important it is to be clear on the language we employ in our research because this determines the discourse which will dominate the interpretation and understanding of the phenomenon being investigated. Clarifying language is not just an analytical technique applied to concepts, but it is also a means for clarifying values or, more correctly perhaps, *what* we value. But sometimes values appear to be absent in research, in particular in clinical and scientific research. Therefore, what advice would you give to education researchers who may assume that values are not relevant to their research, especially if they are mainly attempting what they regard to be purely empirical work? For example, they may be investigating ways that students learn a particular maths approach or English language skill. So

**134** R. Scott Webster and Richard Pring

they're looking for efficiency and effectiveness in teaching and learning strategies. What advice would you give to education researchers who don't see values being present at all in their studies, and don't even recognise any clashing of values?

**RP:** First, no significant research is straight-forwardly empirical. If I can give an example, there's a lot of work now on developing skills necessary for an economic future. So we've got to have a skills revolution (Pring, 2004b). Now what's fascinating about that is if they're claiming that this work is empirical, which they were, then it all depends on what you mean by a "skill". But they don't define skill at all. So then, let's start by asking, "Is a person who cleans the streets, for example, a skilled worker?" They clean the streets very effectively. They're able to sweep up the mess. They're able to put it in the lorry. They're able to drive the lorry. Is that three skills or one skill? In other words, if you're going to add up and subtract and do all that sort of stuff, it depends on what you mean by what it is that you are adding up and subtracting. So what is a skill?

It is similar with apprenticeships. Some politicians and the media go on about how we need another 1,000 apprenticeships. This is based on research, the need for apprenticeships. But if you look at the concept of "apprentice", it's a very woolly one and it has a history. It trades upon the notion of an apprentice from mediaeval times. But now they call people who do a fortnight's training in McDonalds an apprentice.

Before you engage in empirical work, you must ask the question, "What do you mean?" This usually raises a very interesting set of philosophical questions. The concepts need to be defined clearly. They need to be related to the particular "form of life", as Wittgenstein says, through which you are actually describing the world. I don't think you can ever really get away with just pure empirical work where these issues are considered to be unproblematically straight-forward.

A second point about this refers to how you often get research students saying, "I'm going to do quantitative research" or "I'm going to do qualitative research". But beneath each of these approaches lies a whole lot of different philosophical traditions. Obviously you've got strict positivism behind quantitative approaches where you try to reduce everything to that which can be measured. But a lot of quantitative work does not assume that positivist type of background. So it's not straight-forward to assume there are two kinds of research: quantitative and qualitative. These are notions which need to be unpicked until you realise there are different kinds of empirical work, depending upon the nature of the issue or problem that you are empirically investigating. Otherwise you're going to reduce everything to a kind of behaviourism and you don't have to be a behaviourist in order to do quantitative work.

A third issue then emerges: if you ask these questions and you're going to call it educational research, eventually this educational research must have something to do with helping people develop as persons. So you've got to relate your research to what you mean by being a person. If, for example, you're concerned, as a lot of research is, with improving standards, then standards logically relate to the purpose of the activity. Therefore, if the purpose of the activity is not considered very carefully, then your research is not necessarily going to be about an educational issue. Mathematics is quite a fascinating example because what you're getting now is a tightening up of the standards on mathematics, but the mathematicians are saying, "I'm afraid that's got nothing to do with educating people in mathematics. It's got nothing to do with a deeper understanding of what counts as thinking mathematically." It really is learning off [by heart] particular formulae, learning off by heart your times tables. Useful skills; but it's not really understanding mathematics. There was a very good report that came out in this country a few years ago called the Smith report, *Making Mathematics Count.*[2] It was written in 2004. It identified a problem with those who are coming to university, who have got their A levels in mathematics grade A – the crème de la crème when they come to university – but who don't really *understand* their mathematics. In other words, they have been trained in a particular narrow view of what counts as mathematics – to learn off [by heart] the formulae, to learn off [by heart] the various skills – but they have not gained a deeper understanding of the key ideas and concepts. So if one is doing research into mathematical learning, then one can't avoid raising philosophical questions in the philosophy of mathematics aimed at identifying those key ideas, those key concepts, which constitute understanding mathematics. One must therefore realise that coming to understand those concepts is often a struggle, which itself is often removed from the idea of training people to know what the answers are, to be more efficient, to be more effective. So, I don't think you can get away without raising these philosophical questions concerning: "What do you mean?"

## Some differences between "educational" research, compared with research on education

**SW:** I'm wondering if you can highlight the contrast you refer to in your writings between "educational research" and "research on education".

**RP:** Well, I think that educational research means that it's research which is being shaped by *that* question: "What constitutes an educated person?" You must therefore be thinking about the question, "What sort of values are intrinsic to being educated?" How those values are actually entering into the kind of research questions that one is asking, the research approaches and so on. Now, it's quite possible that you could get different researchers, let's say in the sociology department, who really aren't interested in those questions. They will just look at the situation as it is and give a good sociological account of why things happen and why they don't happen. These accounts can be very useful for educational researchers, because in deliberating over educational questions the evidence coming from sociologists and psychologists is quite clearly important. It's a part that has to be brought in to one's overall thinking, but it can't itself give the answers because those answers depend upon broader questions of an ethical kind.

Now this becomes particularly significant when one starts thinking about teachers as researchers and that whole tradition going back to the work of Lawrence Stenhouse (1975, 1985) and John Elliott (1988, 1991) on the teacher as researcher. They argue that it is wrong to think that teachers are suddenly going to take on the research findings of sociologists and psychologists because teachers are actually operating in a classroom which has its own unique features. Moreover, teachers are concerned with the questions about how can *these* youngsters develop as persons in some way – morally, as well as in terms of knowledge and understanding. In order for teachers to do that, they must engage in philosophical deliberation about how their values, which they are trying to implement in the classroom, are affected by what they can see empirically to be the case and what the evidence is. I think a very good example of this in this country [the UK] is what became known as the *Rutter Report* (Rutter, Maughan, Mortimore, & Ouston, 1979). This went against the grain of much of the material coming from America in the 1970s and 1980s, saying that schools don't make any difference to a person's life trajectory, because it's all to do with social class, it's all to do with background. Certainly, when I started teaching back in the 1960s and 1970s that was very much the case: keep these kids happy, because, you know, they come from a working-class background and they'll leave school and do jobs like cleaning the streets. But the *Rutter Report* got 12 schools which were roughly the same in terms of catchment area [in London] and other features, so any differences to emerge were less likely to be caused by social context, etc. – they were matched up very, very carefully – and yet there was a massive difference in terms of what different schools achieved with the children. So there was pretty good evidence [in this report] that schools can and do make a difference. Therefore, a teacher in a school researching how to improve the performance of youngsters would obviously see this to be a very significant finding, coming from psychologists and sociologists who took part, and would feed this into their deliberations. It would mean that those teachers would no longer be saying, "I can't do anything about this, it's all to do with background." No, it's not all to do with background. It's also to do with the interactions which take place within the school. So once again, the teacher is engaging in researching their practice, or the school is engaged in researching its practice, in terms of the sort of values which they have, but also in terms of the kinds of empirical evidence which needs to be taken into account in those deliberations. So, there's an interaction between "research on education" and "researching in education".

## Might doing philosophy, and in particular, philosophy of education, be too much to expect from all researchers?

**SW:** What would you say to researchers who might be confronted by these broader questions regarding personhood, values and living a valuable life, if they say, "Look, I might be a practising teacher but I have no formal philosophy behind me to engage in these kind of philosophical questions in my research"? What advice would you give?

**RP:** Like anything, things can be pitched at different levels of understanding. Philosophy is now becoming a very popular subject in our schools. My 14-year-old grandson has just gone home with a philosophy book of mine because he says this is what he finds most exciting in his school. So I don't think getting people to think philosophically is a terribly esoteric business. It really is something which gets people to raise the question, "What do you mean?" Realising that the further you ask that question, the more you are being pushed down into issues which are normally covered by philosophy of knowledge, philosophy of morality or ethics, philosophy of mind. This all sounds very grand, but it really is something that even children can be trained to be thinking about. Indeed, where this is going on in schools, especially amongst 17 and 18-year-olds, they find it very exciting and they really do take it very seriously. I don't think people should say, "Well, this is not my interest", or "I'm not up to this". I think it's part of that sort of deliberation which ought to be part of the researcher's training. So, for example, here at Oxford University they've brought back, thank goodness, a compulsory course in the philosophy of education for all first-year doctoral students or research students.

I was brought back at my great old age to run seven two-hour seminars on the philosophy of educational research, and it's highly popular. They're still seeing me. I'm spending a fortune in the Rose and Crown running my tutorials.[3] They all appreciated this very, very much indeed. Then I had the final session in the old library at the university where the mediaeval scholastics would have argued about these things in the fourteenth century and so on. So these are issues which have been going on since Aristotle and Plato, and in this particular building where they have the texts of Aristotle and Plato, and all the students were engaged in this. Therefore, I don't think it's a sort of esoteric thing. I think it's a question of getting people to be thinking in those sorts of terms. And I think it ought to be part of the preparation of all research students, to get them to be thinking philosophically like this.

**SW:** On that point, would you say for such students who are considering that kind of engagement with philosophy that there is a difference between philosophy, or pure philosophy, and philosophy of education?

**RP:** I think philosophy of education is asking philosophical questions about educational practice, and getting people to look critically at the things which are often imposed upon them uncritically, such as politicians increasingly dictating

**138** R. Scott Webster and Richard Pring

what students ought to learn. For example, our previous minister for education in England, Mr Gove, decided that he was going to dictate the curriculum for history. He laid it down that every child from the age of five up to 11 should do 1,000 years of history, starting with Stonehenge and moving up to 1066. That's up to the age of 11. Then from 11 to 16 they will cover the next 800 years to the Act of Union. His view of history is just learning these facts. It wasn't until the historian Schama, in a lecture presentation to the Hay Festival,[4] identified Clive of India as nothing other than a sociopathic and corrupt thug that Gove removed Clive from the history syllabus. Now, once you've got to the stage where a politician, on the back of an envelope, can say, "This is what history is and this is what you've got to learn", then you need a teaching profession that is able to look critically at what you mean by teaching history.

We need teachers to be thinking about the nature of education in their work, which will draw them into traditional philosophical areas such as the nature of knowledge. How do we know things about the past? How does knowledge of history grow through that kind of critical examination? Why this history and not that history? There's an argument at the moment about people saying, look, we totally ignore black history in this country. And yet, if you think the British Empire was based pretty much upon going into Africa and into India and so on – a whole lot of things are now emerging historically – should we not actually have a view about the way in which we've exploited these countries? What are the values here? And what should we be doing in order to ensure that black people in this country are not just seen as non-citizens but so they're actually a part of it. These are ethical questions about the teaching of history: the nature of knowledge in history and ethical issues about what is valuable in history and should be taught. All these things are part of the discourse of a good professional and of professional associations. And at heart they're philosophical.

## How do researchers contend with having so many different theoretical frameworks to choose from?

**SW:** Early career researchers are often overwhelmed by the many philosophical frameworks that may possibly apply to their research. What advice would you give them as they attempt to navigate this complex theoretical landscape?

**RP:** I think they've got to do a lot of background critical thinking about the different paradigms. If you were to take feminism, you could say that what the feminist literature has picked out is a traditional bias against the distinctiveness of women's ways of thinking. A very good example of that is the critique of Kohlberg's work (1981, 1984) by Carol Gilligan (1982). She was saying that, in Kohlberg's case, had it been a woman researcher rather than a man, and had that woman researcher chosen young girls rather than young boys, then they might have arrived at a different way of classifying moral development.

Richard Pring on *educational* research **139**

What one needs to do before one picks a particular framework is to have a fairly broad understanding and knowledge, even if it is a bit superficial at first, about what these different frameworks are. Then you are able to say to what extent *that* framework really helps me to understand the issues and the problems which I am interested in addressing.

I think you need to develop a broader picture of the different theoretical perspectives and the extent to which they are mutually exclusive or mutually supportive. So a feminist perspective is of a different logical kind from a positivist one and, say, a phenomenological one, which is at a very different philosophical level. And once again, in this case, they've got to start questioning what is meant by "phenomenological", because it is a word which slips out very, very quickly, without people realising the significance of that word in terms of the work of people like Husserl, and what was assumed in Husserl's writings.

**SW:** So the advice you are giving to researchers would be to develop a broad-brush view of various theories, then decide which theoretical perspective would lend itself to best exploring the problem in question?

**RP:** Yes. Presumably in making that sort of decision they would already have some rough idea of the kind of problems that they're interested in, that they want to research. It is possible they may say, "Look, I'm vague at this moment, but I'm really interested, for example, in how children develop basic mathematical concepts." There would be a relevant feminist perspective here because it was assumed, until very recently, and probably still in many places, that women aren't very good at that sort of thing. So there would be a feminist perspective but by itself this wouldn't be sufficient to get at the deeper understandings of how concepts develop and in which contexts they were developed (for example whether you develop them better through practical engagement in mathematical work or sitting down with a textbook).

They would come, I would have thought, with some rough idea. But even in thinking more deeply about that idea, during the first few months, their ideas would be developing. So they may say, "I started off with that idea, but in pursuing it I realise now it's not the main thing that I'm interested in; or it was but there are other connected, more fundamental ideas, which I'm now increasingly interested in." The deliberation during that first year just seems to me absolutely crucial. As people acquire a deeper level of understanding, they come to think differently about their original question, as they asked initially with a fairly superficial view.

## Ethical issues for researchers and the "educated person"

**SW:** Are there other things you may have wanted to share with us at this time about how you have personally used philosophy, or some examples to unpack theoretical frameworks or methodologies that you use in your own work?

**RP:** I think that one of the issues that permeates almost everything is the concept of standards. If you think about the way in which schools are being forced to meet what are called certain standards of performance, they're being compared with other schools. Then you've got the international league tables and that kind of thing. This notion of standards gets the least questioning from the people who say, "We're going down the league table", or, "There are much higher standards in China than here", without looking behind the statistics at the underlying concepts. Often, what are assumed to be straight-forward facts need to be philosophically critiqued and theorised – and the concept of standards seems to be one of those.

I think that a lot of thought needs to be given to the ethical values, the virtues if you like, of an educational researcher. For example, to what extent does getting grants depend upon the views of the person who's giving the grant? This raises questions about perceived expectations of producing certain kinds of results, which might require twisting things a little bit. So notions like truthfulness and respect. How do you engage in research in such a way as to reconcile getting at the truth to inform practice, and at the same time respecting the people from whom you're obtaining that sort of information? How do you reconcile these two, which very easily contradict each other? Because by telling the truth you might therefore ruin a person's career. But by respecting that person, then your report may not be exactly truthful. There are these very interesting ethical dilemmas which I don't think can be answered in general form, but it's all part of moral deliberation. But moral deliberation has still to be informed by principles of justice and truthfulness.

I think the notion of truthfulness, having that virtue of truthfulness rather than actually altering what you've got to say or write to fit in with what is desirable in terms of your grants or the future jobs you're going to get and so on, is a very real moral difficulty. So I think these ethical issues need to be very much a part of research. I was asked to chair the ethics committee of the university before I retired, in everything but medicine and science. That experience raised some very interesting questions, for example from anthropologists out in Africa, who were supposed to get written confirmation of what they're doing from people who couldn't write. Well, that was dead easy to sort out really. But nonetheless there are other difficult things which are clearly ethical issues.

I do think the perennial issue has been what really counts as an educated person. When I first started teaching I remember I was given class 1X, which was the fifth stream of a five-stream comprehensive school, when there were no public examinations at the end which the students of 1X would take. So they all left school at the age of 15 with no qualifications. Now, they didn't really achieve anything academically in this qualification sense, but are we going to say they're totally uneducated people? Can you imagine an educated person who actually is an academic failure? Are there certain kinds of virtues which develop: qualities of caring, moral sensitivities and dedication to making a better community? There are lots of examples in history where the working-class of England, though they may have been without education, really got together because they were interested in ideas about improving their own community. So what are the characteristics that we ought to put at the centre of our educational system? I think one of the kind of problems is that we identify being educated with academic success, and that distorts the educational experience of a good 50 per cent of the school population, who go away feeling that they are uneducated failures because they have not been part of the group that really do well in their examinations. So, what would it mean for 1X to leave school as really educated people: having an ability to discuss, to think and to have a sense of responsibility? That, to my mind, is absolutely basic.

There was a philosopher, John Macmurray (1992, 1993, 1999) who talked about the form of the person and that notion of what it is to be a person. Absolutely crucial to his sort of educational thinking was how we develop those particular qualities, virtues and skills that go into enabling a person to live a fulfilled life, with personal dignity and worth, contributing to the community, able to engage in personal relationships fruitfully and responsibly. All these things contribute towards gaining a deeper and much broader view of what it is to be an educated person.

Then, of course, if you're going to start talking about the standards going up and down in schools, there is a need to have a much broader set of criteria as to what constitutes high standards in a school, or low standards. You can get the people with very high academic achievements, but if they then devote their academic skills to actually just feathering their own nest and ignoring the good of the community, we are missing something critical. Consequently, we are getting some terrible scandals coming out from the bankers and so on, who are guilty of such conduct — so called "educated people", who didn't even see the immorality of what they were doing. Those are the sort of issues which I think are absolutely fundamental to the philosophy of education.

## Conclusion

Throughout this chapter, Pring has stressed that research which purports to be *educational* research ought to be oriented with an understanding of the nature of education. To pursue this Pring draws significantly from the work of R. S. Peters, an important figure in the analytic tradition of philosophy of education who was at one time Pring's PhD supervisor. Peters' (1966) "criteria for education" are explained in his book *Ethics and Education*. Significant amongst these criteria are: worthwhileness, possessing a "reason why" and coming to care about what one understands. We can see the influence of these principles on Pring's work in his description of the nature of education which involves six main characteristics.

First, education involves activities which are specifically intended to bring about learning. This does not refer to just *any* kind of learning but rather to the sort of learning which enables a broader range of meanings to be understood, reflected upon and evaluated. Such learning involves what Peters' referred to as a "cognitive perspective" (1966, p. 31). This cognitive perspective is Pring's second characteristic of education. Third, education must be worthwhile; not just functional but valuable for its own sake in enabling people to increase and expand upon the possible meanings of their experiences. Educative learning is not the "mere learning" of inert facts but involves understanding and valuing living ideas, which imbue life with richer meanings. The nature of educative learning is not only a cognitive affair but involves the very being or character of the person herself. So, the fourth characteristic of education involves the learner, as a person who is to become more virtuous, being able to bring more critical insight and relate to things learned in a more thoughtful and caring manner. Such transformation of a person, through educative experiences, must involve processes which are appropriate for an educated person. This fifth characteristic distinguishes educative learning from the mere acquisition of information, because the learning involves a more thorough form of understanding, which is reflective of Dewey's preference for "warranted assertions" rather than simply "knowledge" because learners come to understand the warrants that support knowledge claims (1938). Lastly, the sixth characteristic of education which Pring argues for identifies education as the formal and intentional intervention made by a social group, as distinct from informal learning experiences. Therefore, it involves institutions, policies and professional educators, who make a significant contribution to the overall education experienced by a society.

Grappling with questions about the nature of education inevitably requires researchers to engage with the philosophy of education. One of the important aspects for understanding education is to uncover and articulate what we, as researchers, understand by personhood and, in particular, what we mean and value regarding becoming educated persons. This is quite different to the views currently dominating research, which reduce persons who learn to simply those who come to acquire or possess information. Engaging with educational values and ethics, especially with regards to how people are being transformed – for better or for worse – through learning experiences, is often neglected through studies which adopt narrow understandings of 'learning' and which often claim to adopt 'objective' approaches. Pring is one of the few educators who, since the time of Thorndike, reminds us that education cannot be reduced to pure empirical work. Educational researchers must courageously engage with the moral, ethical and political concerns regarding how learning experiences are impacting upon persons individually and collectively. This requires all educational researchers to engage in philosophy of education and this is where Pring's contributions are most valuable.

## Notes

1 For more information on this review, please see: http://www.nuffieldfoundation.org/14-19review
2 For more information on this report, please see: http://www.mathsinquiry.org.uk/index.html

3 The Rose and Crown is a public house near Oxford University which is sometimes used as a meeting place.
4 To listen to this lecture, please refer to: https://www.hayfestival.com/p-6108-simon-schama-and-teachers.aspx

# References

Biesta, G. J. J. (2010). *Good Education in an Age of Measurement.* London: Paradigm Publishers.

Dewey, J. (1938). *Experience and Education.* New York: Collier Books.

Elliott, J. (1988). Educational research and outsider-insider relations. *Qualitative Studies in Education,* 1, 155–66.

Elliott, J. (1991). *Action Research for Educational Change.* Milton Keynes, UK: Open University Press.

Gilligan, C. (1982). *In a Different Voice.* Cambridge, MA: Harvard University Press.

Kohlberg, L. (1981). *The Philosophy of Moral Development: Moral Stages and the Idea of Justice (Essays on Moral Development, Volume 1).* New York: Harper & Row.

Kohlberg, L. (1984). *The Psychology of Moral Development: The Nature and Validity of Moral Stages (Essays on Moral Development, Volume 2).* New York: Harper & Row.

Lagemann, E. C. (2000). *An Elusive Science.* Chicago, IL: The University of Chicago Press.

Macmurray, J. (1992). *Reason and Emotion.* New York: Humanity Books.

Macmurray, J. (1993). *The Self as Agent.* New York: Humanity Books.

Macmurray, J. (1999). *Persons in Relation.* New York: Humanity Books.

Oakeshott, M. (1975). *On Human Conduct.* Oxford, UK: Oxford University Press.

Oakeshott, M. (2001). *The Voice of Liberal Learning.* Indianapolis, IN: Liberty Fund Inc. (Original work published in 1989.)

Oakeshott, M. (2015) *Experience and Its Modes.* Cambridge: Cambridge University Press.

Peters, R. S. (1966). *Ethics and Education.* London: George Allen and Unwin.

Pring, R. (1971). Bloom's taxonomy: A philosophical critique. *Cambridge Journal of Education,* 1(2), 83–91.

Pring, R. (1976). *Knowledge and Schooling.* Wells, UK: Open Books.

Pring, R. (1995). *Closing the Gap: Liberal Education and Vocational Preparation.* Orpington, UK: Hodder & Stoughton.

Pring, R. (1999). Universities and teacher education. *Higher Education Quarterly,* 53(4), 290–311.

Pring, R. (2004a). *Philosophy of Education: Aims, Theory, Common Sense and Research.* London: Continuum.

Pring, R. (2004b). The skills revolution. *Oxford Review of Education,* 30(1), 105–116.

Pring, R. (2007). *John Dewey.* London: Bloomsbury.

Pring, R. (2015). *Philosophy of Educational Research.* (3rd ed.). London: Bloomsbury.

Pring, R. (2016). In defence of pragmatism. In P. Cunningham & R. Heibronn (Eds.). *Dewey in Our Time.* (pp. 144–57). London: IOE Press.

Rutter, M., Maughan, B., Mortimore, P. & Ouston, J. (1979). *Fifteen Thousand Hours: Secondary Schools and Their Effects on Children.* London: Open Books.

Smeyers, P. and Smith, R. (2014). *Understanding Education and Educational Research.* Cambridge, UK: Cambridge University Press.

Stenhouse, L. (1975). *An Introduction to Curriculum Research and Development.* London: Heinemann Educational Publishers.

Stenhouse, L. (1985). *Research as a Basis for Teaching.* London: Heinemann Educational Publishers.

# 10

## PAUL SMEYERS AND A PERSPECTIVE ON EDUCATIONAL RESEARCH

In dialogue with Maurizio Toscano

*Maurizio Toscano and Paul Smeyers*

### Introduction

In academic circles, the word *perspective* is often used to capture the sense of holding, applying or offering a particular world-view. Furthermore, the etymology of the word – with its connotations of looking clearly through something – remains alive and well in the rather clichéd use of the word *lens* to describe a theoretical or methodological research instrument through which one encounters the world. Thus, almost by stealth the word *perspective* seems to have also taken up the burden of scientific instrumentalism. Nothing new is being claimed here. Heidegger, in his essay *The Age of the World Picture* (1977), already famously examined not only what we might mean by concepts like world-view or perspective in the context suggested here, but also how the very possibility of having such a resolute, collective perspective has emerged hand-in-hand with the metaphysics of modernity, resulting in a kind of narrowing of the mind. It is fitting then, that we reflect upon the distinguishing features of scientific and social scientific research in this chapter.

One could argue that the following dialogue with Professor Paul Smeyers deals precisely with those issues in educational research that appear to arise from cultural biases (implicit or explicit) towards the values, methods and approaches of the sciences in ways that simultaneously reinforce the sanctity of a modern, technological view on the world. Indeed, it could be argued that educational research provides insufficient regard for what distinguishes educational research from other modes of inquiry. Smeyers is very keen to caution us against any false hope that the phenomena and problems that are of interest to educational researchers might easily yield to such causal relations as are captured in laws of nature, expressed in terms of independent and dependent variables. Educational research is distinctive, Smeyers claims, because its engagement with its subject matter is more than merely of theoretical interest. Educational research concerns itself with a call to respond practically to an issue or problem that emerges from a particular educational context (schooling, parent–child relations and so on), and especially when such calls appear otherwise neglected or overlooked. This, of course, is not to deny the possibility of scientific methods being used in the service of educational research; rather, it is to suggest that many different approaches may be applied to educational problems and therefore we ought to be discerning when matching these methods to what is called for by the problems and issues at hand.

There is another aspect that Smeyers provides us with in the following dialogue that shifts our attention to a different dimension of educational research that goes beyond the familiar debate about the status and role of science in social scientific research. I think it can be summarised as the following paradox: the nearer you get to something, the more remote it becomes. This paradox captures, as it were, a failure, or perhaps a feature, of *perspective* in the alternative sense in which the word is often used: the masterly use of geometric techniques by artists to realistically depict a three-dimensional spatial world in two-dimensional form. Certainly the great artists of the Renaissance recognised that one could transform a figure in the picture plane to affect our perception of its proper location in the virtual space opened up by the painting. Yet, they were also well aware that an object could be made to vanish, not only by placing it virtually an infinite distance away, but also by bringing it so close to the viewer that all its identifying features are blown apart. Only when the viewer and/or artist adjusts his/her position to properly meet the context of the scene of interest does the kind of space that holds both the proximal and the remote actors and objects within it achieve a balanced unity amongst its parts. Context here is not some abstraction but the richness of what *can, may* and *is* taking place in the world between people and things. Something akin to this kind of perspectival equilibrium is what Smeyers takes as an essential orientation towards the practice of research. That is, doing research that attends sensitively and practically to both the particular and the general dimensions of that which one is examining.

Perhaps the best exemplar of this perspective making – and a visual prelude to the conversation below – is Raphael's *The School of Athens* (1511). The radial geometry of the painting's perspective, its grand architectural features and its bright pallet force our gaze to jump from the countenance of one depicted philosopher to the next in a kind of roll call of the great figures of classical thought. The scene has the atmosphere of a busy market place to someone uninitiated to its back-story. There is a mixture of people attending to their own affairs, many more engaged in personal and intense exchanges with others and still others merely taking in the life and activity filling the space. The genius of the work is that it gives the impression of taking in simultaneously the whole activity-space as well as the individual figures and episodes within it. For Smeyers, educational research must likewise achieve such a balance between the specificity of the problem one is dealing with and the broader landscape that makes it meaningful.

Sadly, Smeyers sees the climate of contemporary research and its dominant modes of scholarship as making such a perspectival balance increasingly intractable. He cites the dominant culture of performativity in which metrics have irrevocably transformed what counts as academic success, the fast-paced channels of communication, the drive for novelty and the increased degree of specialisation amongst academics as especially antithetical to research of this balanced kind. When allied to this is the market preference for research that has international impact, but little to say for local concerns, over research that addresses local issues but lacks global reach. Smeyers sees educational research becoming increasingly the domain of specialists with ever-narrowing fields of expertise. Exacerbating these neo-liberal trends is the decade-long disappearance of theoretical and philosophical subject matter in graduate and undergraduate courses, as they make room for subjects with a greater focus on professional skills. Moreover, the disappearance of these subjects takes with them a deep understanding of, and appreciation for, the application of philosophy and theory in the practical service of educational activity and research.

In spite of Smeyers' occasional tone of doom-and-gloom, his insights reveal two important ingredients for an antidote to the myopia of our times. First, like Raphael, Smeyers offers Aristotle a central position in the Academy. For what Aristotle invites us to do is orient ourselves towards research that is at once the enactment and the pursuit of wisdom. Smeyers notes many times in the following conversation that research in education cannot rely on strictly scientific modes of inquiry, because the kinds of problems education is concerned with require theoretical, ethical and practical forms of wisdom: precisely the kinds of wisdom so powerfully articulated in Aristotle's *Nicomachean Ethics* (1954). Second, there is a point where the mindless application of research techniques and methods is insufficient to draw out what is meaningful in the subject matter of the research. At this point the longer you stare into the abyss of data, the more it stares back at you. For Smeyers this becomes no less than a call to take up personal ownership of one's own ethical and practical stance towards the people, things and phenomena one is researching. This too finds artistic expression in the painting of the Academy in which, almost hidden amongst the greats, is the humble portrait of the artist meeting our gaze and inviting us to find our own place within the world.

## The dialogue

**Maurizio Toscano (MT):**   Let me begin by asking what you see as the object of educational research? Scientific research is directed at nature, its phenomena and its hidden mechanisms. Is there something peculiar about educational research and what it's directed at?

**Paul Smeyers (PS):**   I think most educational research starts from a particular problem that educational practitioners experience, either in classrooms or educational settings, or as a parent or social worker. It's different from, say, archaeology, where you study something just to understand it, but are unable to do something with these results in a straightforward sense. It may be very interesting to know the cause of death in the case of Tutankhamun but there's nothing that follows from this except what is of interest to historians wanting to understand our civilisation.

Paul Smeyers on educational research **147**

There are some issues in educational research that are like that; pursued for a theoretical interest and only for that theoretical interest. Most educational issues, though, start from problems that you are presented with in educational settings. So you look for solutions, or you make some comments or you direct people to issues that you observed but have not been dealt with and that are important and forgotten. It's not a straightforward means and reasoning that I'm proposing, of course. There are all kinds of issues that come up.

The starting point I think is usually a particular kind of problem you want to deal with, or you want to anticipate how these problems can be avoided, or understand new societal conditions. Facebook or technical devices create all kinds of new issues in the context of bullying for instance, and things of this kind. I think you're interested in seeing the various aspects of those problems as a starting point to possibly dealing with them.

**MT:** Do you think that educational researchers can approach a particular educational problem in many different ways? So they could approach a topic scientifically, or psychologically or treat it as an issue of behaviour. Do you think that's an advantage or a disadvantage to educational research?

**PS:** It certainly makes things very confusing. Educational research is very broad in scope. It concerns dealings between parents and children, teachers and pupils. It also concerns educational policy. It concerns how to build a school, what kind of infrastructure you want these days. In that sense, it's quite difficult for two reasons. First, you need to observe a kind of balance, and not focus on just one aspect and forget all the other aspects. You constantly need to see what the particular thing you are trying to understand brings to the whole picture. The second element is that given this wide variety of interests, you can pursue all kinds of methods in the context of educational research. It's in this broad sense that people bring in all kinds of methods used in other disciplines. So I would say that makes it a very confusing situation if you want to observe the balance that I spoke of earlier.

**MT:** Does that make educational research very post-modern in the sense that it has multiplicity and plurality built into it, that you can't reduce it or unify it in any particular way? I know you've worked on issues of post-modernity in education, so I'm wondering whether educational research is actually a good example of post-modern research?

**PS:** Well, yes, of course it's post-modern in terms of plurality of issues, plurality of content and so on. The concept post-modern is itself quite a problematic concept with which to cover different things.

Perhaps it's also interesting to point to something else: that educational research and educational theory are different from physics or chemistry – even from experimental psychology – in the sense that there you look for an answer to a specific problem in terms of the independent variable that you can manipulate in order to have a particular result in terms of your dependent variables. I don't think that particular idea of a theory is the kind of theory that educational research should embrace. Educational research is more like deepening understanding about particular issues. So there's nothing that can be established once and for all. There's nothing like gravity, or things you find in physics or chemistry. It's got to do with a particular situation we live in, the historical context, the variety of things people find important in that particular context and so on. You reflect on those issues.

This is more a sort of Aristotelian wisdom than it is a definite answer to a particular problem in terms of what can we do to solve it or avoid it, which suggests a different concept of a theory altogether. It's more reflection and wisdom in terms of practitioners. Theoreticians are not different in this sense. There is a problem, you reflect upon it, you identify all kinds of issues that are related to that problem and this will help you. It will give you a kind of mirror. It will make you more aware of all the issues that are involved. From there, a lot of things follow for practice, but they don't follow in the sense that you can anticipate all minuscule kinds of things in order to have a certain outcome.

That's not how education works, and so therefore we need a different kind of theory. Some would say there is no theory in the traditional sense of the word because there is no hypothesis that can really be tested. So you bring ethical considerations, you bring ideas about what the human being is, about how society should be and so on; all these kinds of things come together. They do not fall under the traditional notion of the umbrella concept of a theory that can be tested as such.

That makes it confusing. And the result is not a very particular kind of advice. I know, of course, that when I deal with my children or grandchildren or when I teach, I have to make a number of decisions. There are all kinds of things involved in those decisions. However, the position of a researcher, an educational researcher, is a little bit different. The educational researcher does not have to fill in all these kind of elements. He or she has the freedom to stand back, to reflect and to identify what the presuppositions of a particular action are, what the pros and cons of that action are, what the other presuppositions for other actions are and so on. It's all these things that come together.

So yes, there is plurality and in that sense it is post-modern. But I'm not saying that you can't say anything as a theoretician. There is a difference between theory as we traditionally conceive it – in areas such as psychology generally, and experimental psychology in particular, following the model of physics and science of the seventeenth or eighteenth centuries – and what counts as theory in education. In educational research it's very much more thinking about practices in the sense that Aristotle, MacIntyre, Taylor and many others have argued for. You can reflect on those practices – the result of which will help the practitioner to make up his or her mind – but it's not the same kind of problem as determining how to build a bridge in order to avoid it falling apart when there is a 40-tonne lorry driving over it every day.

Education doesn't work like that. It can't be manipulated in that particular sense. After all it's your child, or your pupil or your student who is learning;

you can do all kinds of things to explain your position, give your reasons, but in the end the person is himself or herself. And so that's not something you can manipulate in terms of having dependent variables.

**MT:** Do you think educational researchers perhaps don't appreciate that aspect of their research? That they may think of their research as being scientific in terms of means and ends and finding an answer to a problem; a definitive answer? Will they go looking for a theory and be satisfied with any sort of theory that works for them? I'm thinking of research where one might say, "Well this is the problem I'm trying to solve, here's the research question I'm trying to answer, I just need a theory to justify it so that I can get on with finding the answer." Do you think that's a temptation for the educational researcher?

**PS:** Yes, certainly. It's got to do with tendencies in society to focus on output in order to look for short-term results instead of having a general vision of where exactly we want to go, and all the things that this implies. It's also got to do with the way that research has been done in the last two, three, four decades compared with the past before we were mimicking psychological research: looking for variables that can be manipulated without taking into account aims and the discussion about aims in general, the broader picture in which other kinds of considerations come in. I guess that's a bit cryptic so let me expound a bit more on that.

Research – and philosophy of education is no exception – has become much more specialised. That's got to do with a change of communication channels. It took 35 years before Heidegger's *Sein und Zeit* (*Being and Time*) was translated into English. The book was first published in 1927 – the first translation in English was published in 1962. Of course, some people in England and the United States could read German but most of them could not. So the communication between scholars was a slow process. It appeared in journals for some readers and then people reacted to it.

All of this now goes on with an enormous speed. That means that to be a good researcher, to have good publications, you have to know to publish in certain journals, or to publish books with certain publishers and so on. These are reviewed by experts, so in the end we are at the point where, let's say, 10 of our colleagues over the road read our publications, but we've lost all the other potential readers because they're not at this top level of specialisation in one's area of work.

So everything has become a bit more specialised, and specialising means that you refer to certain things, to a very particular debate, or one sentence or a famous philosopher, and deal with that in about six to nine thousand words in a paper.

Now this process that I've described for philosophy of education is happening in all disciplines and sub-disciplines. The desire to write something new – well some people would argue there's nothing new in philosophy since Plato or Aristotle and in a particular sense there are kinds of problems stated 25 centuries ago that reappear – requires one to take a little element of a problem in isolation. Something like that is happening in empirical research as well, even in qualitative research. It becomes more and more specialised. And if you do that you have to limit the problem you're studying to an enormous extent. So you end up with some minuscule element and no room for raising more general considerations.

Let me say this in a very straightforward way. In order to make an impression on your colleagues and therefore to be able to publish in the good publication channels – and you need to do that for your curriculum vitae and in order to attract funding – you have to play this particular kind of game.

Now this particular kind of game is not very good for theory building. It's very good if you look at short-term results where you focus only on this particular element – and maybe this doesn't do a lot of harm in the context of philosophy or philosophy of education research, but if you do this kind of research in the context of a classroom or when you deal with parent-children relationships, you're likely to forget that so many other issues are involved.

It's a bit like politicians who are elected and worry *not* about what's going to happen in the next four years but whether they will win the next election. It's short term and not long term, because in the long term you will come back to those general insights that most of us will share. So the general climate about efficacy, efficiency, output and performativity is certainly not helpful to doing interesting research in the context of educational problems or in the educational field.

Let's say the climate, the general site or conditions are such that people write a lot; indeed, they are required to write in order even to get a PhD, to get tenure, and so on. It's all identified by parameters. Everyone is writing (no one is reading anymore), and everyone is writing on one particular issue that may be important to have a new look at – a specific problem – and forgetting all the rest.

Of course, what I'm presenting is a kind of caricature. I know that a lot of people are trying to go against this stream, but in general I think that it's a very unfavourable climate to become a scholar in an area like educational research or philosophy of education.

**MT:** Do you see philosophy of education or philosophy in general as a kind of antidote?

**PS:** I think philosophy can help, but first of all we're not living in times where a lot of people are interested in theoretical perspectives. Second, we are not living in a time where a lot of people are looking favourably towards philosophy in general. Philosophy is disappearing from all kinds of courses, not just particular disciplines or degrees, and not just in the context of education; it's the same in law degrees, psychology degrees, etc.

So yes, philosophy could be an antidote, but it is disappearing from the curricula of educational sciences worldwide. I see this happening in Belgium and in the Netherlands. To give you an example: there were 10 places in the Netherlands where philosophy of education was studied 10 or

15 years ago, where you could do a PhD in philosophy of education, and now there are only two places left.

When people are not acquainted with philosophy in general and philosophy of education in particular, when they're studying educational sciences, it's much harder for them to appreciate the possible interesting outlook this could give to educational research.

A lot of people do quantitative or qualitative empirical research in the educational field without having had an introductory course in philosophy. So, if you try to convince these people to consider all kinds of ethical considerations or philosophical considerations that are important to addressing particular problems, they just won't understand you.

Yes, philosophy and philosophy of education are antidotes, but I don't know how to change the current climate. I'm not saying this because these particular considerations will disappear within the societal debate or that they will ever disappear when you think about educational relationships. Rather, I'm saying this because of the way that educational studies are done these days, which is completely different from 30 or 40 years ago when I studied educational sciences first, before I studied philosophy. In the first two years we had five pure philosophy courses out of our 26 subjects. Now students in my own university will still have some philosophy education, but will not have any general philosophy courses.

It's like what might happen to educational research if you took out initial statistics courses: after 10 or 20 years it would look completely different. So, for whatever reason, philosophy has become unpopular. People don't like philosophical considerations; they think it is too theoretical: "What can you do with it? Does it help you?" No, it doesn't help you, it throws you back on your own resources to think about what is involved. Or as Nietzsche claimed, philosophy is a kind of work on the self (Nietzsche, 1974). Education is moving too quickly and for that reason people don't want to engage in the slower pace required by philosophy anymore.

So it is an antidote, but it is a very complicated antidote. As I said, it's got to do with financing universities, with how important research is, how you define what research is and research output. In my university, that's defined in the number of PhD's that are successfully defended and the number of journal articles published, which are far more important than books or chapters in books. The kind of metrics around publication that give them a certain value are the kinds of things that are important to get tenure or to get your PhD or to get funding. Of course, researchers have to play that game whether they like it or not.

To give you an interesting example: my native language is Dutch, not English. But if I publish in Dutch that doesn't count for anything on my curriculum vitae – which is a little bit ridiculous because it is the Flemish community that actually pays my salary and it pays for all the costs of the university. If I do publish something in Dutch – let's say for teacher training,

# 152 Maurizio Toscano and Paul Smeyers

or colleges outside of the university or for teachers – I can do it in university time, but it won't help me to get anything from the university.

Maybe that particular format works for physics or for medicine, but it is very doubtful that it supports development of the best and most interesting research for educational problems. If I write, if I do research, if I think of an issue that is an important issue in the debate now in Belgium, especially in the Flemish speaking community of Belgium, it's very difficult for me to get that particular research published in an international journal because it deals with all kinds of local problems. As a philosopher of education, maybe I'm in a better position than quantitative or qualitative empirical researchers because philosophical problems are, of course, problems experienced worldwide. So it's a bit like theoretical physics, mathematics or such.

There is something very strange with a funding format that's used to subsidise research which is directed at particular kinds of publications that are not local and do not deal with those issues that particular communities are occupied with. They'll subsidise something that has a worldwide impact, but education is different everywhere in the world. Every state has a different educational system and therefore it's confronted with different problems. However, these may not attract the attention of international journals necessarily.

I'm not saying there are no exceptions; there are case studies, etc. I know all about that, but this funding format is now determining the scope of the research we'll engage in. I'm sure there are junior researchers and PhD researchers who will be advised by their supervisors to look for an issue that is heavily debated now, because you have to look for an area that will give you the opportunity to publish your results in a particular kind of journal. That is turning things upside down. You should start with a relevant problem, not necessarily a problem that is particularly publishable in these kinds of outlets.

This may sound like as a Marxist interpretation of what's happening and I'm not ashamed to say that the conditions in which we have to work determine to a much greater extent what we do now than 50 or 100 years ago where there was a kind of freedom to engage in all kinds of problems. We don't have that freedom. You can still work that way if you want to, but you won't have a brilliant university career if you do that. You won't be able to attract a lot of funding. It may get really difficult for you to achieve tenure if you don't worry about these kinds of problems. Of course, all young people will worry about these problems as they will want jobs or to keep a job.

**MT:** Do you see that this obsession with metrics, with quantifying research, is affecting the teaching of research and therefore what we see as valuable in research?

**PS:** We used to have a French model for the university degree, which started with two candidate years followed by two licensee years. That was the standard degree before Bologna[1] in the early 1990s in the European context. We've now got the Anglo-Saxon model: Bachelor and Masters but across a five-year degree. So in Belgium, in the Netherlands and in Germany (as different from the Anglo-Saxon world) you have a Bachelor degree in educational sciences at the university, not directed towards teacher training but as a general degree; much as you have a Bachelor in Mathematics, Psychology or Philosophy, then a two-year Master's degree.

The traditional split of themes in the three candidate years of your course – now called the Bachelor years – will give you an introduction to a number of areas. I'm teaching a course at Ghent University for first-year students, which is philosophy of science and an introduction in philosophy of education. I deal with all kinds of theoretical positions, first of all in science. To give some examples, I deal with critical theory, with phenomenology, with conceptual analysis, with post-modernism and so on.

For these Bachelor years, the candidate years, lecturers were expected to give a kind of introduction that was not necessarily based on their own research. Many people could give that kind of introduction in an area if they were, for instance, in philosophy of education. In the licensee years, the Masters years, lecturers were usually free to determine the content of their course according to the particular research interests they pursued: this person could speak about area A, another person could speak about area B.

That is still the case, but there's much more pressure now than 20 or 30 years ago as groups of scholars – that is, at the faculty level – to intervene in the content taught in the Masters years. So we start from a general Bachelor in educational sciences and then it will split in three directions: teacher training, special education and social pedagogy. There is no Master in Philosophy of Education or History of Education; these don't exist either in Belgium or the Netherlands anymore. So there are these three directions and, again like the Anglo-Saxon context, special education is much more linked to psychology than it is to educational sciences. That's got to do with our continental past and the legacy of Kant and Herbart and so on.

Given how we prepare these students – the current rhetoric is that our students are clients – they have to be prepared for certain jobs in society. They will work in teacher training colleges or in educational institutions, dealing with special education, or in community work, social pedagogy and so on. These particular professions require that our students be prepared for problems that arise in those particular areas. What I'm trying to convey is that the pressure from these applied fields is much more intense now than it was 20 or 30 years ago, and for that reason most theoretical courses have disappeared from the Masters level. You will still find some of them at the Bachelor level, but almost all of them have disappeared from the Masters level because they want to make room/space/time for those courses that prepare you directly for certain jobs later on.

As a result, the space to talk about your own research has been limited; the opportunities to share your work have been reduced to seminars and conferences. To initiate practitioners in your own research area is not impossible, but it's much more constrained now because there are all kinds of things that you have to deal with. When I started my career, basically the professor determined content, the way things were examined, everything. And of course, here and there, there were some problems with that kind of academic freedom. Yet in general it worked fine, and at least the students got initiated in terms of those things that professors or lecturers were passionate about and thought were extremely important. Now, because of all these other demands, there's less room for most theoretical courses and that is not very helpful for research. It's not very good for the scholars. It's only at the international conferences or in seminars that this philosophical and theoretical content can be dealt with.

**MT:** If that kind of education is missing from pathways through university that lead into research, it suggests that research is being impoverished in some way. It also indicates, perhaps, that those who are not going into research, but nonetheless have to do educational research in the sense of solving the kinds of problems they encounter in their professional lives, are also ill-equipped with the kind of philosophical training that might help them when they encounter such problems.

**PS:** I certainly agree with that. I would distinguish a researcher from a practitioner. I think a practitioner needs educational theory. I think educational researchers also need philosophy of education, in addition to educational theory. I'm not sure that a practitioner needs philosophy of education. In the ideal world, everyone would think about important issues such as those Plato or Socrates discussed. But in a more realistic world, I think practitioners should know something about educational theory. Educational theory should be informed by philosophy of education and philosophy more generally. It's the level of abstraction in philosophy of education that I'm drawing attention to.

It goes wrong when there's too much attention towards quantitative experimental approaches, randomised field trials and these kinds of things. There's still a dominance of the experimental paradigm. Whether they agree with that or not, I think they pay lip service to the idea that they accept our qualitative approaches. Quite a few educational researchers, let's say in educational psychology, do something very similar to what experimental psychologists do, and experimental psychologists do something very similar to what's done in medicine. A good example of this is neuroscience. You see worldwide chairs for neuroscience in neuro-education, and they've got all kinds of other labels. So in the end we'll all end up doing something that's very similar to what people do in the context of medicine. They do it there for very good reasons, but if they start talking neuro-education and the brain and all this kind of nonsense, then of course we'll end up with a very good example of experimental research that has a conceptual confusion lying at the bottom of it. The groundwork needs to be done before you can engage in all these kinds of other things. You can never engage in them while bracketing all the very fundamental considerations of what you think of knowledge, ethics, the good life, etc.

For example, there was a psychiatrist a couple of months ago who said we have to do something about children living in poverty-stricken conditions because it affects the development of their brain. So now a major reason we should pay attention to the living conditions of children is because of the effect on a child's brain? No, we have to deal with poor living conditions whether or not they affect the brain. I'm sure poverty will affect a child's brain. Yet some researchers do this kind of research and forget that they're dealing with dodgy concepts, and all kinds of confusions and conceptual mistakes, etc. People did less of this 30 or 40 years ago when they were at least initiated at a basic level in philosophy of education, and philosophy and its different branches.

It's not that I think that a parent will be a better parent if he has a philosophy degree. No. I think practitioners need some input from educational theory. Unfortunately, educational theories in general are now very much characterised by theories coming from empirical research areas, which deal with some important aspects but seem to forget all the rest. I think there's more need for philosophy of education for researchers than there is for practitioners. Of course, practice develops on its own terms, at which point I would say you don't need a theory for your practice, but that doesn't mean that you're not going to have to reflect on your practice.

Given the particular business that theoreticians or researchers are in, they should be aware of such things as the necessary and sufficient conditions for certain consequences, all the technical things from philosophy people have been thinking about for 25 centuries. They are important when dealing with a theoretical enterprise, and of course educational research is a theoretical enterprise; it should feed on philosophical insights, our philosophy of education insights.

**MT:** Do you have any particular advice you would give those involved in research training for example, whether in formal courses or supervising of research students or even for the graduate students themselves or those who are learning about research? Is there some advice or recommendation you could offer in terms of the role of philosophy and theory?

**PS:** Well, let me say something before I answer that question. There is a kind of fascination with methods these days. People look for a particular method. They're either trained in quantitative or qualitative methods, but I think there are *no* methods in philosophy. There are particular strands of philosophy. When you write a piece on the basis of Heidegger or from a Heideggerian viewpoint, you will do things differently compared with writing from a viewpoint based in Marx or Nietzsche.

This preoccupation with methods is wrong-headed in the confines of educational research. It suggests learning a particular idea of method as an algorithm to be followed in order to go from point A to point B. Now as I said at the beginning, there are all kinds of considerations that come in when you deal with research. So, to bracket everything and to follow only this particular method won't get you where you really want to be. To say this more generally, there are many roads to Rome, but then again, not everyone really wants to get to Rome. This is sometimes denied by those educational researchers who say that there is a specific method one must follow in order to get to a certain goal.

There are many ways to get there. You could conduct a reflection that is inspired by the arts that can make a very valuable point in the context of an analysis of an education situation, and yes, there could be an experiment. It all depends upon what your interest is and what exactly you want to do with it. And then there's the "gold standard", as the Americans call it: the causal or quasi-causal experimental randomised field trials. But, as I said, not everyone wants to get to Rome. Not everyone is interested in the same kind of thing.

My advice? I think Masters, or even graduate, students should reflect on methods from a philosophy of science perspective, or a philosophy of educational research perspective, where they will necessarily bring in the very broad picture and all kinds of considerations that can help weigh up a particular problem. At least at the initial stage of their research, that would be very important I think. However, I'm not saying that will change the general research climate. They will still have to perform according to the standards of the top journals. You can't bracket that. You can't change society like that. Maybe one day it will change again. It will go back to a broad theoretical approach. I hope so, but I can't see it yet.

So, my advice would be: don't lock yourself up in a particular method. Don't only do conceptual analysis or even philosophy of education research. Sure, it's very interesting to do conceptual analysis like Ivan Snook does on the topic of indoctrination, but Michael Peters says marvellous things too, and Scheffler also and so on. You have to be broader. You have to bring in Rancière, Agamben, Foucault as well; not that I'm necessarily in favour of those positions, but you have to bring them in to see the broader picture.

I think it would be beneficial for their research, even if what they will publish is restricted by the funding format. At the same time, I think it's very demanding for junior researchers to do that. They have to do both, in a way. They have to play the game of this particular kind of research – otherwise they won't survive – and at the same time make the space to get acquainted with these broader positions to situate the relevance of what they're doing, without the kind of exaggeration one so often finds at the end of articles where you see stated: "We found one thing and now in the future everything will have to be changed and accommodated to these insights." It hardly works like that; where's the input from the broader picture?

Open it up at the beginning. Don't limit it to methods courses, either quantitative or qualitative or a combination of both. Broaden it, have a look at some good research that has been done in the context of the educational field, and what the considerations were in this research. To give you an example, a number of colleagues and myself have edited quite recently *The International Handbook of Interpretation for Educational Research*, published by Springer (2015). It's a 1,700-page, two-volume work with 69 chapters or so and more than 100 contributors, dealing with many aspects of educational research. What you have is an idea of how interpretation is relevant when you use videos to do research; how interpretation is relevant when you do history of education – that kind of introduction. To know what interpretation means and what the various kinds of interpretation are would indeed be helpful, not just for philosophers of education but also for all educational researchers. It is a doorway that opens to the wide variety of what is happening.

You have to be aware of these many elements when you do research; this will make your claims a bit more modest while also helping to give you a picture that is more true to the nature of the area that you're studying. Along the lines of what I said in the beginning, it is deepening our practical wisdom of the areas that we have under consideration.

## Conclusion

In this dialogue, Professor Smeyers has continuously directed our attention to the unique challenges that educational contexts present researchers. The problems that occupy educational researchers cannot so easily be framed within the narrow confines of a scientific approach, nor any overly prescriptive methodological approach or research tradition. The important issues in education to which researchers apply themselves sit within a complex of overlapping social, economic, political, epistemic, cultural, ethical and other dimensions that make careful articulation of research problems, their aims and contexts a necessary condition for the successful enterprise of research. This certainly does not make research of this kind impossible, but it does demand researchers take into account the broader picture, as well as the fundamental considerations that underpin one's research and its objectives. Achieving this level of insight requires more than knowledge or technical prowess. As Smeyers points out, it requires the development and application of a kind of practical wisdom. That research of this philosophically and theoretically informed kind is more difficult to undertake in the present academic climate that no longer has time for it, should not stop us in our search for what matters in education.

## Note

1 This refers to the Bologna Process for the reform of Higher Education in the European Union: http://ec.europa.eu/education/policy/higher-education/bologna-process_en

## References

Aristotle. (1954). *The Nichomachean Ethics* (D. Ross, Trans.). London: Oxford University Press.
Heidegger, M. (1962). *Being and Time* (J. Macquarie & E. Robinson, Trans.). London: SCM Press.
Heidegger, M. (1977). *The Question Concerning Technology and Other Essays* (W. Lovitt, Trans.). New York: Harper and Row.
Nietzsche,. F. (1974). *The Gay Science* (W. Kauffman, Trans.). New York: Vintage Books.
Smeyers, P., Bridges, D., Burbules, N. & Griffiths, M. (Eds.). (2015). *International Handbook of Interpretation in Educational Research*. Dordrecht, Netherlands: Springer.

# 11

# BECOMING A GOOD EDUCATION RESEARCHER

*Lyn Yates*

## Introduction

This book invites us to think about the value and uses of philosophy and theory in education research, and also to think specifically about education. Through the contributors' stories, the book elicits a further perspective as well: the characteristics of those who have made some mark in education. In the dialogue chapters we hear how each of these prominent educationists have entered into and developed their own thinking about education: what they have studied, who and what they were influenced by, and how they began to develop the various kinds of research and diverse contributions to the education field for which they are now well known. Notwithstanding their differences, they talk about the value of theory, philosophy and research with some significant commonalities; their biographies, too, suggest some common characteristics that also speak to the focus of this book. In this final chapter I want to reflect on four themes I see as inherent in these earlier chapters, with a particular focus on implications for graduate students embarking on their own entry into research in education.

## "Theoretical" versus "empirical" as a false binary

Some years ago the question I took up for my own PhD was this:

> What is good educational practice having regard to the characteristics, existing social arrangements and future possibilities of girls and boys?
>
> *(Yates, 1987, p. 2)*

In many ways this is a variant of a central agenda of the field we work in: "what is good education?" But, as a doctoral student, it is necessary to decide what

Becoming a good education researcher **159**

kind of question this is and to develop an appropriate (systematic and defensible) methodology for addressing it (Yates, 2004). So is that a philosophical question? Clearly many philosophers have taken up this question, and in some quite different ways. John Dewey, for instance, has been hugely influential, but he is an example of a philosopher who also engaged in what we might call action research and actually set up a school. Many men (and I say that advisedly) over the years have written about the characteristics of the educated person. In the decade preceding my own study, the analytic philosophy of R. S. Peters and Paul Hirst was popular; they wrote about things like developing discernment, the ability to give reasons rather than be driven by sentiment, and the opportunity to access important realms of human achievement. Later those conceptions were attacked from various perspectives, including by a number of contributors to this volume. More recently again, variants of the theories and arguments (though with significant differences) have resurfaced in the work of the philosopher Gert Biesta (2015) and the sociologist Michael Young (2008). Elsewhere, work on "capabilities" by Armartya Sen (2005) and Martha Nussbaum (2003) began to approach the question of the purpose of education in a different way – in terms of skills, competencies or capabilities necessary for human existence in the twenty-first century – by taking up philosophical questions but also drawing on Sen's work as an economist and Nussbaum's as a humanities scholar of literature, and giving attention not just to wealthy western countries but to all people throughout the world.

Meanwhile a stream of research and theory has interpreted these kinds of questions in quite a different way. Sociologists like Bourdieu (1996) or Foucault (1979) have addressed the question about education purposes, or "good" education, by taking it as an empirical and critical question about what education actually does. For example, Bourdieu's analyses of "distinction", "cultural capital", and "judgement" are intended to show that what is taken as good education contributes to the reproduction of inequalities. Or consider another approach to addressing the question of "what is good education?" that is extremely popular with schools around the world: John Hattie's *Visible Learning* (2008, 2013). These books are not presented as philosophical answers but as evidence-based answers that derive from what has been reliably and empirically established about effective teaching and learning practices. In similar fashion, many people (especially politicians) take the PISA tables and the OECD *Education at a Glance* reports as a definitive manual to where good education is happening.

The question I started with earlier, that asked about "boys and girls" and "existing social arrangements and future possibilities" was located at a time when new ideas, social movements and practices related to gender were beginning to arise. Both that context and the extended form of the question possibly makes clearer the extent to which empirical and non-empirical matters are tied together in thinking about education. New conceptions of inequality and otherness came into being as social movements and changes, and the theories and agendas for education moved from focusing on class to gender to race, colonialism, disability, and poverty. These are about conceptual framings or "theories", not just about "data." And this is not

**160** Lyn Yates

just characteristic of specifically sociological or political concepts such as inequality, or overtly normative and philosophical questions such as "what is good education?" As the current debates about learning and twenty-first-century skills and capabilities makes clear, even a supposedly concrete or empirical concern with "effective learning" is not just an empirical or "evidence-based" question. Rather, the criteria or concepts within which empirical or evidence-based answers are accepted or challenged are connected to views of education purposes and human and social possibilities – and these have changed over time. Even the dictionary definitions of learning have begun to interpret the conception of education and learning in terms of students' future capacities to go on learning and changing in the twenty-first century, alongside, or as replacement of, the old idea of learning that is valued from the past (Yates, 2012).

In one sense, all of the questions we investigate as education researchers are normative (and political), at least in terms of their implied significance and the contexts in which they will be taken up (Yates, 2004), although it is especially evident for my own field of curriculum studies. My thesis question made the dual agendas for *both* conceptual and empirical inquiry more evident than many because it came in the wake of social changes that challenged some taken-for-granted purposes, practices, and outcomes of schooling (in terms of what they did and achieved for girls and women). But *any* questions that education researchers take up presume a stance on what matters, as well as a conceptual stance on what the methodology and empirical data will "prove" or "show."

This awareness of the connection of empirical claims to conceptual and theoretical thinking threads through the chapters in this book. Peter Roberts in his opening chapter (see Chapter 2) refers to this in terms of "slowing down", of the need to pause and consider the ramifications of starting points for research projects and not jump prematurely into methods. John Hattie, best known in education not as a philosopher but for his empirical contributions and meta-studies of empirical research, repeatedly flags the connection of the empirical to these conceptual and normative questions about "what matters." He is critical of psychometricians who become obsessed with tools at the expense of questions that matter to education (see Chapter 6). Paul Smeyers makes a similar critique: without consideration of education purposes, chairs of neuroscience end up doing something similar to that which people do in medicine instead of pursuing educational ends (see Chapter 10). Richard Pring, asked to chair a major government review on education and training for the 14–17-year-olds, is clear that perspectives on personhood necessarily come into this question, and that what counts as a "skill" has altered historically and needs its own conceptual attention. He is quite explicit that "no significant research is straight-forwardly empirical" (Chapter 9).

At the same time, many chapters within this book suggest that even where the writers are themselves engaged in work that might be seen as non-empirical or "philosophical", addressing normative and conceptual questions depends on (or assumes, relates to or can be challenged by) some empirical knowledge. Penny Enslin talks of how her theoretical frameworks changed as she moved from South Africa

Becoming a good education researcher **161**

to the UK; her empirical experiences drove which theory and bodies of theory seemed relevant (see Chapter 5). Michael Apple mourns what he sees as a loss of technical statistical skills among progressive students, because it handicaps their ability to accurately portray empirical realities and to challenge the picture being given by official authorities (see Chapter 3). Michael Peters is critical of other philosophers who pursue analytical philosophy as if nothing has happened since 1972 (see Chapter 8), and Nel Noddings learns from people struggling with empirical research (see Chapter 7). Thinking about directions for education or for schooling presumes some empirical assumptions about the realities of how the world works (about people, learning, schools, teaching, and scholarly and social relationships), and the contributors to this book show respect for good empirical research that tries to build more accurate or effective understandings of these matters.

One background aspect of my own doctoral study, as I noted earlier, was the rise of the women's movement in the 1970s and the development of new books, theories and politics related to feminist thinking. These had implications and challenges for education processes and purposes. However, as someone coming to these questions from several years of graduate studies in education, I was conscious of the naivety of some of the big-name feminist theorists trained in fields other than education when it came to what they said about the possibilities of schooling. Sometimes it seemed that all you needed to do was to decree a new set of messages for curriculum and then students would transform their ambitions as if no other social influences were in play, and as if schools had no role other than to transmit messages about what students should think. A wide array of empirical research has shown that the relationship between what schools set out to teach and what students take from that teaching is, to say the least, more complicated (Yates, 1985, 2013; Kenway *et al.*, 1998).

That is also why it is misleading to think of education research only in terms of one-off studies. Research projects are normally located in programs of research that extend over time, attending at times to more empirical questions and at other times to refining conceptual or theoretical questions. With gender reforms over time, certain patterns of what schools (or curriculum) produced for girls and for boys did change, but not in a simple way. Rather the new purposes generated a lot of new empirical research (and actions), and these in turn spawned yet more new theories and research questions.

## Education research as situated activity

In science and in medical research, knowledge builds over time and in complex ways – theories evolve and change in dialogue with empirical investigation. In the sophisticated technical environment of the twenty-first century, conceptual work and collaborations involved in building methodologies and drawing conclusions from data in such fields is extensive (Knorr-Cetina, 1999; Yates *et al.*, 2017). But education has additional challenges. It is situated temporally and spatially against world (and local) settings that change, it is about purposes not just processes, and

**162** Lyn Yates

it works directly and indirectly by actions of others (namely teachers and policy makers).

When I read the earlier chapters in this book the thing that most struck me was the sense of dynamism and breadth in how these educationists have themselves developed their research careers. Many of the contributors started out with studies in fields they no longer actively pursue (for example physics in the case of Biesta, mathematics for Noddings, and analytic philosophy was a common starting point for many who would no longer see that as their preoccupation). Beyond that, chapter after chapter mentions the writer actively studying or reading in a range of different theories as their sense of the education problems they want to grapple with continues to evolve. They make clear that they think some of this breadth is similarly important for students. They show, through their own practices, an ongoing awareness that their initial knowledge and problematizing of a research project may be limited. They seek out other ways of thinking and other kinds of research that may also be relevant and may give new insights. And they show an orientation to thinking about education as a field of practice, and an alertness to how people will use their research.

Another way of putting this is that there is a problem in what research methodology textbooks recommend, and students rightly find this difficult to grapple with when designing their research projects. Education research (especially at the doctoral level) involves delimiting a problem: designing a researchable question or focus and drawing out some defensible boundaries and methods of working on that question. But there is always the niggling problem of how to see and take account of that which lies outside that frame but may still be pertinent, both in the world and in the other bodies of research and thinking. Most methodology textbooks are clear about the need to build on previous work, and to be able to see how the conceptual as well as empirical framing of the problem has evolved. But the researchers in this volume, I think, show an active awareness that goes well beyond that injunction to "build on the literature." Over time they have continued to actively seek out and explore different theoretical traditions and forms that might give different perspectives on the education matters with which they want to grapple. It is clear that they see research as more than a technical exercise, as more than mastering a particular methodology.

The chapters also show an awareness of education as a field of practice and action by others. Michael Apple laments the ease with which perspectives of those on the Right speak to "common sense" compared with current critical perspectives (see Chapter 3). John Hattie talks of the way his projects are designed with teachers in mind and how he continues to ask his students "what is the story?" (see Chapter 6). This thinking shows attention to the specificities of *education* as a field of research. The theorists here do not come to identical substantive conclusions about practice. They differ in their political stances and in the projects for education with which they are most concerned. But there is a dynamism and continual rethinking that threads through the stories. They show a recognition of the importance of ongoing conceptual thinking about their research and its relationship to education, of standing outside the work to try to think about "where next?" and "what else?"

## "Philosophy" compared with "theory" compared with "concepts": disciplinarity, identity, and policing practices

A number of the chapters in this book speak of the paring down of education foundation studies in graduate programs, lamenting the absence of mandated courses in philosophy in favour of an over-emphasis on "methods" and instrumental purposes. All of the contributors have themselves taken some courses in philosophy, and found it of value even if they later discarded the particular paradigms with which they began. Some talk of the value of philosophy in terms of its specific attention to the big questions about personhood, ethics and the like, that also enter strongly into education. Others value philosophy's interest in argument and logic. But many of the contributors also comment that they prefer to speak of "theory" rather than "philosophy", because they think many students are put off by talk of philosophy, because they do not see themselves as doing formal philosophical work, or because they explicitly reject some of the work associated with "philosophy of education."

In my recent projects I have been interested in disciplines and disciplinarity in the context of school and university practices that now seem to be moving away from using these as the central organizing entities (Yates *et al.*, 2017). As intellectual fields, disciplines are social constructions with historically established foci, boundaries, and traditions carried through professional associations, journals, conferences, and university departments. Disciplines have been important in developing refined ("disciplined") ways of studying things, and have been a source of new insights and theories. But as socially organized forms they are also sources of conservatism. They both effect and constrain understanding of phenomena such as education.

Disciplinary questions, boundaries, and methods change as a result of developments internal to their focus and also through exogenous forces. What it means to be doing philosophy in education evolves and changes over time and place. This is seen in the earlier chapters, as the accounts talk about "analytic" compared with "continental" philosophy, or about "Marxist" compared with "post-structural" approaches. Change has also taken place as boundaries between sociology and philosophy become blurred as they take up similar questions (for example, about curriculum), draw on the same theorists, and work collaboratively, or as those trained as philosophers work on projects with empirical dimensions, and begin to be seen not as "philosophers" but perhaps as "policy theorists" or "curriculum theorists" and the like.

Nevertheless, although disciplines are not static, it is useful to consider what disciplines do. Disciplines sensitize you to certain kinds of questions and methodologies, and to taking up questions in particular ways. They create identities that you take into your further work. In my own case, for example, I see myself as someone who works with philosophical theories but not primarily as a philosopher. My own initial training was in history, and I have taken on some of the discursive and

**164** Lyn Yates

grounded modes of that field of study. So my own interest in theories (for example, curriculum theories of different kinds) is not just in whether they are logical, rational, or have good questions, but with why, historically and contextually, those ideas make sense or were meaningful. Similarly, I get impatient with theories that stay too long in the realm of abstraction and do not use enough empirical reference points or use only over-simple, empirical "straw man" examples rather than paying enough attention to difference and specificity.

In terms of foundations and underpinnings, what is potentially lost when "philosophy" disappears and courses become problem-centred, or approached through other lenses, is that some sensibilities or sensitivities (to specifically philosophical kinds of questions, methods or purposes) are replaced with others. Sometimes this may be an appropriate response to a new conception of problems and modes of thinking about them, for example as inter-disciplinary work spawns its own new approaches. However, the losses from losing disciplinary training and affiliation, such as foundation courses in philosophy, can also produce more superficial approaches, less diversity of approach, and a reduction in the tools we have available with which to approach education problems (Yates *et al.*, 2017). I am aware when working alongside colleagues whose background is philosophy rather than history that we do bring some different orientations to our joint work and graduate supervision that can be very useful – a point that is often made in the literature on interdisciplinarity, but seems to be more recognized currently in the sciences than in the humanities.

## Practical matters: using theory in education research

The contributions in this book are helpful in making a case for *why* researchers need to work with theory and they are also useful in setting up some sense of *how* to work with theory – showing what it means to work effectively and ineffectively with theory. From teaching doctoral seminars over a long period of time, I think many students in education begin with the wrong idea about what it means to work with theory or philosophy. Some consider theory as not relevant to their own quest. They say they are setting out to do a qualitative inquiry, for example, to provide rich descriptions of a classroom, or they are aiming to test the effect of a particular innovation. The problem here is that without critical attention to some fairly philosophical issues, such work may end up hopelessly arbitrary or banal (not showing anything that a casual observer would not also say). It is important to be aware of embedded theoretical issues, whatever the research focus. What is involved in making an inductive claim from your observations? Are the assumptions you bring to your conclusions actually tested in the thesis or coming from a different source?

This is the point that contributors to this volume make very strongly, and that I discussed earlier in relation to the necessary dialogue between empirical and non-empirical questions. It is a particular issue in the field I work in: curriculum research. Critical sociological theories, for example, often take the form of concluding that having exposed, say, the sexism or racism of curriculum, they have provided the answer as to what curriculum should do. But just understanding what is going wrong only provides part of the answer to what might or should be done.

One point that is repeatedly made by researchers of quite different types in these chapters is the need to "slow down" or stand back and look seriously at the concepts, definitions, and history of development of the problem, and not take at face value the form in which the problem is initially named or understood.

Other students come to doctoral work aware that they need theory of some kind, but do not have a good sense of working with theory. They treat theory in a way that is quite at odds with the breadth, dynamism, and reflectiveness evident in the stories in these chapters. One ineffective way of working with theory is where students name a theory as the framework for the research and then leave it just sitting there with little connection to what they actually do in their investigation. For example, qualitative or post-structural accounts may begin by rehearsing at length the theme that truth is relative, but then go on to treat the object of their inquiry as if the interpretation speaks for itself, and as if the value of doing their particular research project (if everything is relative) needs no further rationale.

At the other pole, but similarly ineffective, some students use theory as a kind of straightjacket or god-like truth that frames all of the research design and analysis of findings and cannot be questioned. In this case, research projects are positioned within the work of a big "Theorist" (think Foucault, Bourdieu, Vygotsky, etc.) and the remainder of the thesis treats that theoretical work as a template or bible that is a given truth to be illustrated, rather than a study where the new research project provides *further insights or new knowledge* on both the empirical findings and the theoretical starting points in the light of each other. A good thesis which works with theory or theories should end up not only using those theories to focus and provide ways of making progress and critical perspective, but also with something to say about those theories (their adequacy, their limitations, and what else might be needed).

A related issue was touched on by some contributors in their criticisms of some of the internal camps, debates, and "policing" within philosophy (which also applies to other social science fields). One of the requirements of setting up a thesis or other type of research program is to identify the program of research (the literature) on which this is grounded and to which it is expected to contribute. But if this is interpreted simply as a "naming which camp I belong to" and not having to further explain and reflect on the assumptions with which you are working, this closes down rather than opens up the research.

Seeking out theoretical differences in how concepts and problems have been understood can, itself, be a very practical strategy for a beginning researcher. For example, to go back to my own (now ancient) doctoral thesis (Yates, 1987), the question with which I began ("What is good educational practice having regard to the characteristics, existing social arrangements and future possibilities of girls and boys?") might seem so broad as to be: (a) not a good "researchable" topic, and (b) hard to set up methodologically (given that one of the requirements of a doctoral thesis is that it proves one has an understanding of what it means to do

**166** Lyn Yates

a systematic piece of research) (Yates, 2004). Potentially my topic "Curriculum theory and non-sexist education" could be addressed as primarily a philosophical inquiry, or as emphasizing sociological questions of particular kinds. But I embarked on it from what was potentially a more manageable starting point: by seeking to understand how different kinds of theories understood curriculum, what kinds of questions they asked about curriculum, and what these ways of seeing might alert us to or blind us from seeing about new questions about gender. I similarly looked at how different kinds of feminist theory understood gender, and what these might alert us to or fail to understand about curriculum and schooling.

Education research brings together different kinds of questions and disciplinary approaches. For some, "theory" (in the sense of abstract models) is the ultimate aim of all research. For others, "evidence" and "proof" is what matters and the fact that what is being tested has some theoretical or conceptual beginnings recedes into the dim background. My own background in history means that while I work with theory in the sense of the first of these senses, my aim is not to create a new theory but rather to discursively take up education issues to show what is happening and discuss the sources, problems, possibilities, and specificities, not to build an abstract model (theory) as the highest end point of research. The differences of purpose in different kinds of research means that the weighting and the form of explicit consideration of theory or philosophical questions will vary. But all good research in education will need some attention to philosophical, theoretical and conceptual questions.

## Conclusion

As we have seen throughout this book, "theory" and "philosophy" in education are ambiguous and diverse concepts. They elicited broad reflections in the foregoing chapters about education and its purposes, and other more specific reflections about the processes and practicalities of addressing education problems through empirical and non-empirical research projects. They also elicited reflections on specific strands of educational philosophy and theory, sometimes for their value, other times for criticism of their limitations (often understood retrospectively). But the commonality that flows through the book is, I think, about the importance of thinking about *the questions the research is addressing*. In many different ways, contributors here returned to some similar themes:

- do not take education problems or your starting question at face value;
- do not let research tools dominate the purposes of research in education; and
- be prepared to find ways of standing outside and reflecting on your research, which often involves reading and learning other kinds of theories than the ones you started with.

The answers most of these contributors would give to the question "why study theory and philosophy?" is threefold. First, because the nature of the field we work in requires that kind of thinking. Education (and even schooling to take Biesta's important distinction) is not just about "what is the case?" – aims and purposes, questions about what is valued, and encounters with ethical issues are unavoidable. Research that fails to think about this will be the poorer. Second, theory and philosophy are of practical use in education research, in guiding the researcher to more subtle thinking about a problem and in working against naivety in the treatment of methods, data, and evidence. And third, I would add, because these kinds of questions and thinking, and the interchanges with others across different fields, are exciting, stimulating, important – and part of the necessary conversation that makes up the education research field.

## References

Biesta, G. (2015). What is education for? On good education, teacher judgement, and educational professionalism. *European Journal of Education*, 50(1), 75–87.

Bourdieu, P. (1996). *Distinction: A social critique of the judgement of taste*. London: Routledge.

Foucault, M. (1979). Governmentality. *Ideology and Consciousness*, 6, 5–21.

Hattie, J. (2008). *Visible learning: A synthesis of over 800 meta-analyses relating to achievement*. London: Routledge.

Hattie, J. (2013). *Visible learning for teachers: Maximizing impact on learning*. London: Routledge.

Kenway, J. & Willis, S., with Blackmore, J. & Rennie, L. (1998). *Answering back: Girls, boys and feminism in schools*. Sydney: Allen and Unwin.

Knorr-Cetina, K. (1999). *Epistemic cultures: How the sciences make knowledge*. Cambridge, MA: Harvard University Press.

Nussbaum, M. C. (2003). Capabilities as fundamental entitlements: Sen and social justice. *Feminist Economics,* 9(2–3), 33–59.

Sen, A. (2005). Human rights and capabilities. *Journal of Human Development*, 6(2), 151–166.

Yates, L. (1985). Is girl-friendly schooling really what girls need? In J. Whyte, R. Deem, L. Kant & M. Cruikshank (Eds.). *Girl Friendly Schooling*. London: Methuen.

Yates, L. (1987). *Curriculum theory and non-sexist education: A discussion of curriculum theory, feminist theory, and Victorian education policy and practice 1975–1985*. (Unpublished doctoral dissertation). La Trobe University, Victoria, Australia.

Yates, L. (2004). *What does good educational research look like? Situating a field and its practices*. Maidenhead, UK and New York: Open University Press.

Yates, L. (2012). My school, my university, my country, my world, my google, myself … What is education for now? *Australian Education Researcher*, 39(3), 259–274.

Yates, L. (2013). Revisiting curriculum, the numbers game and the inequality problem, *Journal of Curriculum Studies*, 45(1), 39–51

Yates, L., Woelert, P., Millar, V. & O'Connor, K. (2017). *Knowledge at the crossroads? History and physics in the changing world of schools and universities*. Singapore: Springer.

Young, M. (2008). *Bringing knowledge back in: From social constructivism to social realism in the sociology of education*. London: Collier MacMillan.

# INDEX

abduction 7–15, 21n5, 92–3, 97, 99n8
absolutes 105, 113
abstraction 18, 145, 154, 164
academic status 53, 145–6
accountability 44–5
activism 37, 46–7, 49
activity, situated 161–3
Adorno, T. 36, 40
aesthetic judgment 16–19
affective education 104
Africa 73, 77
*Against Method* (Feyerabend) 118
Agamben, G. 156
*Age of The World Picture, The*
     (Heidegger) 144
aid-tourism 73
*aisthesis* (prejudice) 16
alliances, building 45
alternative theoretical framework 53, 56
Althusser, L. 71, 75
Althusserian Marxism 70
analytical philosophy 39–40, 76, 116–19,
     125, 161
Anglo-American tradition 53, 58
Anglo-Saxon degree model 152–3
anti-foundationalism 115
anti-Semitism 120
anxiety 29–30
apartheid 69, 71, 75–6
Apple, M. 18, 20, 123, 161–2; *Can Education
     Change Society?* 43, 46; *Educating the Right
     Way* 43; *see also* praxis
apprenticeships 134

Arendt, H. 37, 40, 56
Aristotle 37, 137, 148; *Nicomachean
     Ethics* 146
artists and perspective 145
Asia 73
assessment 26, 88–90, 89
assumptions xix, 161, 164–5
attention 29–30, 106–8
Austin, J. L. 39
Australia 26, 42, 46, 74, 77
autonomy 41, 68–9, 71–2, 74

balance in research 147
beautiful, concept of 62–3
*Beautiful Risk of Education, The* (Biesta) 60–4
Beauvoir, S. de 32
behaviour 95–6
behaviourism 110, 132, 134
*Being and Time (Sein und Zeit)*
     (Heidegger) 149
Belgium 149–51, 153
Benjamin, W. 36, 40
Biesta, G. 18, 20, 93, 159; *The Beautiful
     Risk of Education* 60–4; *see also* thinking
     philosophically
black people 46, 138
Black Swan problem 117
Bohr, N. 92
Bologna 152–3, 157n1
Bourdieu, P. 44, 159
brain, the 95–6, 154–5
Brazil 45
Brexit Referendum (2016) 71

**170** Index

Brighouse, H. 47
British Empire 138
Bruner, J. 110
Buber, M. 102, 104–6

Campbell, D. T. 87
*Can Education Change Society?* (Apple)
    43, 46
capital, global 75
care/caring 101–13; background 101–2;
    concepts 107–8; feminism and 106;
    measurement of 102–3; teaching and
    learning 108–13; theories 102–7
*Caring* (Nodding) 105–6, 111
Carr, D. 59
Cartesian dualism xx
case studies 152
catering *see* theory in research
Cavell, S. 17
charity 72–3, 81n5
children 55, 59, 69, 71, 76, 96, 154
China 46, 77–8
Chomsky, N. 93
citizenship/civics 53, 55, 71, 73
clarity 31, 126
class 41, 159
Clive of India 138
cognitive perspective 142
coherence 9, 16, 18–19, 31, 75
cohesion 17, 31
collaborative research 78
Collège de France 121
colonialism 70, 72–3, 79, 159
Columbia University 38, 45
commitment 27–9, 32, 37–9, 49, 64, 69,
    85, 140
communication 3, 5–6, 62, 122–3, 146, 149
community service learning 73
competition 27, 71–2, 109–10
complexities of inquiry 1–3, 16
compromises 45
concepts: analysing 77; of attention 29–30;
    of beautiful 62–3; care/caring 105,
    107–8; communication 107; contested 71;
    genealogical 119; Kant on xix; learning
    129; of omnipotence 65; of praxis 37,
    39, 49; real life 45; of rights 42; standards
    140–1; teaching 48; understanding 135
conceptual analysis 119–20
confession 85–6
confirmation bias 94
*Conjectures and Refutations* (Popper) 116
Connell, R. 46
consolidation 96
consumers of education 132

context 32, 76–7
continental philosophy 40–1, 53–4, 58, 76
controversies 110
conversations 122–3, 133
cosmopolitanism 72–4
Counts, G. 46
criticisms 36–9, 42–3, 49n5
cuisines 16–20
cultural diversity 69
curriculum 37–8, 56, 132, 137, 160–6
curriculum vitae 150–1

data 146; analyses 23–4, 79, 88–93;
    collection 78, 98, 102; Dewey on
    14; evidence 60, 86; interpretation
    of 88–90, 92, 94, 161; Popper on 2;
    Roberts on 19
data-driven teaching 61
death of God 119
decentred unities 45
decolonisation 46, 73
deduction 7–15, 92, 97
degrees, university 151–3, 156
democracy 42–3, 55–6, 71, 73, 124
*Democracy and Education* (Dewey) 7
Descartes, R. xx
Developmental Studies Center 108, 112n4
Dewey, J. 2, 46–7, 123–4, 142; on
    deduction 13–14; as dominant white
    voice 46; educational theories of 39–40,
    104, 129–30, 159; on experience 9;
    on failure 15; on inference 10; on
    reflection 7–8; on trial and error
    method 8–9, 15
Dewey, J.; works of: *Democracy and Education*
    7; *Essays in Experimental Logic* 7; *How We
    Think* 7; *Logic: The Theory of Inquiry* 7;
    *Studies in Logical Theory* 7
diasporic people 46
disability 159
disciplines 53–4, 79–80, 125, 149, 163–4
discourse 17, 28, 41–2, 119–22
discovery 114–15
displacement 106–7
Dostoevsky, F. 32
dualisms xx, 24, 130
Du Bois, W. E. B. 40, 46, 49n4

eclecticism 31, 93
educated persons 139–42
*Educating the Right Way* (Apple) 43
education: conceptions about 18; criteria
    for 141; nature of 130; open 123;
    philosophy of 137–8; right to an 42; risks
    of 60–3; study of 57–8

education, philosophical work in 23–35, 125–6; background 23–5; considerations regarding 30–2; expertise in 48; living 27–30; policy, politics and research 25–7
*Education, Philosophy and Politics* (Peters, M. A.) 116
*Education at a Glance* reports (OECD) 159
*Educational Philosophy and Theory* (journal) 77
Educational Policy Studies (UW) 47
educational research 129–43; background 129–30; compared with research on education 135–6; and ethics 131–3, 139–41; expectations for researchers in 137–8; theoretical framework choices and 138–9; values and 130–5; *see also* perspectives on educational research
Einstein, A. 103, 122
Elliott, J. 136
embodied cognition 118
emotions 11–12, 43
empirical research 55–7, 60–1, 78–9, 133–5, 160–1
England 42, 131
English-speakers 54, 57, 60
engrossment 101, 106–7
Enslin, P. 18, 20, 69–70, 160–1; *see also* liberal feminism
epistemology 39, 46, 49, 110, 118, 122
*Erziehung* (educative teaching) 54
*Essays in Experimental Logic* (Dewey) 7
essentialism 41
ethics 24–5, 73–4; of caring 101–2; living 27, 32; and research 95, 97, 131–3, 139–41, 146, 151; virtue 105
*Ethics and Education* (Peters, R. S.) 125, 141
Europe 71
evidence xviii, 60, 93, 97, 129, 166
evolutionary cosmology 122
excellence 93
Excellence in Research for Australia 26
experiments 9–10, 15, 87–8, 124, 154, 156

fable 121
Facebook 123, 147
facts xviii, 8–10, 12–15, 14, 114, 117–18
fads 80
failure 8, 15, 88, 116, 140–1, 145
false dichotomies 41
falsifiability 86, 88, 90–1, 97, 99n2, 116–17
feelings 7–8, 12, 16, 111
Feigl, H. 117
feminism 45–6, 74, 105–6, 138–9, 166
Ferguson, P. F. 17

Feyerabend, P.: *Against Method* 118
Foucault, M. 41, 70–1, 75, 119, 120–1, 126, 156, 159; "Nietzsche, Genealogy, History" 114
foundational subjects 47
France 42
Frankfurt School, The 40, 49n5
Fraser, N. 40, 42, 45, 76
Frege, G. 116, 118
Freire, P. 23, 31, 36–7, 39–40, 47, 48
fundamentalism 124
funding 5–6, 26, 43–5, 47–8, 61, 151–2

Gadamer, H.-G. 16, 18
Gardner, H. 93
Gauss, C. F. 111
gender 41, 74, 159, 161
genealogy 114–15, 119–20
generalisations 116–17
German Marxism 49n7
German-speakers 53, 57–8, 60
Germany 42, 117, 153
gestalt switch 118
Ghent University 153
gift of teaching 64
Gillard, J. 74
Gilligan, C. 102, 138; *In a Different Voice* 105
global financial crisis (2007–8) 71
global interconnectivity 122–3
global justice 69
global North, the 77
God 119, 124
Gödel, K. 116, 122
good education researchers 158–67
Gordon, L. 45
Gorz, A. 36, 42, 49n7
Gottingen 111
Gove, M. 138
grace, theology of 64
Gramsci, A. 36, 37, 39, 42
Greek thinkers 28
Greene, M. 40
guessing 12, 14

Habermas, J. 36, 40, 123–4
Hadot, P. 27–8; *Philosophy as a Way of Life* 121
Haig, B. 92
Hall, S. 43
Hanson, N. R. 12–13, 117–18
Hattie, J. 19–20, 160, 162; *Visible Learning* 159; *see also* interpretation
Hay Festival 138
Hegel, G. 125
hegemony 18, 45

**172** Index

Heidegger, M. 37, 119–21, 155; *The Age of The World Picture* 144; *Nietzsche* 120; *Sein und Zeit* (*Being and Time*) 149
Heisenberg, W. 122
Herbart, J. F. 153
Herrnstein, R. J. 110
Hilbert, D. 111
Hirst, P. H. 57, 159
history curriculum 138
holism xxi
*How We Think* (Dewey) 7
Huebner, D. 40
humanities, the 60, 122
Hume, D. 111, 116
Husserl, E. 139
hypotheses xviii, 8–15, 20, 117, 148

ideas 14, 18–20, 27, 29, 120
identities 43, 45, 58
ideologies 18, 71, 75
implications 13
*In a Different Voice* (Gilligan) 105
incommensurability 124
incompleteness theorems (Gödel) 116, 122
India 46, 77
indigenous music 79
Indigenous people 46
individualism 26, 69, 105
indoctrination 156
induction 7–15, 97, 116
industrialism 126
inequalities 36, 38, 72–3, 159
inference 7–15, 21n5
information 89, 97, 140, 142
inquiry 2–3, 7–15, 24
Institute of Education (London) 47
intellectual kinship 26–7
interdisciplinarity 54, 111–12, 164
*International Handbook of Interpretation for Educational Research, The* (Springer, publisher) 156–7
International Test Commission 89
Internet 126
interpretation 85–100; background 85–8; demand for 89–90; and falsifiability 88; genealogy and 114; measurement 88–9; purpose of 90–2; research 89, 94–8; tools 92–4
intricacies of research 7–16
investigation 3
Item Response Theory (IRT) 88

Jewish Holocaust, the 111
journals 77, 81n6, 103, 121, 149, 151–2, 156

judgments 2, 16–17
justice 27, 42, 68–71, 74–5
justification 115

Kant, I. xix, 105, 120, 153
Kaufmann, W.: *Nietzsche* 120
keywords 43
Klein, F. 111
knowledge 130, 142, 161
Kohlberg, L. 138
Kuhn, T. 2, 116–17; *The Structure of Scientific Revolutions* 117

language 37, 39, 42–5, 59–60, 119, 132–3
language-games 121
Laudan, R. 18
learning 60–5, 129, 141–2, 160
*Learning to Trust* (Watson) 108
Left, the 45
liberal feminism 68–84; background 68–70; defined 74; philosophical issues regarding 72–8, 80; policies 71–2; research on 70–1, 78–81
liberalism 41–2, 69, 75–6, 80–1, 81n2
lies 105
linguistic philosophy 119
listening 106–7
literary sources 31–2
literature: building on the 162; critical pedagogy 37–9; current 129; feminist 138; political philosophy 55–6; psychological 107–8; reflective 90–1; and theoretical understanding 32
logic 61, 116, 117
*Logic of Scientific Discovery, The* (Popper) 116
*Logic: The Theory of Inquiry* (Dewey) 7
Lorde, A. 44
Lyotard, J.-F.: *The Postmodern Condition* 26

MacIntyre, A. 148
McDonald's 134
Maguire, T. 87
*Making Mathematics Count* report 135
Malawi 69, 72–3
management 132–3
manipulation 148–9
Maoridom 46
Marcuse, H. 36, 40
marginalised groups 69
market preferences 146
Marx, K. 41, 42, 75, 155
Marxism 39, 41, 70, 75–7, 152
mathematics 14, 103, 111–12, 135
Maughan, B.: *Rutter Report* 136
meanings 9

measurement 87–9, 97, 102–3, 108
Melbourne University 46
memory 96
men, gender roles of 74
mentors 109
Messick, S. 89
*metapherein* (carrying over) 1
metaphysics 114
methodologies 16–20, 30–1, 46, 76, 97, 119–20
methods: analytic 116–19; mixed 98; over-emphasis on 163; preoccupation with 155–6; research 24, 70–1
methods anxiety 30
metrics 145, 151–3
misogyny 74
mobilisation 42
Modern Educational Thought (course) 77–8
monism xx
moral deliberation 140
*Moral Questions in the Classroom* (Simon) 107–8
morality 114–15
Mortimore, P.: *Rutter Report* 136
motivational displacement 106–7
Mouffe, C. 56
*Mrs Beeton's Book of Household Management* 12–13
multiculturalism 69, 75–6
Murdoch, I. 32
Murray, C. 110
Musgrave, W. 88
music research project 78–9

narrative 44–5
National Assessment Program - Literacy and Numeracy (NAPLAN) 89
nationalism 72–3
Nazis 117, 120
neoliberalism 26–9, 36, 39, 41–5, 48–9, 75–6, 146
neo-liberal/neo-conservative agenda 49
neo-Marxists 36, 41
Netherlands, the 56–7, 149–50, 153
neuro-education 154
neuromyths 95
neuropsychology 95
neuroscience 95–6, 154, 160
New Right 36
New School, The 40
New Zealand 26, 77, 88
Nietzsche, F. 29, 91, 114–15, 119–21, 126, 151, 155; *On the Genealogy of Morality* 114, 119–20
"Nietzsche, Genealogy, History" (Foucault) 114

*Nietzsche* (Heidegger) 120
*Nietzsche* (Kaufmann) 120
Nodding, N. 18, 20, 161; *Caring* 105–6, 111; *see also* care/caring
non-reformist reforms concept 42, 49n7
non-Western traditions 46–7
normal science 117
North, the 46
North America 77
novelty 146
Nuffield Foundation 131
Nussbaum, M. 42, 69, 159

Oakeshott, M. 133
objectivity 114–15, 121
observation 108, 116–18
OECD (*Education at a Glance* reports) 159
Okin, S. M. 69, 74
*On the Genealogy of Morality* (Nietzsche) 114, 119–20
open globalism 123
openness 18, 115–16, 122–5
Otago, NZ 88
other, the 46, 95, 107, 159
Ouston, J.: *Rutter Report* 136
outputs 26, 149
Oxford philosophers 119
Oxford University 137

paradigm change 117–18
paradoxes 123–4
Paris Declaration for Philosophy (UNESCO) 80, 81n10
pedagogy 36–7, 120–1, 126
peer-to-peer interactions 123
Peirce, C. S. 2, 7, 9–16, 39, 92, 99n8, 124
pensions 41
perception xix, 16–17, 144
performance 26, 140
Performance-Based Research Fund (Tertiary Education Commission, 2016) 26
performativity, culture of 145–6
persons 131–2, 134, 137, 139–42, 160
perspectives on educational research 97–8, 139, 144–57; approaches to 147, 149–50, 154–5; background 144–6, 153–4; philosophy of 150–2; and post-modernism 147–9; recommendations for 155–7
Pestalozzi 97
Peters, M. A. 18, 20, 156, 161; *Education, Philosophy and Politics* 116; *Selected Works* 119, 121–2; *see also* science theory
Peters, R. S. 57, 141, 159; *Ethics and Education* 125, 141
phenomenology 60, 101–2, 139

**174** Index

philosophers 24–5, 28, 121
philosophy: as antidote 150–2; avoidance of term 79–80; defined 24–5; of education 25, 39, 47, 125–6, 137–8; pedagogical 120–1; as a way of life 27–30, 121
*Philosophy as a Way of Life* (Hadot) 121
*Philosophy in History* (Rorty) 122
*Philosophy of Educational Research* (Pring) 130
Piaget, J. 110
pig farming image 61–2
PISA tables 159
Plato 42, 97, 137, 154
plurality 147–8
policies 61, 71, 147
policing 165
political correctness 72, 76
politicians 131–2, 150
politics 25–7, 40, 45; of benevolence 72; of representation and recognition 42; traditions in 48
pondering 12
Popper, K. 2, 86, 88, 91, 93, 98, 99n1, 116–17, 123–4; *Conjectures and Refutations* 116; *The Logic of Scientific Discovery* 116
positivism 44, 134, 139
post-colonialism 70, 72–3, 79
post-holocaust Europe 40, 49n5
*Postmodern Condition, The* (Lyotard) 26
post-modernism 75, 147–9
post-structuralism 75, 77
poverty 154, 159
power 54, 64, 75, 119–20, 124
practitioners, education of 154–5
pragmatism 7, 39–41
praxis 36–52; background 36–9, 49n1; and feminism 45–6; and non-Western traditions 46–7; research philosophies 40–5, 47–8; and rhetoric 39
prejudices 16–18
preparation 2–3
presence 101
presentation 3
presuppositions 148
Pring, R. 18, 20, 24, 160; *Philosophy of Educational Research* 130; *see also* educational research
private/public dualism 70
problem solving 7–8, 147–8, 151–2
professional development 91
progressives 36–7
proof 166
psychology 94–5, 96, 136
psychometrics 87, 89, 160
publishing 149–51

qualitative research 98, 103, 108–9, 134
quality education 69, 76
quantitative research 43–5, 57, 87, 134, 152–4
Queensland, Australia 89
questions 4–7, 30, 58–9, 134–5, 158–67
Quine, T. 117

race 18, 110, 159
Rancière, J. 56, 156
randomised field trials 156
Raphael: *The School of Athens* 145–6
*Rashomon* (film) 108–9, 112n5
Rawls, J. 70, 74–5
realist epistemology 122
reason 111
reasoning 8–9, 13–14
receptive attention 106–7
reciprocity 86
recognition 42
redistribution of resources 76
reflection 7–8, 156
rehearsal 96
Reichenbach, H. 117
relational analysis 38
relationship to others 29, 63, 72, 101–5, 108–9
relativity theory 122
relevance 59–60, 74–5, 78–9, 133, 139, 152, 156–7
Renaissance, the 145
representation 42
Research Assessment Exercise (2008) 26
research defined 86, 91, 125–6
Research Excellence Framework (2014) 26
researchers, good education 158–67
resources 58, 76
respect 140
revolutionary science 117
rhetoric 37, 39
Right, the 36–7, 39, 43, 45, 49
rights discourse 42
risks of thinking philosophically 60–3, 86
Roberts, P. 19–20, 160
Rogers, C. 93
Roman thinkers 28
Rorty, R. 123; *Philosophy in History* 122
Rose and Crown 137, 143n3
Russell, B. 116, 118
Rutter, M.: *Rutter Report* 136
*Rutter Report* (Rutter, Maughan, Mortimore, & Ouston) 136
Ryle, G. 119

Sartre, J.-P. 32
Schama, S. 138

Scheffler, I. 39, 156
Schick, M. 117
scholar-activists 37, 46–7, 49
*School of Athens, The* (Raphael) 145
School of Philosophy (Australia) 76
schooling 59, 69, 130, 136, 161
Science of Learning Research Centre 95
science theory 114–28; background
114–16; genealogy of 119–22; method
116–19; and openness 122–5; and
philosophy in education 125–6
Scotland 78
Scotland-Malawi Partnership 69, 72, 81n5
*Sein und Zeit (Being and Time)*
(Heidegger) 149
*Selected Works*, (Peters, M.A.) 119, 121–2
SEM (Structural Equation Modelling) 88
sematic ascent strategy 119
Sen, A. 159
sensitivity 86
service learning 73
Siegel, H. 111
Simon, K.: *Moral Questions in the Classroom*
107–8
skills 47, 134, 159, 160–1
Skinner, B. F. 93, 110
Skype 122
slow theory 29–30, 32, 165
Smeyers, P. 19–20, 91, 129, 160; *see also*
perspectives on educational research
Smith, L.T. 46
Smith, R. 129
Smith report 135
Snook, I. 156
social injustices 36
social justice 27, 42, 68–9
social liberals 69
socialisation 55
socialist feminists 45
sociology 136, 165–6
Socrates 126, 154
Soltis, J. 38–9
South Africa 69, 71, 76, 78–9
Southern theories 46
special education 153
special relationships 72
specialisation 146, 149–50
Spinoza, B. xx, 25
spirituality 27, 121
Stalinism 41
standardized testing 36
standards, concept of 140–1
Stanford 105, 108–9
*Stanford Encyclopedia of Philosophy, The* xviii
Stanley, J. C. 87

state interference 68, 70
statistics 24, 37, 44–5, 87
Stenhouse, L. 24, 136
Stolz, S.A. *see* thinking philosophically
stories 86–8, 97, 105, 108
Structural Equation Modelling (SEM) 88
structural modelling 92
*Structure of Scientific Revolutions*
(Kuhn) 117
students 55, 63–4, 90, 97–8, 109, 137–8, 153
*Studies in Logical Theory* (Dewey) 7
subjectification concept 56
subjectivity 115, 120–1
suffering 29
suggestions 7–8
suturing 43
systems 116, 122

taste 171
Taylor, C. 148
teachers 41, 70, 90–2, 110, 132–3, 135–6
teaching and learning 60, 63–5, 108–13,
134, 159
tenure 47, 103, 152
terror management 95
testing 61, 89–90
textbooks 162
texts 121–2
theoretical frameworks 16–20, 24;
alternative 53, 56; choosing 130,
138–9; defined 2, 30–1; Enslin on 70–9;
outlining 38–9
theories 19–20, 92; care/caring 102–7;
contesting 94; defined 24–5, 148;
justification for 149–50; for practitioners
155; relativity 122; research 23–5, 75;
using 164–6; verification 117;Visible
Learning 88, 91, 93, 99n3
theorists 19, 31, 36
theory in research 1–22; background 1–2;
complexities 2–3; generation 7–15;
methodologies 16–20; questions 4–7
theses 20, 31, 121
thinking 9–10, 85–6, 96, 97, 133, 161–3
thinking philosophically 53–67; background
53–5; empirical research and 55–7; risks
of 60–3; teaching and learning from
63–5; thinking about 57–60
Thomas, L. 109
Thorndike, E. 129, 142
Tillich, P. 104
time, struggle with 29
Tolstoy, L. 32
tools 92–4, 97, 160
*Tractatus* (Wittgenstein) 116

**176** Index

traditions: academic curriculum 38; of charity 72; culinary 17–18; family 38; Marxist 75; non-Western 46–7; philosophical 18, 28, 40–3, 48–9, 53–4, 134, 138; pragmatic 2, 7
training researchers 97–8
transforming, inquiring as 7–8
treatise 121
trial and error method 8–9, 11, 15
Trump, D. 48
trust 109
truth 115, 116, 124, 140
Tutankhamun 146

Unamuno, M. de. 24–5, 32
uncertainty principle 122
UNESCO (United Nations Education Scientific and Cultural Organisation) 80; Paris Declaration for Philosophy 80, 81n10
United Kingdom 26, 77
United Nations 42
United Nations Education Scientific and Cultural Organisation (UNESCO) 80
United States 41–2, 46, 49, 74
universalism 76
University of Canterbury 116
University of Manchester 47
University of Wisconsin 47
unscheduled castes 46
usefulness 108

values 118–19, 133–5, 140
variables 144, 147–9

verification theory 117
Vienna Circle of Logical Empiricism 117–18
virtues 140–1
*Visible Learning* (Hattie) 159
Visible Learning theory 88, 91, 93, 99n3
Vygotsky, L. 94

warranted assertions 142
Watson, M.: *Learning to Trust* 108
wealth distribution 68–9
Weil, S. 29, 102, 106–7
Western theories 78, 121
Williams, R. 43
wisdom 27, 148, 157
Wittgenstein, L. xix, 16, 39, 42, 117–21, 124, 126, 134; *Tractatus* 116
women 41, 45, 48, 69–70, 76, 106
wonder 12
Woodson, C. 46
Woolf, V. 102, 107
words 16–17, 30, 43–4
Workers Party (Brazil) 40
world views 93, 95, 97–8
World Wide Web 123
world-apparatus complex 92
writing 30, 121–2, 149–50
wrong, being 86, 88, 92–4, 97

Yates, L. 20, 158–67
Young, M. 159
young people 54–5, 58, 62, 132–3